Prophetic Visions
and
Economic Realities

Prophetic Visions
and
Economic Realities

Edited by

WILLIAM B. EERDMANS PUBLISHING COMPANY

Protestants, Jews, and Catholics Confront the Bishops' Letter on the Economy

Charles R. Strain

GRAND RAPIDS, MICHIGAN

For Dianne

Copyright © 1989 by Wm. B. Eerdmans Publishing Co.
255 Jefferson Ave. S.E., Grand Rapids, Mich. 49503

Library of Congress Cataloging-in-Publication Data

Prophetic visions and economic realities: Protestants, Jews, and Catholics
  confront the bishops' letter on the economy / edited by Charles R. Strain
      p.   cm.
  ISBN 0-8028-0065-3
  1. Catholic Church. National Conference of Catholic Bishops. Economic
justice for all. 2. Economics—Religious aspects—Catholic Church.
3. Catholic Church—Doctrines. 4. Sociology, Christian (Catholic). 5. United
States—Economic conditions—1981-   . 6. Economics—Religious aspects—
Christianity. 7. Economics—Religious aspects—Judaism. 8. Sociology,
Christian. 9. Sociology, Jewish. 10. Judaism—Doctrines.   I. Strain, Charles R.
BX1795.E27P76   1988
261.8'5'0973—dc19   88-25842
                                                                      CIP

Contents

Acknowledgments   viii

Abbreviations   x

Contributors   xi

Introduction   1
Charles R. Strain

PART 1 | EVANGELICAL PROTESTANT PERSPECTIVES ON
AMERICAN ECONOMIC LIFE   11

1 | Evangelical Protestant Perspectives on
American Economic Life   13

2 | Thinking about the Poor:
What Evangelicals Can Learn from the Bishops   20
Richard J. Mouw

3 | A Lesson in Constructive Theology   35
Robert K. Johnston

4 | Wealth and Well-Being:
The Bishops and Their Critics   48
Eugene R. Dykema

5 | The Bishops and Third World Poverty   61
Mark R. Amstutz

Contents

PART 2 | JEWISH PERSPECTIVES ON
AMERICAN ECONOMIC LIFE   75

6 | Jewish Perspectives on American Economic Life   77

7 | The U.S. Catholic Bishops' Pastoral Letter on
the Economy and Jewish Tradition   81
Byron L. Sherwin

8 | The Bishops and the Poor: A Jewish Critique   93
Arnold Jacob Wolf

9 | The Prophetic Tradition and
Social Transformation   103
Frida Kerner Furman

10 | Bishops, Rabbis, and Prophets   115
Leonard Fein

PART 3 | MAINLINE PROTESTANT PERSPECTIVES ON
AMERICAN ECONOMIC LIFE   127

11 | Mainline Protestant Perspectives on
American Economic Life   129

12 | The Morality of Power
and the Power of Morality   134
Larry Rasmussen

13 | Graceless Poverty and the Poverty of Grace   146
Timothy F. Sedgwick

14 | Poverty and Policy: The Many Faces of the Poor 156
Rebecca M. Blank

15 | The Churches and the Corporations   169
Paul F. Camenisch

PART 4 | ROMAN CATHOLIC PERSPECTIVES ON
AMERICAN ECONOMIC LIFE   183

16 | Roman Catholic Perspectives on
American Economic Life   185

17 | Beyond Madison and Marx: Civic Virtue,
Solidarity, and Justice in American Culture   190
Charles R. Strain

Contents

18 | New Experiment in Democracy:
Blueprint for Political Economy?   203
Dennis P. McCann

19 | Women and Dignity: Vision and Practice   216
Ann O'Hara Graff

20 | Individualism, Interdependence, and
the Common Good: Rapprochement between
Economic Theory and Catholic Social Thought   229
Charles K. Wilber

Notes   242

Acknowledgments

I wish to acknowledge DePaul University's College of Liberal Arts and Sciences, Dean Richard J. Meister, and the Center for the Study of Values in Modern Society for significant support for this project.

The Center, established in 1985, directs DePaul University's Catholic and Vincentian commitment to questions concerning the role of values—religious and moral, cultural, political and economic—in modern society. It coordinates faculty research on these questions and promotes public discussion with the intention of contributing to the democratic pursuit of the common good. The Faculty Research and Development Committee of the College of Liberal Arts and Sciences provided summer grants to Ann O'Hara Graff, Frida Kerner Furman, and Dennis P. McCann to work on this project.

I am especially grateful to the Lucius N. Littauer Foundation, which provided a generous grant to sustain this project, and to its president, William Lee Frost. Fuller Theological Seminary provided travel funding for Richard Mouw so that he might join the project. Spertus College of Judaica and Dr. Byron Sherwin graciously hosted several meetings of the various teams.

Sharing many of the editorial duties with me were Richard Mouw, Frida Kerner Furman, Paul Camenisch, and Dennis P. McCann, leaders of—respectively—the evangelical Protestant, Jewish, mainline Protestant, and Roman Catholic teams. They were also responsible for drafting and revising the respective introductions to each section of the book. I am deeply indebted to them for their assistance.

Special thanks go to Jon Pott of Eerdmans for his support for this project, and to Mary Hietbrink, also of Eerdmans, for her careful review and revision of the manuscript.

Finally, I am most grateful to Ms. Kelly Johnson for her cheerful and unstinting labors in typing the manuscript and shepherding it with me through its multiple revisions.

To all of these individuals and institutions, to fifteen of the most cooperative scholars whom I have ever met, and to my always-patient wife and sons, my deep thanks.

Charles R. Strain

Abbreviations

All biblical references use standard abbreviations and appear in parentheses in the text; a variety of translations have been used. All references to *Economic Justice for All: Catholic Social Teaching and the U.S. Economy* by the National Conference of Catholic Bishops appear in parentheses in the text. These citations are indicated by the abbreviation *par.* and the paragraph number of the cited text—for example, (par. 45). References to the Pastoral Message preceding the pastoral letter itself are likewise indicated by the *par.* abbreviation and the paragraph number of the cited text, followed by the designation "PM"—for example, (pars. 3-5, PM). All citations are to the final draft of the letter as published in *Origins: NC Documentary Service* 16 (27 Nov. 1986): 409-56. All other citations appear as endnotes.

Contributors

MARK R. AMSTUTZ is Professor and Chair of Political Science, Wheaton College. He is the author of three books, including, most recently, *Christian Ethics and U.S. Foreign Policy* (Zondervan, 1987).

REBECCA M. BLANK is Assistant Professor of Economics and Public Affairs, Woodrow Wilson School of Public and International Affairs, Princeton University. Recent publications include "Macroeconomics, Income Distribution and Poverty," in *Fighting Poverty: What Works and What Doesn't* (Harvard University Press, 1986).

PAUL F. CAMENISCH is Professor and Chair of Religious Studies, DePaul University. He is the author of *Grounding Professional Ethics in a Pluralistic Society* (Haven, 1983).

EUGENE R. DYKEMA is Professor and Chair of Economics and Business, Calvin College. He is a contributing author of *Earthkeeping: Christian Stewardship of Natural Resources* (Eerdmans, 1980) and *Responsible Technology* (Eerdmans, 1986).

LEONARD FEIN is the author of *The Ecology of the Public Schools* (Pegasus, 1971); *Israel: Politics and People* (Little, Brown, 1967); and *Where Are We? The Inner Life of America's Jews* (Harper & Row, 1988).

FRIDA KERNER FURMAN is Assistant Professor of Religious Studies, DePaul University. She is the author of *Beyond Yiddishkeit: The Struggle for Jewish Identity in a Reform Synagogue* (SUNY Press, 1987).

Contributors

ANN O'HARA GRAFF is Assistant Professor of Religious Studies, DePaul University. She is a member of the advisory board of the *Chicago Call to Action Newsletter* and its Women's Committee and a former member of the Chicago Archdiocesan Pastoral Council Task Force.

ROBERT K. JOHNSTON is Dean and Professor of Theology and Culture, North Park Theological Seminary. He is the author of *The Christian at Play* (Eerdmans, 1983) and *Evangelicals at an Impasse: Biblical Authority in Practice* (John Knox Press, 1979), and the editor of *The Use of the Bible in Theology*.

DENNIS P. MCCANN is Associate Professor of Religious Studies and Director of the Center for the Study of Values in Modern Society, DePaul University. He is the author of *Christian Realism and Liberation Theology* (Orbis, 1981) and *A New Experiment in Democracy* (Sheed & Ward, 1987), and co-author of *Polity and Praxis: A Program for American Practical Theology* (Winston Press, 1985).

RICHARD J. MOUW is Professor of Christian Philosophy and Ethics, Fuller Theological Seminary. He is the author of *Called to Holy Worldliness* (Fortress Press, 1980); *Political Evangelism* (Eerdmans, 1973); and *Politics and the Biblical Drama* (Eerdmans, 1976). He is also an editor of *The Reformed Journal*.

LARRY RASMUSSEN is Reinhold Niebuhr Professor of Social Ethics, Union Theological Seminary. His numerous publications include *Dietrich Bonhoeffer: Reality and Resistance* (Abingdon Press, 1972) and *Economic Anxiety and Christian Faith* (Augsburg, 1981).

TIMOTHY F. SEDGWICK is Associate Professor of Christian Ethics and Moral Theology, Seabury-Western Theological Seminary. He is the author of *Sacramental Ethics* (Fortress Press, 1987).

BYRON L. SHERWIN, an ordained rabbi, is Vice-President for Academic Affairs and Verson Professor of Jewish Philosophy and Mysticism at Spertus College of Judaica in Chicago. Dr. Sherwin is the author of nine books, including *Mystical Theology and Social Dissent* (Oxford University Press, 1985).

CHARLES R. STRAIN is Associate Professor of Religious Studies and Director of the Master of Arts in Liberal Studies Program, DePaul University. He is the co-author of *Polity and Praxis: A Program for an American Practical Theology* (Winston Press, 1985) and co-editor of *Techno-*

logical Change and the Transformation of America (Southern Illinois University Press, 1987).

CHARLES K. WILBER is Professor of Economics, University of Notre Dame. He has shaped eleven books, either as author or editor, including *An Inquiry into the Poverty of Economics* (University of Notre Dame Press, 1985) and *Capitalism and Democracy: Schumpeter Revisited* (University of Notre Dame Press, 1985). Wilber was a consultant to the U.S. Bishops Committee on Catholic Social Thought and the U.S. Economy.

ARNOLD JACOB WOLF is the rabbi of K.A.M. Isaiah Israel Congregation, Chicago, Ill. He is the author of *Rediscovering Judaism: Reflections on a New Theology* (Quadrangle Books, 1965), among other works, and a founding editor of *Sh'ma: A Journal of Jewish Responsibility*.

Introduction

Charles R. Strain

Signs of the Times

"The economy is a human reality," begins the pastoral letter of the U.S. Catholic bishops, *Economic Justice for All: Catholic Social Teaching and the U.S. Economy* (par. 1). Signs of hope and grim scars of failure mark the face of this human reality. While sustained by hope, the bishops clearly labor with the pain of those scars. The reality of 33 million Americans below the poverty line. The reality of soup lines in a nation of abundance. Of unemployment and economic insecurity tearing at the fabric of American family life. Of farmers losing not just their farms but a way of life. And "beyond our shores," confronting the bishops in all its starkness, "the reality of 800 million people living in absolute poverty" (pars. 3-4, 16).

The bishops are not alone in their anguish. Recent statements by the Presbyterian Church (U.S.A.) and the United Church of Christ begin with similar litanies.[1] Who is not troubled by the human face of our economic life? Each of us can make our own sketch of this human face, supplying our own lines of hope and the shadows of hopelessness. So, a normally conservative economist, writing in *Newsweek*, focuses on recent statistics of the U.S. Census Bureau: in 1986 the median family income rose 4.2 percent while 13.6 percent of the American people had incomes below the official poverty line. "Here's a statistical snapshot of a two-tiered society," he grimly concludes, "a general prosperity sitting atop a stubborn poverty."[2] Or two social critics find the visible evidence of the human costs of

1

economic change in the lament of an unemployed steelworker's wife—"When I look out the door of my house . . . , I see my mother's house across the street, my sister-in-law's down the block, and the neighborhood full of people I have known all my life. Everywhere I look there is love, and now we have to move."[3] Or I, as I walk the main avenue of my Chicago neighborhood, am stunned by the feat of entrepreneurship—unimaginable to my fourth-generation American mind—of Asian immigrants creating a bright bazaar out of the dead and empty storefronts. Yet I also daily pass a huddle of the homeless, our human discards, to reach my university, which is located in one of the most affluent neighborhoods in the city. One more sign of the times. In Chicago, the First World and the Third World live side by side.

What do we make of these signs? More importantly, how should those of us who have the remarkable audacity to think of ourselves as religious people think through these contradictions? What are we called to do? Or are these questions wrongheaded? Is economic life best left to the experts and executives? Is it the business of America's religious leaders, like the National Conference of Catholic Bishops and the study groups formed by other denominations, to intrude upon our daily business? Does the ark of the covenant belong in the marketplace?

Of Markets and Squares

The sixteen authors of this book have wrestled with these questions during a year-long series of meetings. We first met as a group in December 1986, immediately following the publication of the bishops' pastoral letter on the economy. As a group focusing on public policy issues, we are distinct in two ways. We represent a variety of academic disciplines, yet we are consciously organized into four teams representing major religious traditions in America—Roman Catholicism, Judaism, evangelical Protestantism, and mainline Protestantism. Whether we write as systematic or political theologians, as business or social ethicists, as economists or political scientists, we think out of the traditions that have shaped us. The protracted opportunity we had to test our ideas against the perspectives of other traditions and other disciplines left none of our positions unaltered. Each of the four teams wrestled with the diversity of its own tradition in confronting the challenge to discover the distinctiveness in its own religious tradition's vision of economic life and to express it in the prefatory chapter that opens its section of the book.

We began, like the bishops, with two basic premises. If the

economy is a human reality, it has an ineradicable moral dimension. More importantly, the very questioning of the appropriateness of the ark in the marketplace betrays a profound misunderstanding of the nature of religion. We cannot "immerse ourselves in earthly activities as if these latter were utterly foreign to religion and religion were nothing more than the fulfillment of acts of worship and the observance of a few moral obligations." No religious community can tolerate "a tragic separation between faith and everyday life" (par. 5, PM).

To be sure, these premises are frequently contested. A few years ago Lutheran pastor Richard John Neuhaus worried through a long book that Americans would acquiesce in the creation of what he called "the naked public square, . . . the result of political doctrine and practice that would exclude religion and religiously grounded values from the conduct of public business."[4] To enter this sanitized arena, to engage in public debate over public policy, all individuals and groups would have to strip themselves of the particular religious beliefs and values that shaped their deepest commitments. At the gates of this square, Neuhaus sensed, we would each be admonished: You may fight for your interests, but you may never speak of what lies at the bedrock of your motivation nor hint at the grounds for the hope that is in you.

Some things, however, have changed since Neuhaus's jeremiad. Listen to the bishops once more:

> We want to make the legacy of Christian social thought a living, growing resource that can inspire hope and help shape the future. We write, then, first of all to provide guidance for members of our own church as they seek to form their consciences about economic matters. No one may claim the name Christian and be comfortable in the face of hunger, homelessness, insecurity and injustice found in this country and the world. At the same time, we want to add our voice to the public debate about the directions in which the U.S. economy should be moving. We seek the cooperation and support of those who do not share our faith or tradition. The common bond of humanity that links all persons is the source of our belief that the country can attain a renewed public moral vision. (pars. 26-27)

A new firmness of tone can be heard in the voices of these religious leaders. We are in the public square, the Catholic bishops seem to be saying—robes, miters, crosiers, and all. We will not be abridged of our rights as American citizens because we are religiously committed. We will not be removed. Nor silenced. Nor stripped of our deepest convictions. This determination is matched by the equally confident ring that can be heard in the words of leaders of denominations across the spectrum of American life.

"The public square," Neuhaus insisted, "is not limited to Government Square."[5] In the modern world the political sphere and the economic sphere have interpenetrated to create complex forms of political economy. Instead of a public square located some distance from the marketplace, we inhabit something like the Athenian agora where political and economic institutions together order the swirl of activities.

Religious voices have always been raised in this arena. Religious evaluations of American economic life are staples of American rhetoric. One tradition was inaugurated as early as 1606, when British poet Michael Drayton described America as "earth's onely paradise," a land God provided for industrious heroes precisely to enable them "to get the pearle and gold."[6] Another tradition, beginning with John Winthrop, the first governor of the Massachusetts Bay Colony, has worried constantly about the fate of a nation under God and has, therefore, fought over the nature, the purpose—indeed, over the very meaning—of "commerce" in this land. Would we be "seduced and worshipp other Gods, our pleasures and proffitts, and serve them," or would we "avoyde this shipwracke" by following the call to justice issued by the prophet Micah? To reach the latter end, Winthrop continued,

> We must be knitt together in this worke as one man, . . . we must be willing to abridge our selves of our superfluities for the supply of others necessities, we must uphold a familiar Commerce together . . . as members of the same body. . . . Therefore lett us choose life, . . . cleaving to him for hee is our life and our prosperity.[7]

Today erstwhile prophets crowd every corner of the public square. Pronouncements by the score are heaved into the swirl of the agora. A new danger emerges: we honor our prophets as confirmations of our free way of life, then return to business as usual. Having rejected multiple forms of religious and ideological absolutism, most of us consent to the transformation of the public square into the equivalent of London's Hyde Park. As Wayne Booth puts it with supreme irony, "Here all are free to speak because no one is listening."[8]

How do those who provide religious perspectives on economic life manage to get a hearing? Can we avoid the transformation of these perspectives into merely ritual demonstrations of how wonderfully tolerant we are in America? How do we sort through the clamor of voices in the no-longer-naked public square? Is it possible for me to be transformed by a voice speaking out of a different religious tradition without compromising the integrity of my own perspective on our common life?

Religious Discourse in the Public Square

The authors of this book share these questions even when we find no consensus on the answers. But we do hold at least four convictions in common about religious perspectives on public policy. *First*, we insist that there is no political Esperanto. That debate in the public square could occur without frequent recourse to the vital and particular sources of belief and value is a myth of the first order. Everybody brings some ideology—whether religious or secular—to bear in arguing questions of public policy. By organizing ourselves along the lines of America's salient religious traditions, we make explicit the roots of our own ideological convictions. Each of our teams, representing a particular balance of unity and diversity, creates its own perspective on the economic order. Each thereby invites response from others within and outside its tradition.

Whatever our criticisms of the bishops' pastoral letter on the economy, and they are many, it has indeed established a new benchmark for religious contributions to the debate on public policy issues. It has provided us with an excellent foil for conversations both within and among our four groups. We intend not to fault the bishops for this or that perceived failure but to use their accomplishment to hone our own religious perspectives on economic life. With the bishops, we hold, as our *second* major point of agreement, that any such perspective must trace a complex and difficult "movement from principle to policy," recognizing the fallibility of the judgments that mark each stage of the process (pars. 134-35).

Given the complexities of modern economic life, we require something more than Karl Barth's theologian armed with a Bible in one hand and a newspaper in the other. Those who articulate the biblical, theological, and moral vision of their religious communities cannot work in isolation from cultural historians, economists, and political and social scientists—hence the variety of disciplinary skills included in each of our four teams.

More importantly, the complex movement from principle to policy is reflected in the diversity of inquiries that make up this book. Let me give you some indication of that complex movement and those diverse inquiries.

To begin, clearly the Bible dictates no particular form of

5

economic life. Or should we say it can be made to suggest too many forms? Getting a grip on the complexities of the biblical vision of economic life and justice, urges Richard Mouw, is the initial step across a complex terrain. Just how difficult this step will be is illustrated by Arnold Jacob Wolf. What are we to make of the Torah's formulation of the law of God with its provisions for a sabbatical year and a jubilee year, with its prohibitions of interest-taking? "Judaism," Byron Sherwin argues, quoting Abraham Heschel, "is based upon a minimum of revelation and a maximum of interpretation." Sherwin proceeds to demonstrate this principle, showing in the process just how hard it is for our four traditions to come to any sort of common reading of the Bible we share.

Robert Johnston argues that theologians, needing to fuse biblical sources with the resources of the religious tradition in addressing the modern setting, have their own complicated task to perform. The bishops have much to teach evangelical Christians and others about doing theology in the marketplace. But how, he asks, do we accomplish this task without losing our souls? One way, Timothy Sedgwick maintains, is to resist the tendency of theology to become the rationale for a socially optimistic moral idealism. A theology of the economic order no less than any other form of theology must underline our need for perpetual conversion.

Like Johnston, Ann O'Hara Graff is concerned that theology interact with experience. Abstract visions, however sublime, can mask oppression. What does human dignity mean, she asks, for a welfare mother or, for that matter, a middle-class woman, who is compelled by both economic necessity and personal choice to juggle the demands of love and career, to work two shifts?

Sedgwick's concern for the spiritual life of the converted community and Graff's for the specific struggles of women for human dignity force ethicists no less than theologians to reconsider whether their abstract principles preserve the nuances of our actual situations. Simply resorting to the rhetoric of prophetic criticism, Frida Kerner Furman implies, will not do either. The appeal to the tradition of the Hebrew prophets—so tempting in its fusion of biblical, theological, ethical, and ecumenical motifs—demands strenuous reflection to be authentic. How do we carry forward this tradition without simply subordinating it to our political commitments of the moment?

Others, too, try to broaden our sense of what is entailed in developing our economic ethics. Paul Camenisch believes that careful attention must be given to the issue of moral agency as well as to moral principles. Unless we make American corporations, especially the transnational corporations, the unredeemable villains of a morality play, we must ask ourselves, What are the moral responsibilities of these immensely powerful actors on the world scene?

Larry Rasmussen asks a similar question: What does effective moral agency mean in the case of religious communities? Would even moral consensus, were that possible, be sufficient to transform American economic life? What will religious communities do when entrenched power, of whatever sort, nods gravely at their moral admonitions and persists resolutely on its unjust course?

Neither must we demonize American culture, as Charles Strain and Dennis McCann illustrate. If religious communities must maintain their integrity—must avoid, as Johnston puts it, a form of cultural captivity—must there not also be some engagement with what the bishops refer to as the unfinished business of American democracy? At what precise points do cultural values, economic forces, and the religious imperative for justice converge? Another aspect of that engagement involves breaking down cultural stereotypes. Rebecca Blank does just that, using empirical data to answer the question, Who are the poor?

Other economists and political scientists join Blank to examine the assumptions that underlie our reigning economic models. Charles Wilber explores one after another of the economic cul-de-sacs to which individualist assumptions lead. He also has another model in mind based on the assumption of human interdependence. Eugene Dykema questions whether the economic model of a market ruled by an "invisible hand" can be made to square with a Christian economic model oriented to the public good. Mark Amstutz, on the other hand, sees the Christian's calling to co-creation as a mandate to enhance economic productivity. The searching debate of these two over the relative merits of wealth creation versus the redistribution of wealth as a means to achieve greater justice is a practical illustration of the manner in which we have followed the bishops' lead. We too say without qualification, "This document is not a technical blueprint for economic reform. Rather, it is an attempt to foster a serious moral analysis leading to a more just economy. . . . We believe that differences on complex economic questions should be expressed in a spirit of mutual respect and open dialogue" (pars. 133, 135).

Finally, Leonard Fein reminds us that there are practical questions tied to each and every one of our theoretical inquiries. Perhaps most important is the one with which he struggles: How does a religious community move beyond good intentions and charitable commitments into the realm of political action, seeking economic justice for all?

To be taken seriously, religious and moral discourse in the public square must trace the movement from principle to policy. It follows equally that excluding anyone who makes this effort from the public dialogue undermines the conditions for democracy. This leads directly to the *third* conviction that we came to share as a group: the bishops' call for a public dialogue had to be worked into the structure of this book. How do different religious traditions maintain their distinctive voices while managing to address common issues in ways that might reach others as well? The problems that evangelical Christians have with the notion of a religious magisterium, as indicated in the introduction to the section of this book by the evangelical Protestant team, and the problems that Byron Sherwin and Arnold Jacob Wolf, articulating a Jewish perspective, found in the very form of the pastoral letter—these illustrate very well the difficulty of even beginning such a dialogue. This book itself, I believe, reflects a precarious balance reached between those who would strengthen the authentic voice of their own traditions and those who—to paraphrase Frida Kerner Furman's interpretation of the Jewish mystical concept of *tikkun*—gather divine sparks of holiness across traditions in an effort to mend a torn world.

Speaking across religious traditions is as necessary as it is challenging and enlightening. This interaction led us to a *fourth* conviction: each of our traditions belongs in the public square, but none of them owns it. We based our project on the premise that public discourse in a democratic society depends upon an explicit acknowledgment of the limitations of all perspectives, religious or secular, upon the common good. A plurality of religious perspectives on a given moral issue is not only an inevitable development but a desirable characteristic of the struggle to attain religious and moral clarity. All must learn from the wisdom of each.

Thus the only alternative to compromising the integrity of our religious commitments that is compatible with the maintenance of democratic pluralism is mutual transformation. Yet, as Charles Wilber argues, it is always easier to abandon responsibility for the public realm than to achieve the consensus, the synthesis of opposing positions, necessary to sustain it. The false haven of a withdrawn communal life remains a great temptation to each of our traditions.

The authors of this book hold that temptation to be fatal to the religious life of our communities as well as to the commonweal. Whether we speak of desperately poor evangelical and Catholic Christians in the Third World, as Richard Mouw and Mark Amstutz do, of the poor as a sacrament of God's presence in the world, as Timothy Sedgwick does, or of those whose fast will not cease at the close of Yom Kippur, as Leonard Fein does, we face an inescapable challenge: What is at stake in the confrontation of prophetic visions and economic realities is nothing less than the reality of religious community in any conceivable meaning of the term. Ultimately, this is why we write and, we hope, why you read. We are concerned about the fate of a society whose power and wealth is an ambiguous given. It becomes increasingly obvious that the struggle to transform that society is an also inescapable condition for the redemption of our own religious communities. If the salt should lose its savor . . .

Part 1 | *Evangelical Protestant Perspectives on American Economic Life*

1 | *Evangelical Protestant Perspectives on American Economic Life*

When journalists discuss the conservative evangelical community in the United States, they often work with a figure of forty or fifty million people. It is possible to raise quibbles about that estimate. For one thing, the same journalists like to offer generalizations about the social attitudes of this group of Christians—evangelicals are militaristic, unenthusiastic about racial justice, devoted to civil religion—that hold up only if one works with a somewhat more modest estimate. For example, to get to the forty or fifty million count, several black denominations as well as a few "peace church" groups must be included within the scope of conservative evangelicalism.

There is something journalistically intriguing about the fifty million figure, though. This puts evangelicalism in roughly the same numerical position as Roman Catholicism as a voting bloc in the United States. With two groups of that size, both so inclined to express public policy opinions that ruffle the feathers of secularist pundits—well, the "religious angle" can usually be counted on to provide good reading when a political campaign starts to get a little dull.

But the high visibility of both evangelicals and Roman Catholics in public debates is not the mere product of journalistic creativity. We can quibble about the numbers, but there can be no doubt that leaders in both camps have a way of attracting attention to their pronouncements about societal issues. And on some topics their views are quite similar—on abortion, for example, as well as on several other matters relating to family and sexuality. However, despite the fact that evangelicals see Catholics as important allies in controversies about public morality, conservative Protestants have been less than enthusiastic about the two major pastoral letters issued by the bishops in the last several years.

The bishops' pronouncements on peacemaking and economic justice have been difficult for evangelicals to cope with. On the practical level, the Catholic hierarchy has endorsed policies and attitudes that are not popular among evangelicals. Peacemaking simply isn't a strong suit among the vast majority of evangelical Christians. Nor are conservative Protestants inclined to spend much time promoting "a preferential option for the poor."

The discomfort also appears on the theological level. We evangelicals take pride in our own self-proclaimed love of "sound theology." We regularly complain that liberal Protestants don't take theology—"real" theology, the kind heavily sprinkled with biblical references and citations from the Christian past—seriously enough; liberals have forsaken the theological moorings of the Christian tradition for a lot of "modern social analysis."

In the two pastorals the Catholic bishops say many of the things that we associate with the Protestant Social Gospel movement. But they cannot be accused of not taking theology seriously. The bishops go on for pages with their theological reflections on war and peace and on economic life. In the process they work closely with biblical materials, and they quote frequently from Christian thinkers of the past—an impressive marshaling of theological resources for their magisterial task.

It is difficult for evangelicals to dismiss this as not properly theological or as "modernist" in tone. If we are going to respond critically, it will have to be with a different and better theology. The bishops have, in effect, met us on our own turf.

Or have they? The bishops' turf, the place where careful theology gets done with a focus on issues like peacemaking and poverty, really isn't ground that's all that familiar to evangelicals. For all of our celebrations of sound theology, we have done very little thinking about these sorts of issues. Some of the reasons for this are dealt with in the essays that follow. But there can be no denying the fact that when evangelicals have discussed political and economic issues, we have been less likely to engage in calm theological reflection and more likely to mouth clichés and proof texts and on occasion to appeal to conspiracy theories and elaborate "Bible prophecy" schemes, to say nothing of questioning the motives of those with whom we disagree.

There is yet another reason why evangelicals are uncomfortable with the bishops' pastorals: we have difficulties with the very notion of a *magisterium* as it relates to these areas of concern. This is a matter that was touched on explicitly in the report of the group of evangelical and Roman Catholic leaders who engaged in a seven-year "dialogue on mission." The group discovered

> some tension concerning the allocation of responsibility for social service and action. Roman Catholics accept the legitimacy of involvement by the Church as a whole, as well as by groups and individuals. Among Evangelicals, however, there are differences between the Lutheran, Reformed and Anabaptist traditional understandings of Church and society. All would agree that Christian individuals and groups have social responsibilities; the division concerns what responsibility is assigned to the Church as a whole.[1]

There are legitimate concerns at stake here. This is not the place to engage in a lengthy discussion of what the "evangelical" label comes to. But it is important to observe that the groups which have come to be associated with the conservative evangelical movement in North America all place a strong emphasis on the Bible's supreme authority in the Christian life and on the need for individuals to develop a personal relationship with Jesus Christ. This celebration of the Christian life as centering on a personal appropriation of the biblical "evangel" is often clearly related to a suspicion of any system of thought that places much weight on ecclesial authority. Almost every evangelical group has a story to tell about a specific struggle against a very real *magisterium*.

Again, there are important matters at stake here for evangelicals. But the evangelicals' expression of genuine theological worries about a strongly centralized *magisterium* can also serve to divert attention away from issues that are equally important. There is certainly nothing in any evangelical ecclesiology that would prohibit church leaders from sponsoring a broad-ranging dialogue about the ways in which our attitudes on military and economic policies ought to be shaped by the claims of the gospel. Even if one believes that bishops have no right to issue official proclamations on such matters, there is much that evangelicals can learn from the dialogic process that the bishops sponsored as a way of preparing those proclamations. Furthermore, whether or not one accepts the pastoral letters as proper exercises of ecclesial authority, they do contain discussions that are provocative, instructive, and worthy of evangelical consideration. More importantly, they can serve as helpful models of how people who care about the Bible and the Christian tradition can wrestle with crucial issues of peace and justice in the contemporary world. Evangelicals need such models if they are going to think more deliberately and clearly about such matters.

Actually, there is often an informal *magisterium* at work in evangelical communities when it comes to these sorts of issues.[2] More often than not, the insistence that the church has no business "meddling" in politics really means that evangelicals do not want their *de facto* consensus on such matters to become a matter of open discussion. In the absence of a clearly defined magisterial office, evangelical social and economic attitudes have often been shaped by cultural mores that have not been subjected to critical scrutiny.

But the case for a more articulate evangelicalism on these subjects must not be formulated in only remedial terms. Evangelical Christians have a unique contribution to make to the larger theological dialogue about the nature of political and economic witness.

For one thing, evangelicals have extensive scholarly resources to draw upon. There exists in North America an elaborate system of evangelical liberal arts colleges, Bible institutes, and seminaries, many of them with large student bodies and impressive faculties. Evangelicals have actually been very good at creating scholarly networks: organizations of evangelical scholars exist for almost all of the academic disciplines, and they bring together persons who teach at evangelical institutions with evangelicals from the larger academic community. The possibilities (some already being realized) for a broad-ranging discussion of societal perspectives and issues are exciting, especially since evangelicals have nurtured an interest in the integration of faith and learning that extends far beyond the theological disciplines.

Perhaps even more important are the communal *experiences* that evangelicals can bring to such deliberations. There are certain ways in which evangelical actions have been much better than evangelical words on social issues. This is the case with the matter of poverty. The evangelical community has long sponsored its own "Mother Teresas": women and men who have devoted their lives to the unspectacular task of feeding the hungry and providing shelter for the homeless in urban rescue missions, to say nothing of those evangelicals who have played their musical instruments on cold street corners in order to fund the Salvation Army's important skirmishes with the forces that make for poverty and oppression.

Nor should we forget the intense evangelical commitment to foreign missions in this regard. The theology and spirituality of the Christian poor of the Two Thirds World (that two-thirds of the world's population living in situations of poverty, powerlessness, and oppression) seldom show any affinities to "liberal Protestantism": most of the impoverished followers of Jesus are either Roman Catholic or evangelical. This means that we North American evangelicals cannot continue our pretensions about being apolitical for too much longer; we are already being evangelized on this subject by our own converts.

But it would be misleading to suggest that evangelicals are suddenly being forced to take seriously the poor and oppressed of the earth. The situation is much more intimate than that way of putting it would suggest. In North America many evangelicals *are* poor and oppressed. Here too the parallel to Roman Catholicism is instructive. Hispanic people now constitute one-third of the American Catholic community; in the near future they will be the majority. Hispanics are no longer the invisible faces in Catholic pews. And the same holds for evangelicalism: if Hispanic Christians are not Catholics, they most likely belong to a Pentecostal congregation.

Given the fact that 27.3 percent of all Hispanics in the United States live below the official poverty line, their presence in the Catholic and evangelical churches means that those churches are increasingly becoming two-tiered communities. And the strongly evangelical tone of much black Christianity makes the evangelical situation even more pronounced in this regard. Among both Catholics and evangelicals, the newly attained affluence of many white Christians co-exists with the poverty of many fellow church members. The message should be clear: those with whom we share the Table of Fellowship, those whose shoulders we rub as we squirm under the Word of God, are the others whose precarious existence on the bottom tier we have no eyes to see, no ears to hear.

This means that evangelicals must re-examine their traditional patterns of "ministering to the disadvantaged." Evangelical outreach to the poor and the oppressed—much more extensive than is often acknowledged by the critics of conservative Protestantism—has often been intended as a "mere means" to "personal evangelism." And this has been, in its own way, a very real commitment to offering the cup of cold water in Jesus' name. But the time has come for evangelicals to think more clearly about what they have been doing.

The essays that follow are obviously evangelical in their tone and focus. They are concerned about how a community that regularly proclaims its *sola scriptura* convictions can approach the issues of economic theory and practice with a perspective that is shaped by the biblical witness.

The essays of Richard Mouw and Robert Johnston focus primarily on the ways in which the Bible is properly handled in attempting to formulate a Christian perspective on economic life. Mouw notes that both evangelicals and the Roman Catholic bishops give special emphasis to the creation-and-fall motif in dealing with economic obligations. But Mouw also argues that agreement on the importance of this motif does not preclude serious disagreement about important questions about the roles that poverty and wealth play in God's world.

If evangelicals are going to be more aware of the extrabiblical factors that influence their choice and use of biblical themes, they must pay closer attention to questions of theological method. Johnston highlights some of the important issues that must be attended to here, arguing that the legitimate evangelical emphasis on "the Bible alone" as the source of theological reflection does not rule out the necessity of drawing upon both cultural analysis and churchly tradition as providing the setting and the resource (respectively) for the theological task. Johnston not only shows how evangelicals can learn from the bishops on issues of methodology, but also suggests ways in which the bishops might improve their case by engaging in more extensive biblical reflection.

The question of how we move from biblically based theological reflection to economic policy formation is addressed by Eugene Dykema and Mark Amstutz. Their treatments display some important disagreements among evangelicals, disagreements that are similar to those which have surfaced among Catholics in the debate over the bishops' pastoral. Dykema expresses serious misgivings about any attempt to make "wealth creation" the centerpiece of Christian economic theory. Like the bishops, he believes that economic agents should consciously aim at "the public good," which is understood as requiring a concern for human dignity that goes beyond the pursuit of wealth-creating private goods. Economic choices often come "down to a crunch between wealth creation and moral rectitude"; to recognize this is to see the need for viewing economic practice as an area where the development of a full range of virtues must be promoted.

Amstutz has more sympathy for a wealth-creation approach and for "the modernization thesis" that undergirds it. According to his view of things, economic production is shaped primarily and extensively by noneconomic factors—for example, by cultural conceptions of work and obligation. Consequently, schemes such as those set forth by the bishops, which place a strong emphasis on redistribution rather than on production, are bound to fail.

Significantly, however, both Dykema and Amstutz insist on qualifications and nuances that serve to shorten the distance between their positions. The virtues that Dykema insists on linking to economic practice include many of the traits valued by those who celebrate the market system. And while Amstutz oppposes many development schemes, he strongly favors "humanitarian aid" to those who suffer from economic hardship. Furthermore, in their shared opposition to a thoroughgoing statism, each of them reaches into the Christian past for a perspective that provides a much-needed supplement to present-day formulations: Dykema appeals to the "sphere sovereignty" notion of Dutch Calvinism, and Amstutz calls for a recognition of the wisdom contained in Catholic teaching regarding "subsidiarity."

In short, these essays display a much-needed evangelical wrestling with crucial issues of economic discipleship. To be sure, the thoughts expressed in these explorations do not comprise a coherent "magisterial" package. But they are presented as some evangelical probings, engaged in with a sense of ecumenical openness, in the course of a spiritual journey that is far from over.

2 | *Thinking about the Poor: What Evangelicals Can Learn from the Bishops*

Richard J. Mouw

The Roman Catholic bishops are convinced that the gospel provides us with a solid case for the "preferential option for the poor." And to some of us, their conviction on this matter seems so appropriate that it is difficult to imagine how any Christian might set out to deny their point.

There are Christians, however, who do deny it. Many Protestant evangelicals, for example, would find it strange to read a pastoral document that expresses such consistent sympathy for those whose lives are enmeshed in poverty. While they may not actually argue that the Bible expresses a systematic bias *against* the poor, they certainly don't think that the biblical writers tell us to judge the merits of economic policies by considering their impact on "the poor and powerless."

This lack of sympathy for the poor is not just a popular reflex; it also comes through clearly on occasion in more systematic discussions of the biblical data. A good case in point in this regard is John Eidsmoe's discussion of the "temporal causes of abundance and poverty" in his 1984 book entitled *God and Caesar: Biblical Faith and Political Action.* Eidsmoe, a professor at Oral Roberts University, is one of the more thoughtful advocates of the "Christian New Right" perspective, and, unlike many other conservative Protestants, he is sensitive to the need for developing a nuanced discussion of the complexities of poverty.

But Eidsmoe seems hard put to come up with any reason why God might be adamantly opposed to the very existence of some forms of poverty. He argues that just as some societies are poor because of their misuse of natural resources or their refusal to organize their economies in obedience to the divine will, so some individuals "are constantly poor because of unwise stewardship, irresponsible management, or a failure to develop and use their God-given abilities. Others are poor simply because other things are more important to them than wealth."[1]

Fair enough. These kinds of factors do deserve to be included in a comprehensive survey of the things that make for poverty in the world. There is even some legitimacy, as I shall soon explain, in appealing to the biblical witness in alluding to such factors. But surely these patterns do not exhaust the causes of poverty. Eidsmoe rightly acknowledges that there are other matters which must be taken into account, not the least being the fact that some people are poor because of injustices being perpetrated against them. But he cannot allow even this minimal admission to stand without an immediate qualification: "Still others may be poor because of some type of injustice at the hands of other men, though God always has some purpose in allowing this."[2]

While this may be a more nuanced account of poverty than is usually offered by New Rightists, it is not the stuff of which a "preferential option for the poor" is made. Eidsmoe's message to the poverty-stricken is unmistakable: your poverty is most likely your own fault, and if it should turn out that your impoverished condition is not something that you have, in effect, chosen, then it is a state of affairs that God has chosen for you. In Eidsmoe's scheme it is difficult to find any grounds for the poor to raise legitimate complaints about their situation.

There is nothing shameful, Eidsmoe says, about being poor, nor is it a bad thing to be rich. To be sure, the wealthy are required to provide for the needy. But the provisions for the poor mandated by the Bible have nothing to do with governmentally sponsored programs of redistribution or "spending" schemes. Rather, they require acts of individual charity along with support for a free enterprise system that promotes the kind of productivity where "each man profits as he benefits society."[3]

This kind of perspective on economic life—as exemplified here in Eidsmoe's comments on wealth, poverty, charity, and free enterprise—is certainly not the exclusive property of conservative Protestantism. Similar themes have been employed by those Roman Catholics who have been very critical of their bishops' economic views. But even though arguments about economic perspectives that take place in the Roman Catholic community may have strong similarities to arguments that are waged among evangelicals, the theological positions set forth in the debates are never exactly the same. And ecumenical sensitivity requires that we take the differences seriously, especially when those differences are shaped by alternative spiritual traditions.

Alternative Economic Spiritualities

The ecumenical study of alternative economic spiritualities can be a fascinating and illuminating task. By "economic spirituality" I mean the way in which an individual or group views the religious meaning of economic activity. None of us goes about our economic dealings in a purely unreflective way. We operate with an understanding—with varying degrees of explicitness and coherence—of what it means to produce and consume, buy and sell, in healthy ways.

A Christian's understanding of economic meanings will inevitably be related to Christian beliefs and values. "God helps those who help themselves" may seem to be a cliché as it passes over the lips of middle-class Americans. But it is not a *mere* cliché. There are very real and important links between the ways in which we understand economic patterns and our grasp, however rudimentary, of God's "economics." Our language about divine creation and redemption is, after all, laden with the metaphors of production and exchange. A Marxist may find evidence in this fact for the ideological character of theology. But there is also good precedent for viewing the situation in quite different terms. If we are beings whose lives are very much taken up with economic activities, and if we are also beings who are created in the image and likeness of our divine Maker, then it would be very strange if there were not at least some analogy between our understanding of this crucial area of our lives and our grasp of the character of the God whom we are called to serve.

It seems plausible to expect, then, that economic spiritualities will differ from group to group in the Christian community. Differences in theology will likely have implications for the ways in which we construe economic meanings.

Differences in economic spirituality have an important bearing on the evangelical Protestant assessment of the kind of theology that the Roman Catholic bishops set forth in their economic pastoral. On one level there are some clear similarities between the ways in which the theology of the pastoral is evaluated in the two communities. Some evangelical leaders would have strong sympathies with the document, while many laypersons, like their Roman Catholic counterparts, would prefer a stronger defense of the "free enterprise" system.

But the worries of the evangelical laity would, if fully articulated, take a somewhat different shape than the Roman Catholic worries. Consequently, evangelicals who wish to build on the bishops' case in order to lead the evangelical community into a fuller understanding of the economic implications of the gospel must think about how best to communicate that case to the evangelical context.

For one thing, evangelicals need some preparation simply to get to the stage where they are ready to receive theological *teaching* on the subject of economics. Not that Roman Catholics are generally well-prepared for this kind of thing. Archbishop Weakland has recently observed that the detailed Catholic social teachings of the past one hundred years have not been "formative of the thinking of a new and important generation of Catholics in the United States." Weakland argues that this failure to assimilate magisterial teachings regarding the marketplace has much to do with factors that are "at the heart of the immigrant American experience up till the middle of this century." For a long time Roman Catholics were struggling with the need to preserve their core Catholic identity in a predominantly Protestant environment. Because of their minority group status, they saw no "need to prepare themselves for leadership in the larger societal structures." Now that many of them are in those positions of leadership, they find little in official church teaching about the marketplace with which they can strongly identify.[4]

There are interesting parallels between the Catholic experience as described by Archbishop Weakland and the situation of many evangelicals. Evangelical Christians have also begun to "arrive" culturally in recent decades, after many years of alienation from the status quo. Many groups within the broad evangelical coalition have made remarkable ascents on the ladder of social mobility in a rather short period. White Southern fundamentalism, long viewed by elites as a faint echo from a primordial past, can now boldly proclaim itself to be the vanguard of an emergent "moral majority." And a number of ecclesiastical groups that were once without exception situated on the poorer side of any town's tracks—the Assemblies of God and the Church of the Nazarene, to cite just two prominent examples—are now more often than not the sponsors of the most affluent and flourishing congregations in the suburbs.

Like their Roman Catholic counterparts, many of these evangelical layfolk would find little to applaud in the bishops' economic deliverances. However, for Roman Catholic laypeople, as Archbishop Weakland has argued, the rejection has to do with a failure to assimilate their church's detailed economic teachings. Evangelical Protestants, on the other hand, cannot be accused of ignoring a body of economic teachings, since there is usually nothing there for them to ignore.

Evangelicals have not been inclined to develop detailed theological views about this area of human interaction. Not that there are no available resources for doing so. The conservative ecclesial community of North America is a coalition representing a number of confessional traditions: Baptist, Wesleyan, Reformed, Mennonite, "free church," and the like. The study of these traditions reveals that there were times in the past when these communities had a much more thoroughly articulated theological basis for economic interaction than is the case today. The writings of Calvin and Wesley are a good case in point.

Evangelicals in contemporary North America have not nurtured their communal theological-economic memories. Instead they have been content to work with the bare minimum of theological articulation regarding economic matters. This minimalist account gets expressed in the form of slogans and biblical "proof texts" such as "You get what you work for," "There are no free rides in life," "If you don't work, you don't eat," and "The poor we will always have with us."

But we must not be misled by the apparent superficiality of this cliché-studded approach to economic thought. The evangelicals' sloganeering pattern does embody a relatively coherent system of economic meanings. There is a kind of economic "worldview" at work in the evangelical community, one that is beginning to be set forth in a more articulate way, as in Eidsmoe's discussion and in other more extensive writings that have been produced in recent years.[5]

When I refer to an operative evangelical "worldview" vis-à-vis economic matters, I do not mean to suggest that there is no diversity of economic thought among evangelicals. The sorts of views set forth in several periodicals such as *Sojourners* and *The Other Side*, to say nothing of the case that Ron Sider has detailed in his well-known writings,[6] represent self-consciously evangelical formulations that have much in common with the views developed in the bishops' pastoral. But this is a minority strain of evangelical thought that stands alongside a more dominant perspective. And it is this majority viewpoint that I am focusing on here, giving special attention to the ways in which poverty is understood.

Theological Bases for Economic Spirituality

There are different possible theologies of poverty, depending on what theological categories are employed or featured in thinking in an intentionally Christian manner about what it means to be poor.

For example, some Christians in recent years have utilized eschatological notions in dealing with the meaning of poverty. They have argued that in the present age God is at work preparing the world for a new and exciting future in which a very different economic order will obtain. And they believe that the poor, or "the poor and the oppressed," are in an important sense the vanguard of this new economic order.

This way of making the case has some obvious parallels to the Marxist scheme, in which the proletariat is viewed as the universal class whose groanings and yearnings are in fact shaped by desires that prophetically anticipate the post-revolutionary age. And many Christian proponents of liberation theology have been directly influenced by Marxism in spelling out their understanding of the special eschatological status of the poor and the oppressed.

One can also argue, of course, that in developing his understanding of the proletariat, Marx himself was secularizing a theme that originated in the teachings of the Hebrew prophets. However that argument about actual historical influences might go, the notion that the poor have a special kind of eschatological status in the biblical scheme is one that can be entertained quite apart from any sympathies for Marxist dogma. The biblical witness makes it clear that there is an important sense in which the poor are "blessed," and that those who hope to participate in the joys of the future kingdom must cast their lot with the poor and the suffering in the present age.

This is not the sort of theological emphasis that will appeal much to most evangelicals. While we have not been immune to a fascination with elaborate eschatological schemes—witness the "Bible prophecy" speculations of Hal Lindsey and company—evangelical interest in such matters is never far removed from a desire to preserve what we evangelicals view as the important biblical distinction between the "saved" and the "lost." Any scheme that would give the impression of romanticizing "the poor" as a generic class will be treated—and, as I see it, rightly so—with much suspicion. It is not "the poor" in some unqualified sense whose desires point us to the coming reign of justice; rather, it is those people who in their experience of poverty and oppression consciously yearn for the coming of the divine Savior. The blessedness of the poor, biblically speaking, resides in the awareness that God can bring genuine liberation from all that oppresses our sinful race.

Another theological concept that is often given prominence in accounts of poverty is the Incarnation. Christ is viewed as being present in a special way among the poor and suffering ones. Since

Christ himself has told us (see Matt. 25) that our actions toward "the least of these" are indeed actions directed toward him, obligations to the poor are viewed as obligations to Christ. Incarnational emphases have played an important role in various economic spiritualities— Franciscan piety is an obvious example—and it is impossible to discount the relevance of this theme for a proper Christian understanding of poverty, as the bishops themselves note (par. 55).

However, incarnationalism by itself cannot provide us with an adequate theology of poverty. Critics of Mother Teresa's self-consciously incarnationalist ministry often complain that the call to "personal presence" avoids difficult but important questions about the structural causes and patterns of poverty. That sort of complaint is misguided if it is intended to disparage the important work of the Missionaries of Charity. But it is a necessary reminder that the spontaneous, unadorned imitation of Christ must be supplemented by systematic reflection on the complex realities of poverty and oppression, as well as the development of programs that are designed to cope with those complexities.

Yet another way of organizing theological reflection about poverty is to employ the creation-and-fall motif. This theme is very basic to the economic perspective that the bishops set forth in their pastoral letter. The first item dealt with under the heading "Biblical Perspectives" is "Created in God's Image." Here the bishops lay out the themes that serve as the fundamental theological reference-points for the rest of their discussion. Men and women are created in the divine image, called by God to "share in the creative activity of God" and "to care for the earth" so that "by their labor they are unfolding the Creator's work" (par. 32). But sinful human beings have attempted to overturn God's creation designs by denying their creaturely status. By turning away from the love and service of God, they have introduced idolatrous patterns into the created order, "such as the quest for unrestrained power and the desire for great wealth." Thus "sin simultaneously alienates human beings from God and shatters the solidarity of the human community" (par. 33).

The bishops believe that an awareness of the realities of creation and fall is foundational for a proper understanding of the Bible's teachings about economic justice:

> Every human person is created as an image of God, and the denial of dignity to a person is a blot on this image. Creation is a gift to all men and women, not to be appropriated for the benefit of a few; its beauty is an object of joy and reverence. The same God who came to the aid of an oppressed people

and formed them into a covenant community continues to hear the cries of the oppressed and to create communities which are responsive to God's word. God's love and life are present when people can live in a community of faith and hope. These cardinal points of the faith of Israel also furnish the religious context for understanding the saving action of God in the life and teaching of Jesus. (par. 40)

Poverty is one of the ways in which created human beings are kept from participating in the tasks associated with their status as the images of God. To work for a just order is to seek "the establishment of minimum levels of participation in the life of the human community of all persons" (par. 70). That kind of pursuit of justice honors God's creation intentions and aligns us with the redemptive ministry of Jesus.

It should be obvious that this creational perspective, which provides the theological basis for the economic spirituality that the bishops advocate, does not preclude the other theological concepts we have mentioned. Indeed, the bishops do make some explicit use of eschatological and incarnational themes, and their account could easily be extended to incorporate those motifs: the new economic order promised as a part of the coming transformation is the flowering of the creational design that looms so large in the pastoral letter, and Jesus' incarnational identification with "the least of these" in our broken world is a manifestation of God's pledge to bring the creational-redemptive plan to fruition.

Like the Roman Catholic bishops, evangelical Christians are inclined to give special emphasis to the creation-and-fall motif when dealing with wealth, poverty, and the issues of economic justice. But they employ this theme for very different ends. The bishops' account of creation functions as the basis for a warning against the dangers of wealth and a reminder of God's special concern for the poor and the lowly. They see sin as very quickly becoming woven into the structures of human interaction, an emphasis that makes it equally natural for them to speak of poverty as primarily a matter of "exclusion and powerlessness" (pars. 49-50, 78).

Not so with the evangelical defenders of the free market. While they too begin by detailing how God's creation purposes bear on economic activity, their subsequent account of the sinful distortion of these divine purposes does not move them to think of the poor as victims of "exclusion and powerlessness."

Brian Griffiths' use of the creation-and-fall motif is instructive in this regard:

In the context of Genesis the fundamental affirmation which any Christian must make is that the world in which we live is God's world. He created it and he created us. We bear an integral relationship to the material world and it is because of this that the business of creating and using wealth is a natural activity for mankind. Life itself demands that we be continually involved in the process of wealth creation. The basic necessities for living are not provided like manna; the land has to be cultivated, the sea has to be harvested, minerals have to be extracted, the city has to be supplied with services. God created us with the capacity and the desire to do all these things. Life itself, therefore, demands that we use what God has given us to provide the necessities.

But God intended far more than that. We were not created to live our lives in hunger or on the breadline, in a state of poverty using only the barest minimum. God intended us to enjoy his world. The land which he promised to Israel was to be flowing with milk and honey. No Christian should feel a sense of guilt from living in a decent house, driving a solid car, wearing a proper suit of clothes or eating a good meal. If we take seriously the fact that this world is God's world, then the business of creating wealth has a Christian foundation.[7]

Note that the initial formulation here regarding God's creating intentions is not all that far removed from the bishops' account. Each discussion begins with an emphasis on the need for human beings to develop the God-given material environment.

But the acknowledgment of the fact of poverty seems to have a very different role in Griffiths' discussion than it does in the bishops' pastoral. The bishops say that since God did not want poverty to occur, we should all look at our patterns of economic activity to see how we can correct this sinful condition. Griffiths says that since God did not intend poverty, we should not feel guilty if, as a result of our labors, we are enjoying the blessings associated with material abundance.

How is it that two groups who are inclined to approach economic issues with the same theological categories can so quickly diverge in their assessments of the fact of poverty? Is there anything significant going on here?

Well, there is undoubtedly much that is going on that has little to do with theology. But there are also some important theological factors at work here. And even though my own assessment of the fact of poverty is similar to that of the bishops, I am concerned that the typical evangelical case not be dismissed out of hand. To wrestle with the issues here is both ecumenically and pastorally important, since the dispute at this point is one that we must all address if we are to develop a more effective economic spirituality for the North American context.

Here it is important to identify three factors of a theological nature that have shaped the ways in which many evangelicals formulate their views on basic economic issues. Not all of them are of equal weight, but each of them has to be taken into account if we are going to be clear about these matters.

The first factor has to do with the specific biblical data to which evangelicals appeal when they talk about the issues of wealth and poverty. There is a significant strand in the Bible that emphasizes a connection between poverty and personal indolence. This strand seems especially prominent in wisdom literature, as in Proverbs 6:9-11:

> How long will you lie there, O sluggard?
> When will you arise from your sleep?
> A little sleep, a little slumber,
> a little folding of the hands to rest,
> and poverty will come upon you like a vagabond,
> and want like an armed man.

This is the kind of biblical emphasis that informs many of the cliché-ridden responses of evangelicals when they discuss the causes of poverty. What they are expressing is not mere platitudes but bits of American popular wisdom that are in turn shaped by the popular "wisdom" of the Hebrew Scriptures.

A second factor is the strong volitionalism of evangelical religious thought. Indeed, it is this volitionalist pattern that influences the choice of the biblical materials just cited as the central data for evangelical thinking about economics. Evangelical religion is very much a religion of "wills." Choice is crucial to the evangelical scheme of things; thus the strong evangelical plea for "a personal decision for Christ," and the correlative resistance to a strong sacramentalism that would separate grace from choice. The implications for economic thought should be obvious. Economic life is a matter of choices, of decisions.

Suppose there is a ghetto in one's city where thousands of poor people live. How are we to explain their poverty? Is it the fault of middle-class evangelicals? No; when did they make choices that resulted in the poverty of their neighbors? Is the fault, then, to be traced to the choices of corporate decision-makers? It is difficult to locate such an "hour of decision." So the options finally boil down to those that Eidsmoe discusses: poverty is either the result of choices made by the poor themselves or the result of divine choice. In either case we non-poor do not have to try directly to reverse the situation. Rather, we must encourage the poor to make different choices or to accept the divine decision that their low estate is a necessary thing.

A third factor is a fondness for an "either-now-or-never" assessment of the way God deals with unfortunate situations. The fact of this fondness struck me clearly one evening when I was asked to lead a group of evangelical business leaders in thinking about "the gospel and the poor." Most of my audience was not very happy with my views on the subject. In the general discussion they began by arguing that things weren't all that bad; poverty simply was not the sort of complex problem that I made it out to be. Fortunately, I had a few articulate allies in the audience, and it finally became clear to the group that the optimistic view would not prevail. So my critics switched to a very different approach: things are so bad, they argued, that there is nothing we can do about it.

The pattern was clear: either poverty is so desperate that we need not do anything about it, or it is not desperate enough for us to do anything about it. The one conjunction of claims that they refused to accept was that poverty was a very desperate thing and that we must do something about it. Thus the evangelical insistence on the quick fix: either-now-or-never, which in effect becomes "now is out of the question, so never."

This is no trivial issue. Evangelicals have a difficult time maintaining what Robert Bilheimer has called "a spirituality for the long haul."[8] Those Pentecostal and neo-charismatic preachers who are presently proclaiming a "name it and claim it" approach to healing and prosperity are, in a significant sense, manifesting a deeply rooted evangelical propensity.

Roman Catholicism, on the other hand, is very much a "long haul" religion. The God of Catholics takes a long time to accomplish things; the Catholic God even seems to prefer extended and deliberate processes. For example, God seems to enjoy "the *development* of dogma." Witness also the incomprehension that most Roman Catholics experience when they encounter evangelical enthusiasm for "scientific creationism"; Catholics find it easy to believe that God could have created the world *and* have taken a long time to do so—utilizing the processes of evolution if that was the divine preference. On the other hand, one reason why many evangelicals cannot tolerate "theistic evolution" is—if my hunch is correct—that it takes too long.

To be sure, evangelicals are selective in applying their "either-now-or-never" pattern to the issues of life. There is much to be explored in analyzing this pattern of selectivity. But there is no question in my mind that economics is one area where it is clearly at work. Thus the bishops' entreaties that we not be put off "by the magnitude and complexity of these problems," and that while we cannot expect utopian solutions in the present, we must proceed with the confidence "that God's providence is not and will not be lacking to us today" (par. 364)—these "long haul" urgings are not likely to trigger evangelical enthusiasms.

An Evangelical Economic Spirituality

Now I must explain why these factors that shape the economic spirituality of evangelicals should not simply be dismissed out of hand, even by those of us whose sympathies lie more with the bishops on these matters.

To begin with, the evangelical focus on the connection between poverty and indolence is defensible to an extent. Since the Bible itself does point to this connection, we cannot fault evangelicals for bringing it to our attention. There *are* poor people who do need to hear warnings against laziness.

The problem with the evangelical focus on laziness as the cause of poverty is that it takes one legitimate theme and makes it function as the sole organizing principle for understanding the problems of the poor. People who think in this reductionist manner need to be challenged by the larger perspective on these matters that the Bible presents.

A similar case must be made with regard to evangelical voluntarism. The Bible does call people to make a decision about God's offer of redemption. Human choices should be respected as important factors in God's dealing with the creation. It must even be noted that among those who have paid so much attention in recent years to the Bible's emphasis on liberation for the poor there is a regrettable tendency to downplay the important biblical insistence that the poor must receive "good news." Ultimately, the crucial problems of the human condition can be solved only if human beings hear and *believe* the gospel, repenting of their sins and accepting in a personal way God's offer of eternal salvation.

But to acknowledge the important volitional aspect or "moment" of God's gracious dealings with the creation does not mean that all of the problems of the poor would go away if they would "only believe." The reality of poverty has to do with more than individual choices. Evangelicals rightly see injustice as beginning with the personal rebellion of our first parents. But it has come to be woven into the very *textures* of human interaction. Poverty is also—and in a significant sense—a "systemic" reality, a fact that evangelical volitionalism has a difficult time accounting for.

There is also something good to be said about the "either-now-or-never" syndrome. It has produced all kinds of good things by instilling a sense of the urgency of proclaiming the gospel and an awareness of the ever-present possibility of a manifestation of the signs and wonders of the Spirit's power. A theology that features a God who *always* works slowly leaves much to be desired.

The problem with evangelicalism is not that it is sensitive to the present manifestations of the reign of Christ but that it assumes that what is not "now" must be classified under "never." More evangelical attention must be given to both the "now-or-later" and the "now-and-later" possibilities.

But we have not done enough with these three points if we simply call for a more balanced appraisal of them. North American culture has deep currents with which we must reckon, and evangelical Christians have solid instincts for tapping into them. Anyone who wants to develop an economic spirituality that connects with uniquely American "habits of the heart" would do well to study the patterns of evangelical piety. This is certainly true when it comes to the spiritual underpinnings of North American economic thought and practice. The strong sense of the importance of work, the emphasis on individual integrity and agency, the spirit of self-reliance and entrepreneurial optimism—all of these are deeply rooted in the American psyche. And evangelicals have known how to speak to and for a culture whose psyche is shaped by such thoughts and attitudes.

Those of us who sympathize with the account of poverty offered in the bishops' pastoral have not yet been especially successful in communicating our vision to ordinary Christian people in North America. What the Roman Catholic bishops need to think about is the fact that many of their own parishioners have by now embraced an economic spirituality that is not far removed from that which typifies much of evangelicalism. Many Catholic families for whom the memories of immigration are still very real have come to resonate to many of the deep traits that evangelicals find it so easy to laud: the sense of self-reliance, the "Protestant" work ethic, and the celebration of entrepreneurship.

Of course, to speak to these themes in a proper Christian

manner is not to accept them as normative. But it is to realize their power while at the same time we probe these spiritual currents to see if there is confusion and ambivalence at work that we might be able to address in edifying ways.

The Roman Catholic bishops obviously sensed a need to speak about economic issues in an edifying way. Pastoral letters are usually meant to address pressing problems, and it is clear that the bishops viewed themselves as speaking to critical questions of contemporary life.

They are not alone in viewing present-day economics in terms of spiritual and moral crisis. Nor is this shared perception something that is easily dismissed as a "leftist" delusion. In his book *Two Cheers for Capitalism,* published in 1978, the "neo-conservative" Irving Kristol argues in a convincing manner that "the accumulated moral capital" that our society has inherited from traditional religion is almost depleted, with the result that we are increasingly vulnerable to moral "nihilism." And the sad thing is that many staunch proponents of capitalism have greeted this nihilism as if it were just one more money-making opportunity: "For them, it is 'business as usual.'"[9]

The failure here, Kristol argues, is a defect of vision: "In the end, you can maintain the belief that private vices, freely exercised, will lead to public benefits only if you are further persuaded that human nature can never be utterly corrupted by these vices, but rather will always transcend them." The naiveté of this view is due to the fact that "the secular, 'libertarian' tradition of capitalism—as distinct from the Protestant-bourgeois tradition—simply had too limited an imagination when it came to vice."[10]

Kristol is right to distinguish between secularist and Christian traditions of capitalism. Too often this distinction is not acknowledged, and as a result any serious criticism of the assumptions that prevail in the market economy is automatically categorized in some quarters as "leftist socialism." It would certainly be wrong to attempt to pin such a label on the U.S. bishops. A careful reading of their pastoral letter reveals that they are calling for a revival of themes and practices associated with the Christian tradition of capitalism to which Kristol points.

The bishops are aware of the fact that this tradition needs to be updated in important ways. But it also offers much important moral capital for the underwriting of a healthy market system. Not the least of its contributions is the sensitivity that Kristol finds so obviously lacking in the secularist strain: a realistic awareness of human vice. This sensitivity has continued to be cultivated in the theologies of both Catholicism and evangelicalism, and a special effort must be made to retain this awareness in the corresponding economic spiritualities.

An insistence on the very real phenomenon of human sin will require Christians to be more restrained in their enthusiasm about the unregulated pursuit of economic "self-interest" than is typical of the more romanticist notions of secular capitalists. But it will also make them wary of "statist" solutions to the problems of economic injustice, since the designs of governmental authorities are no less susceptible to the strong influence of human vice. Instead, Christians will insist upon pursuing the more difficult path of moral reform—not the simple-minded "changed hearts will change society" kind of moral reform to which evangelicals have often reverted, but a more nuanced approach that recognizes that structural injustice must be dealt with by structured communal efforts on the part of Christians and other persons of goodwill.

Both evangelicals and Roman Catholics can find precedents in their own communal histories for creative attempts at linking social reform with movements of spiritual renewal. Evangelicals have some special advantages in this regard, since some of their best efforts have been made in England and North America—Puritanism and Wesleyanism are obvious cases in point. These past experiments, which embodied important strains of economic spirituality, continue to be relevant to the present situation in a culture whose legacy of public symbols draws heavily on Anglo-American religious sources.

Indeed, evangelicals even have some potentially significant "mediating structures" already in place for expediting the retrieval of reformist memories. Evangelical laypeople have established an impressive array of vocationally oriented groups in recent decades: the Full Gospel Businessman's Fellowship, the Fellowship of Christian Athletes, and similar groups among, for example, farmers, airline personnel, and medical and legal professionals. Interestingly, the membership of such groups also includes growing numbers of Roman Catholics. To be sure, these groups presently focus on issues of personal piety and personal evangelism. But they also have the potential for promoting new patterns of economic spirituality.

The present-day crisis in economic life cannot be dealt with properly unless very ordinary Christian people begin to think and act and feel in a manner that is shaped by a genuinely full gospel. Only the Holy Spirit can bring a true revival of Christian discipleship. But the widespread appropriation by Christian laity of the sort of teachings set forth in the bishops' economic pastoral is a process that seems one likely way for the Spirit to grace us all with a new vision for economic obedience.

3 | A Lesson in Constructive Theology

Robert K. Johnston

Ten years ago I heard the Protestant theologian José Míguez Bonino describe the development of his own theology using the experience of his Roman Catholic colleague, Gustavo Gutiérrez. He described how Gutiérrez felt called by the gospel to minister to the poor in Lima, Peru. There Gutiérrez came to three conclusions, conclusions that were at once experiential, theological, and political. First, in living with the poor, he found it necessary to discard the notion that poverty is ennobling. It is evil; it dehumanizes people. Second, as he tried to understand the nature of this poverty, he discovered that poverty is structural. It is not largely the consequence of people's sins. Third, Gutiérrez concluded that ministry, if it is to express concretely the love of Christ, must necessarily involve working to alter oppressive social structures. Nothing less is an adequate expression of the gospel.

Such a process of moving from the pastoral to the political while incorporating the pastoral within the political is evident as well in the U.S. bishops' pastoral letter on the economy. In proclaiming the gospel for these times, the bishops have begun with "the hurts and hopes of our people": "We feel the pain of our sisters and brothers who are poor, unemployed, homeless, living on the edge. The poor and vulnerable are on our doorsteps, in our parishes, our service agencies and our shelters" (par. 10). Consequently, the bishops have felt compelled to speak out on behalf of a more human economic structure, one that both fosters the "faith, good will, and generosity of our people" and furthers the American dream of "liberty and justice for all" (pars. 11, 9).

Prior to Vatican II, Catholic social teaching might have turned to notions of natural law for theological support; now it is more directly the gospel that both motivates and grounds the bishops' discussion. The result is at times eloquent, as the bishops' critique of U.S. food and agriculture policy shows:

> A world with nearly half a billion hungry people is not one in which food security has been achieved. The problem of hunger has a special significance for those who read the scriptures and profess the Christian faith. From the Lord's command to feed the hungry, to the eucharist we celebrate as the bread of life, the fabric of our faith demands that we be creatively engaged in sharing the food that sustains life. There is no more basic human need. The gospel imperative takes on new urgency in a world of abundant harvests where hundreds of millions of people face starvation. Relief and prevention of their hunger cannot be left to the arithmetic of the marketplace. (par. 282)

At other times, the bishops struggle to find the relationship between church and world, gospel and culture. Moral and theological considerations do not always open up to specific solutions (see par. 258). Nevertheless, the document remains remarkable; it has rightfully captured the attention of both church and society.

An Evangelical Response

Evangelicals can learn much from the bishops' letter on the American economy. Only recently have evangelicals recognized the need for doing such constructive theology. Too often, whether in our colleges' policies for hiring faculty or in our pulpits' witness, we have wrongly assumed either that biblical exegesis is coterminous with theology, or that historical theology (the theology of Luther or Calvin or Wesley) is a sufficient constructive theology for today. The results have been predictable and unfortunate. Too often our theology has remained disincarnate, theoretically well-shaped but lifeless and abstract.

For example, we have sometimes elevated our notion of Scripture even over our view of Christ—the abstract over the concrete.[1] It is the battle *for* the Bible that has captured our attention, not our battle with the Bible on behalf of Christ and his kingdom. Kierkegaard's biting critique of the church in his day might well be applied to segments of modern evangelical Protestantism. He tells of a lobby that has two doors. Over the one is a sign that says "heaven," and over the other is a sign reading "lecture about heaven." The church people of his day, chides Kierkegaard, consider the options and then choose the lecture.

Given an analogous situation in some quarters today, evangelicals find themselves in a position to benefit from the bishops' pastoral. In particular, we must take seriously the obligation to work for the transformation of society. The theology of Paul without the witness of James is no longer adequate. In its call for effective Christian action lies the heart of the pastoral's *message*. But evangelicals can also learn from the pastoral's *method*. If we are to once again both think and act Christianly, we must recover the way to do the theological task. As evangelicals seek the renewal of both church and society, we can learn from the bishops that our theology must be integrative, interactive, and public.

An Integrative Theology

The bishops state their methodology at the outset: "This letter is based on a long tradition of Catholic social thought, rooted in the Bible and developed over the past century by the popes and the Second Vatican Council in response to modern economic conditions" (par. 25). They understand themselves to be consistent with Pope Paul VI, who insisted that Christian communities have the responsibility "to analyze with objectivity the situation which is proper to their own country, to shed on it the light of the Gospel's unalterable words and to draw principles of reflection, norms of judgment and directives for action from the social teaching of the church" (par. 26).

Such an awareness of the plurality of theology's resources informs the economic pastoral from beginning to end. The bishops propose an ethical framework that is "both faithful to the Gospel and shared by human experience and reason" (par. 61). They believe their convictions have "a biblical basis" and are "supported by a long tradition of theological and philosophical reflection and through the reasoned analysis of human experience by contemporary men and women" (par. 28). One example will illustrate the point. In their argument that society needs to have a special commitment to the poor, the bishops root their belief biblically in "the radical command to love one's neighbor as self" (par. 87). They then turn to the teaching of the church for support, quoting both Paul VI and John Paul II. Finally, they argue that such a position is reasonable because it is not adversarial, pitting one group against the next. All benefit when all are able "to share in and contribute to the common good" (par. 88).

In *Evangelicals at an Impasse: Biblical Authority in Practice,* I argued that evangelicals need to recognize in the theological task a triad of interactive resources: Scripture, tradition, and the world. "Theology is the translation of Christian truth into contemporary idiom with an eye toward biblical foundations, traditional formulations, and contemporary judgments."[2] Although evangelicals are committed to biblical truth, we too often seem unable to formulate this truth in adequate Christian thought and action. We struggle with how best to interrelate and combine theology's potential resources. Consequently, the bishops' letter is instructive because it provides the evangelical community with a successful model.

In a recent collection of essays, Andover-Newton professor Gabriel Fackre sketched the contours of an adequate method for evangelical theological reflection. Interestingly, it is a method consistent with that found in the pastoral.[3] Fackre argues that it is the world—both our cultural analysis and contemporary experience—that provides theology its setting. Culture gives theology its language and modes of rational discourse. Our experience raises questions afresh and offers intimations of truth. Within this context, the church through its tradition, whether living or ancient, supplies theology with a valuable resource. Through creed, catechism, and proclamation, the church provides theology its perspective.

If the world is theology's *setting* and the church with its tradition is theology's *resource,* Fackre understands Scripture to be theology's *source.* The *substance* of the biblical record is the gospel story. Its authority, one might even say, rests in its testimony to the decisive events in the faith narrative. These events must be judged by a final *standard,* Jesus Christ himself, both as he speaks through his Spirit, providing illumination, and as he provides an objective norm against which to judge all truth in light of his full, historical self-disclosure. Thus there is in any theological investigation a movement from the wider culture through the Christian tradition to the biblical record with its definitive good news of Jesus Christ as revealed through his Spirit.

Moreover, there is not only the need for theologians to penetrate through the circles of culture, church, and Scripture in order to understand the full implication of the gospel of Jesus Christ. There is also the corresponding need for theologians to take their Christian perspective back through a reading of the biblical text and an understanding of the church past and present to the world, where theology will be expressed afresh in each new time and place. Fackre's own diagram illustrates this obverse relationship of the movement of theological *investigation* and that of theological *presentation.*[4]

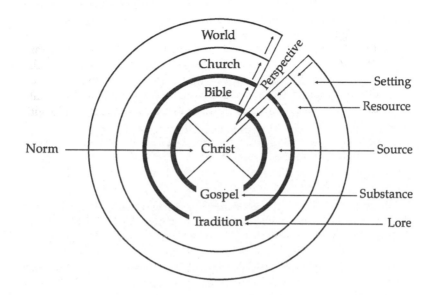

Theology finds its center in Jesus Christ, but both its starting and finishing points will be the culture in which we live. The outline of the pastoral provides evidence of such an understanding. The letter is introduced with the bishops' description of U.S. economic life (Chapter 1). Next it turns to explore a biblical perspective (par. 29) centering in Jesus Christ and then provides basic Catholic social teaching (Chapter 2). After applying this Christian moral vision to selected economic policy issues, the document calls for "A New American Experiment: Partnership for the Public Good" (Chapters 3 and 4).

The presentation of each of the theological resources is thorough. *Biblically,* the pastoral is well-informed, presenting a vision of creation, covenant, kingdom, discipleship, and hope. The critical discussion of the Gospel of Luke is representative, revealing in Jesus' life a pattern of Christian living that raises up the poor (pars. 48-49). Rooted biblically, the ethical reflection is also "shaped by the rich and complex *tradition* of Catholic life and thought" (par. 56). The document draws its inspiration from papal social pronouncements— *Rerum Novarum* (1891), *Quadragesimo Anno* (1931), *Pacem in Terris* (1963), *Gaudium et Spes* (1965), *Populorum Progressio* (1967), and *Laborem Exercens* (1981)—as well as from a host of other classical sources.

Applied *contextually* to the U.S. economy, this social vision proves powerful. The bishops are pragmatic, focusing their exploration of the economy on those aspects where reform seems realistic and Catholic social teaching relevant. Thus, in light of their biblical and theological investigation, the bishops turn from a general awareness of the U.S. economy and its current crisis to a detailed social-scientific analysis of four issues: employment, poverty, food and agriculture, and the international economic order. They are aware of the differences of opinion present in society. They are also cognizant of their own lack of expertise. Yet they realize that theology cannot remain disincarnate. Guidelines for action are demanded.

An Interactive Theology

In his commentary on the economic pastoral, Charles Curran notes that in the last two decades a shift has occurred within Roman Catholic theology "from a static and deductive methodology to one more inductive."[5] The bishops' original mandate for the pastoral on the American economy was a letter on "Christianity and Capitalism." Because the bishops began their task inductively, going out to the people and listening to their experiences, they ended up changing their focus. They realized that they had to ask what Catholic social teaching could contribute to current issues in the U.S. economy. This experiential starting point was lost sight of in the first draft of the letter, which moved logically from the more general biblical and traditional analysis to the more specific cultural application. The result was both misleading as to process and ponderous in effect. Recognizing this, the bishops did some reworking, placing cultural analysis at the beginning of the letter both to interest the lay reader and to show the interaction between reflection and experience that actually took place in the document's formation (see pars. 1-21).

The bishops are sensitive to the criticism that they have made a mistake in entering the "secular" arena of employment rates and international economics. "Yet the affairs of the world," they conclude, "including economic ones, cannot be separated from the spiritual hunger of the human heart" (par. 327). Thus the reality of U.S. economic life compels the bishops to explore "the biblical vision of humanity and the church's moral and religious tradition as a framework for asking the deeper questions about the meaning of economic life and for actively responding to them" (par. 327). The bishops move back and forth from theory to practice and from reflection to a call for action. In almost Protestant language, the bishops challenge their readers to accept their Christian vocation—"praise of God and . . . concrete deeds of justice and service" (par. 327). There is, in other words, a two-way traffic between culture and Christianity that is both necessary and desirable.

Here again evangelicals have much to learn from the bishops. Fearful of replacing revelation with relevance, evangelicals have often failed to connect their theology with life. Speaking for one wing of evangelicalism today, Clark Pinnock states, "I see the current tendency to relate theology to struggles of the present day, while commendable if it were to represent a desire to apply the Scriptures, to be a recipe for Scripture-twisting on a grand scale."[6] This fear of Scripture-twisting has kept most evangelicals from adopting an interactive theological method. At best, cultural analysis has been limited to theological application. That is, correct doctrine is deduced first from Scripture, then applied culturally.

Gordon-Conwell theologian David Wells presents the two major theological options governing the relationship of theological reflection and its cultural context: "In the one understanding of contextualization, the revelatory trajectory moves only from authoritative Word into contemporary culture; in the other, the trajectory moves both from text to context and from context to text, and in the midst of this traffic the interpreter, rather like a police officer at a busy intersection, emerges as the sovereign arbiter as to what God's Word for our time actually is."[7] While Wells' pejorative description of the second alternative clearly underscores his preference for the first alternative, the bishops have recognized—I believe rightly—that they have no other choice but to accept the historical challenge of full and open interaction between church and culture.

If our goal is to make the power of the gospel operative, then assessment of the structures and practices of the economy must help shape the theological dialogue. "The soundness of our prudential judgments," the bishops recognize, "depends not only on the moral force of our principles, but also on the accuracy of our information and the validity of our assumptions" (par. 134). And this mutual interaction will be ongoing. Understanding will result from as well as precede obedient action. A dialectic between word and deed and between church and society must be established. Thus, without fear and without oversimplification, the bishops call for "a conversion of the heart" that will issue forth in "a holiness in the world." They challenge both church and society to become models of participation and collaboration (par. 358).

Such an interactional theological model reflects a recognition of the bishops' historical consciousness. They shy away from offering "a technical blueprint" (par. 133); they limit themselves to questions and recommendations (e.g., pars. 148, 215). They recognize that there is "room for diversity of opinion in the church and in the U.S. society on *how* to protect the human dignity and economic rights of all our brothers and sisters" (par. 84). Their economic recommendations lack the authority of formal church teaching and invite debate. Yet they also call for faithful action. The vision must "be translated into concrete measures" (par. 19, PM).

A Public Theology

The bishops write to provide members of their own church with guidance for responsible action. But they also note that "at the same time, we want to add our voice to the public debate about the directions in which the U.S. economy should be moving. We seek the cooperation and support of those who do not share our faith or tradition" (par. 27). Desiring "a renewed public moral vision," the bishops appeal "both to Christians and to all in our pluralistic society" (pars. 27, 61).

In order to strengthen their public appeal, the bishops turn not only to Catholic social teaching but also to "traditional American values" (par. 7). It is "the American dream" (par. 9, PM; par. 14), "the American promise of liberty and justice for all" (par. 19), and "the unfinished business in the American experiment in freedom and justice for all" (par. 9; cf. pars. 296, 322) that become a common refrain in the letter. The bishops appeal to the American commitment to work ("It is a deep conviction of American culture that work is central to the freedom and well-being of people") and even to the advantages of the market system in the United States (pars. 141, 8).

Behind such patriotic rhetoric is the conviction that "human understanding and religious belief are complementary, not contradictory" (par. 61). "What the Bible and Christian tradition teach, human wisdom confirms" (par. 65). The best of Christian conviction and American values correlate. Thus, in arguing for the continuation of family farms, the bishops state, "Both Catholic social teaching and the traditions of our country have emphasized the importance of maintaining the rich plurality of social institutions that enhances personal freedom and increases the opportunity for participation in community life" (par. 235). Again, in concluding the letter, the bishops turn first to the American dream of making this world "a better place for people to live in," and then to the fact that as members of a "catholic" or universal church, they must "raise their sights to a concern for the well-being of everyone" (par. 363). This correlation of human wisdom with Christian truth even prompts the bishops to comment that one can find in John XXIII's encyclical *Peace on Earth* both an expression of the gospel and an echo of the U.N.'s Universal Declaration on Human Rights (par. 80).

There are problems in conflating public virtue and Christian faith, problems that I will discuss in the following section. The ideological captivity of the church is an ever-present danger. But there are also real strengths in this approach. Since the 1920s American evangelicals have wrongly turned inward in their theology and church life, neglecting the public arena. Unable to develop a corporate ethic for an increasingly industrialized, urban environment, frustrated with their failure over Prohibition, and ridiculed for their unscientific attitudes in such debacles as the Scopes trial, evangelicals retreated. Often members of marginal immigrant groups and disproportionately less affluent and well-educated than their fellow Americans, evangelicals in the twentieth century have failed—until recently—to engage American society in meaningful ways. According to David Moberg, this has been the period of "the great reversal."[8] Evangelicals have turned away from an earlier concern for the whole person, for evangelism and social witness, for the life of the church and life in the world; they have fled from the political, concentrating instead on the spiritual life.

Thankfully, this period in evangelical church life is ending. Evangelicals, from the Moral Majority to the community that publishes *Sojourners*, are recognizing the need for a whole gospel that is engaged in all of life. One will not always agree with a particular political position, but one should applaud this new resolve. As Carl F. H. Henry wrote prophetically in 1947 in *The Uneasy Conscience of Modern Fundamentalism*, "If historic Christianity is again to compete as a vital world ideology . . . it must offer a formula for a new world mind with spiritual ends, involving evangelical affirmations in political, economic, sociological, and educational realms, local and international."[9] The bishops have provided us with an important model for challenging the world mind.

Ongoing Concerns

I am writing this chapter while on sabbatical in Sweden. My Swedish colleagues observe that in the English language, it is important to listen for the "but." What precedes this conjunction can often be discarded; what immediately follows is the central concern. Although I go beyond the affirmation of the bishops' theological method as integrative, interactive, and public, I do not wish to be interpreted as chiefly critical of their document. Evangelicals have much to learn from this bold attempt at collaborative, constructive theology. Nevertheless, we must direct questions to the bishops *for the sake of our common theological task.*

First, any *public* theology must acknowledge the truth in the claim made by Latin American liberation theologians that "theology without ideology is dead." Theology must be incarnated. The gospel message must find a concrete means of expression in any given place and time. Too often the doctrine of the church has remained ethereal and lifeless. There is, nonetheless, an important corollary: theology must never find itself in ideological captivity. Liberation theologians attempt to walk this ideological tightrope by desacralizing all ideology. For them, ideology is only a secular tool, however necessary. It remains relative, a social agenda to be used in conjunction with theology. The American bishops would, I suspect, agree. But there remains in their document a fundamental ambiguity about whether Christian ethics and the American moral order provide common or distinct norms. Mustn't we insist on two standards, the human and the divine? Should they ever be conflated? Are the theology of Amos and the theology of Abraham Lincoln, for example, really synonymous?

The shadow of ideology has been all too present in evangelical circles: one need only consider the Moral Majority. Too many evangelical churches, for example, view America's commitment to material success as a central tenet of the gospel. Yet it seems to me that such a theology of success is nothing but an alien American ideology holding captive certain Christian teachings (e.g., the blessings for the righteous in Proverbs). In a similar way, I suspect that the bishops might find more that is problematic in the American work ethic if they would look at it more closely. For example, isn't Horatio Alger's version of the American dream more individualistic than corporate? A transformation of society—not just a fulfillment of its unfinished business—seems more consistent with the theology of creation, covenant, and discipleship that the bishops set forth so well.

As I see it, there is a fundamental tension in the pastoral between two models of theology's relationship to culture. On the one hand, the bishops have maintained their basic trust in human culture; on the other, they seem to call for the radical transformation of society. The first tendency is more typical of a pre–Vatican II predilection for what H. Richard Niebuhr called a "Christ above culture" model. This model presupposes a fundamental harmony between the underlying ideals of society and the Christian vision of humankind's ultimate end. The second and, I believe, more valid approach is closer to Niebuhr's "Christ the transformer of culture" model.[10] Although this model recognizes that the reign of God must find concrete expression in the world in which we live, it just as clearly sees that the underlying ideals of society must be fundamentally changed if they are to accord with the Christian vision.

Second, the bishops reflect a certain ambiguity about theology's *interactive* nature. Historically the Catholic Church has demanded more doctrinal uniformity than economic or political agreement. Desiring to be the church universal, the church for all peoples, it has recognized social pluralism as a necessary given. This has been true even within societies, not just between societies. William F. Buckley, Jr., and Governor Mario Cuomo share a common Catholic faith, but little else. Diversity within the church on complex economic questions has always been welcomed or at least tolerated. (It is thus consistent that the first person mentioned as having appeared before the bishops at their public hearings during the drafting of the pastoral is Michael Novak, a Catholic layman from the American Enterprise Institute for Public Policy Research and a critic of much of what the bishops drafted.)

Nevertheless, an ecclesiology that stresses the unity of the church and opens itself to a diversity of social opinion can impede the adoption of a social ethic that seeks specific reform. The priestly and the prophetic dimensions of the gospel exist in tension. Seeking to avoid schism, the bishops present social policy "pastorally," as suggestion. Needing the conversion of society, they are reduced to offering guidelines for action within a framework of ongoing debate. It seems unlikely that their letter will prompt strong action. Instead, it will elicit more discussion.

On the other hand, the bishops' document is, from beginning to end, progressive in its economic policy. It is something most European Social Democrats would applaud. There is little diversity or pluralism in its projected public policy options. Even while allowing that "an assessment of economic practices, structures and outcomes leads to a variety of conclusions" (par. 128), the letter itself sets forth a consistent, moderately liberal agenda. Having used the pastoral twice in classroom settings, I have found it telling that political conservatives have been both unconvinced and critical of its theological approach while political liberals have found the arguments both sound and convincing. Although the bishops state that moral values do not dictate specific solutions (par. 134), although they say "it is not the church's role to create or promote a specific new economic system" (par. 129), although they call for "political debate" (par. 123), the political and economic position of the bishops is clear.

It seems that the document is both too specific (those disagreeing with the bishops' political posture are prone to discard the whole document prematurely as "liberal sentiment") and not specific enough (the discussion invites more discussion rather than concerted action). The "action-reflection" circulation that is basic to any interactive theology has been cut short. Specific plans for action that might then produce new situations calling for further theological reflection and thoughtful action have been avoided.

Central as well, and perhaps most damaging to their intention, is the bishops' reluctance to advocate the use of power to overcome systemic evil and sin. They seem to have an unwarranted optimism about the use of human reason and moral persuasion. The bishops almost believe that if we know the good, we will do it. But this is not the case. Having presented moral argument and offered economic suggestion, the bishops need to deal more forthrightly with strategies for implementation. How is human greed checked? How is political decision-making accomplished? The bishops issue a call to conversion but neglect to develop strategies for dealing realistically with competing interests between industries, communities, and nations.

Third, although the bishops attempted to fuse creatively biblical, traditional, and cultural analysis, a truly *integrative* theology will wish to go further. After three-and-one-half pages of helpful biblical discussion, the letter rarely returns to Scripture in the following twenty-nine pages of text. Instead, the bishops take this initial biblical discussion and boil it down to the assertion of the fundamental dignity of all human beings. Moreover, this assertion of human dignity is said to be equally an axiom in the general culture. There, "dignity is manifest in the ability to reason and understand, in their freedom to shape their own lives and the life of their communities, and in the capacity for love and friendship" (par. 61).

In other words, both the secular individual and the Christian should be able to agree "on the respect and reverence owed to the dignity of every person" (par. 61). Since this is the fundamental biblical contribution of the document, the letter turns out to offer little by way of specific Christian warrant. As Yale economist James Tobin ironically observes, "The values expressed in the pastoral letter are presented as derived from Catholic theology. I, a non-Catholic and indeed an unrepentant 'secular humanist,' find them of universal appeal, striking responsive chords among persons of all religious faiths and of none. The ethics of equity and equality are very American."[11] Yet Scripture has much to contribute to the discussion, and I am not at all convinced, as Tobin is (and perhaps even the bishops are), that Christian economic values are "very American." As Reinhold Niebuhr correctly observes, the positive Christian contribution to an understanding of justice is found "in strengthening the inclination to seek the neighbor's good, and in the contrite awareness that we are not inclined to do this."[12]

Conclusion

The preceding criticisms are not intended to diminish the strengths of the pastoral. Through it the bishops have sought to provide instruction for American Catholics and all of goodwill who seek "to live their faith in the marketplace" (par. 3, PM). Evangelicals should applaud such an effort at applied Christianity. They can also learn from the theological integration that is basic to it. In particular, while not questioning the formal or material principles of the Reformation, evangelicals can recognize in this letter the truth of the Scholastic distinction between the *Ordo Cognoscendi* and the *Ordo Essendi*. That is, the order of knowing need not duplicate the order of being. The Word of God, both incarnate and written, is primary. But such a word is not always heard first through traditional biblical interpretation or church tradition. Rather, it is often necessary to listen first to the culture in which we live and to discover God there.

The strength of the pastoral lies in the care with which the bishops first listened to their people and to the wider American society and then sought to offer help based on Catholic social teaching.

> "For I was hungry and you gave me food. . . . I was naked and you clothed me. . . ." Then the righteous will answer him, "Lord, when did we see thee hungry and feed thee . . . or naked and clothe thee? . . ." And the King will answer them, "Truly, I say to you, as you did it to one of the least of these my brethren, you did it to me." (Matt. 25:35-40)

4 | *Wealth and Well-Being: The Bishops and Their Critics*

Eugene R. Dykema

The U.S. bishops' pastoral letter on the economy has stirred an old controversy with new authority, bringing the argument out of the halls of academia and into the parishes and homes not just of Catholics and Christians but of other Americans as well. The letter is addressed to consciences. If it stopped there, it would not be very controversial, but it also calls for action, including political action. For its vision of the good economic life and the actions that make it good, the letter has received major criticisms.

Controversy is nothing new to economics. Debates both esoteric and mundane are stock-in-trade to economists. The letter enters this arena by arguing for its own "images of economic well-being" and its own methods for achieving them. Even in a society noted for its pragmatism, this ought to get people's attention, especially when it enters the charged debate over capitalism versus socialism. Accordingly, although professional economists and others have undoubtedly supported the bishops' position, the attacks on the letter by some critics have received the most press. The views of Michael Novak, an articulate spokesman in the Catholic camp, and several evangelical economists of the "wealth creation" school such as Brian Griffiths will figure prominently in what follows.

The Domain of Economics

One response to the letter has been the suggestion that the bishops are in over their heads. The charge itself is a key to understanding part of the issue of domain. "Religion cannot produce grain," argue some critics,[1] implying that stewards of religious matters ought not to presume to address matters of economic production. The reverse is also frequently held to be true: Economics should be independent from religion. Each belongs to a separate sphere of life, each has its place, but there is no intrinsic relationship between them. The fertile plains of economic experience, perhaps unexciting, are places where people may dwell without ever seeing the mountaintops of religious experience. A journey to the mountains is voluntary, and while it is exhilarating for some, it is merely dangerous for others.

The bishops reject this view. In the pastoral message that introduces the final draft of the letter, they argue that it is a tragic error to separate faith and everyday life (par. 5, PM)—indeed, that it cannot be done in economics: "Economic life is one of the chief areas where we live out our faith" (par. 6, PM). Even when Christians agree with the bishops, they break ranks over the possible ways in which people might live out their faith in economic life, or over the specific demands that religion can place on the economic sphere. Before we can address this issue, however, we must focus more closely on the nature of economic activity.

The Nature and Purpose of Economic Activity

Why do we engage in economic activity? What do we want from an economic system? What should economics do for whom? I won't run through a primer on suggested answers; instead, I'll focus on the issues as they emerge in the debate between the bishops and their critics. The letter focuses on economic activity primarily as a way of meeting human needs. The test of good economic activity, we hear, is its effect on people—especially the poor and the family—and on the "common good." Stewardship of resources and care for the environment are mentioned less often, but care for the creation can also be included as a criterion. Surprisingly, the notion of economic activity for the sake of God's glory is virtually absent from the letter. Only in the closing lines do we hear that emphasis: "The fulfillment of human needs, we know, is not the final purpose of the creation of the human person" (par. 365). Even then the language is primarily that of the "divine goal of the human family," a rather muted way to express the joy and delight of honoring and glorifying God through economic activity well done. God's love for his creation and his desire to see it rendered fruitful make economic activity far from dismal or mundane. Such activity renders daily offerings to the Lord of the creation. Here the critics offer a fair criticism of the letter. Novak, for example, emphasizes the Catholic doctrine of co-creation to get at this point.[2] But that in turn leads to a different understanding of the purpose of economic activity.

Novak's understanding, widely shared in slightly differing versions by conservative Protestants, centers heavily on the task of wealth creation. In this perspective little is allowed to hinder the achievement of this objective. But in another sense, economic activity is clearly seen as a lower form of human endeavor. Little is expected of human moral action when individuals engage in economic activity, and the pitfalls to human morality are likewise not seen as very great in this sphere. Brian Griffiths, for example, quotes Keynes to the effect that it is good to have economic activity as an outlet for "dangerous human proclivities" that would hurt society far more if they came out in other ways.[3] The economic sphere functions as scapegoat: unload all your sins on it and be purged. So wealth is important, instrumentally at least, but the kinds of things that go on in markets to create wealth are presumed to exist at a relatively low level of human virtue. Human beings' participation in God's creative work in this area doesn't seem very pretty, at least not to those who are sensitive or hold high standards of moral virtue. In fact, the relevance of moral virtue to economic activity is one of the main issues of disagreement.

The relationship between economics and ethics has been much debated. The trend has been to presume that in a market system at least, economics can get along with a minimum of moral virtue. The world of economics is seen as a world of practical action, one where pragmatic habits of mind predominate and where "practical compromise" rules the day. In Novak's terms, this means that there is no need to reach agreement on metaphysical, religious, or intellectual implications of economic activity in order to get on with business. Those who fail to see that this world of wealth-creating action is not the same sort of world as that of faith, vision, theory, and ideal are, according to Novak, quixotic and self-destructive.[4]

Novak's view, of course, has much in common with Adam Smith's view, in which the market is the social device where "even the selfishness of individuals can be stimulated ... and transmuted into a powerful instrument of social change."[5] For both Smith and Novak the transmutation of private interest into the public good occurs as the result of unintended consequences, not as the result of intentional moral acts. Novak's agenda is also similar to Smith's in its overall view of the relationship between ethics and economics: both look for the minimum of moral standards necessary for an economic system to function. For both, "to function" means primarily to create wealth. Wealth is the payoff of the practical and minimally moral practices in the economic sphere; it is the silk purse fashioned from the sow's ear of selfishness by the magic of the market.

The bishops are not content with this picture of the nature of economic activity. Risking being labeled quixotic and self-destructive, they look for economic activity that is characterized by more than wealth creation, in which virtues are more fully practiced. For example, they call upon business owners and managers to make choices that reflect a commitment to the public good, not simply to the private good of their firms (par. 111). Typically they see proper economic activity as permeated by the moral demands that stem from biblical ethics, demands that are good for all because all people are created in God's image. This difference in viewpoint raises the issue of where markets fit with the rest of life.

Markets and the Rest of Life

Michael Novak argues that capitalism must be understood not just as an economic system but as a triad of economic, political, and moral-cultural systems. Each has its proper place and role, each needs the other, but each must respect the other as well. Failure to respect boundaries frequently gets us into trouble in Novak's view, a failure he finds in the bishops' approach to the economy, among others. As noted, Novak sees the job of the economic system as the fostering of wealth creation—in his most rhapsodic moments, he refers to the market system as "conferring wealth" as if it were a benevolent mechanism showering wealth upon those whom it favors.[6] But undertaking wealth creation requires values from outside the economic sphere—and it is the task of the moral-cultural system to provide those values. Thus Novak's argument is at once insightful and shortsighted.

Novak's position has some analogies to a theory called "sphere sovereignty." The concept was articulated by the Dutch Calvinist theologian and statesman Abraham Kuyper and later refined by—among others—the philosopher Herman Dooyeweerd, Kuyper's countryman.[7] Although this theory sees society as an organic whole, it also identifies within this whole various spheres such as the family, business, science, art, and so forth. Each sphere is characterized by its own norms and responsibilities, which are separate from and not derived from those of the state. In short, each has its own place in the social scheme and is thus "sovereign" with regard to the state, the church, and the other spheres. Novak employs a similar scheme in which the economic, political, and moral-cultural spheres are distinct and have limited relationships with each other. But be-

Eugene R. Dykema

yond this point Novak's use of the argument bears only a superficial relationship to the sphere sovereignty argument and ignores one of its fundamental principles.

The Kuyper-Dooyeweerd concept of sphere sovereignty is, despite its misleading name, two-pronged. It holds to a limited version of sovereignty, not to autonomy. The sovereignty of any social sphere is limited by the requirement that it maintain proper relationships with all the other spheres. For example, business operating in the economic sphere has its own economic norms to fulfill, but according to the principles of sphere sovereignty it may not do so in a way that destroys the proper functioning of, say, families. Similarly, every sphere must meet the internal requirement of justice. For example, parents operating in the sphere of the family may not treat their children unjustly (e.g., by depriving them of life's necessities). Each sphere must be faithful to its own mandate, but it must likewise responsibly understand and reckon with the domain and needs of all the other spheres. If it fails to do so, the state, as keeper of public justice, must step in to restore proper functioning.

This principle of limited sovereignty, qualified by proper respect for and upholding of the other spheres (sometimes referred to as a "simultaneity" principle, implying an interconnection), is frequently ignored or truncated by modern borrowers of the sphere sovereignty idea. The Christian right, for example, emphasizes the autonomy of the spheres to the exclusion of their interconnection. Novak, for his part, narrows the concern for interconnections to fit his own version of democratic capitalism. His view shows some concern for connections, but it is curiously one-sided.

Novak sees that the market has its own values, the chief of which is efficiency. But it needs more, he argues, to maintain its existence. It is the moral-cultural sphere that provides the values that make economic activity in a market system possible. He's right, I think—and one reason that he's right is that the economic system is not even theoretically self-sustaining on the presupposed motivational ground of self-interest. More is needed to sustain a system of exchanges.[8] In Novak's view it is the role of the moral-cultural system to pour in *via individuals* (an issue postponed for now) the values needed to sustain the system.

Herein lies the blatant irony in Novak's position, because many of these values find no particular honor in the marketplace. People motivated by concerns for the neighbor, for the poor, for future generations, and for the sustenance of creation frequently find themselves in tension with "economic" values such as profit maximization and growth of the enterprise or market share. One of the reasons that the moral-cultural system has to be busy pouring values into the economic sphere is that the economic sphere chews them up, sometimes along with the value-holders. The economic sphere is a consumer of the cultural values that it undercuts. My instinctive reaction is to invoke the principle of fair exchange, demanding that the market system obey its own supposed internal logic—giving as good as it gets. What does the market give in return for this stream of values necessary for its own existence? Why, wealth, of course, the material underpinnings of social existence. The market pays in its own currency.

This raises the question of whether wealth really pays its way, or whether, like the bargain Esau struck, a mess of pottage doesn't go as far as one first thinks. But there is another side to the issue of value relationships between the spheres that I want to take up. In Novak's view of markets, the values flow one way, from the moral-cultural system to the economic system. But what of the other direction? Doesn't market behavior teach people values? Doesn't it reward some values and denigrate others? Doesn't competition sometimes "weed out" precisely those attempting to practice Christian values? Doesn't market behavior alter the values held in the moral-cultural sphere? I think so, and so do the bishops, but the critics are remarkably silent on the matter. They don't seem to see that the limited morality of self-interest, competition, and gain-seeking isn't likely to be compartmentalized in the economic sphere but spills over into family life, political life, and religious life—in other words, into all of the other spheres. Our everyday economic activity is a powerful shaper of worldviews and value systems. One example is the tendency to treat all human relationships as transactions—self-interested exchanges—not allowing for gift relationships (which are fundamentally a one-way transfer of some good) or relationships of commitment.

Many of those who see the market system as having drifted from its moorings in the Judeo-Christian ethic, as floating free from the moral-cultural system that gave it birth, want to re-embed the economic system within the moral-cultural sphere. But they are sometimes frustrated because the cultural system itself seems to lack what is needed to straighten out the economic sphere.[9] A reason for this may well be that the ethic of the marketplace has eroded the broader cultural ethic: there is no home to return to.

What is needed is a view of the spheres richer than that provided by Novak, one that fully recognizes the role of interconnections. The exchanges between the economic and the moral-cultural spheres as well as the political sphere either support or erode the value base of each. Novak supposes that people with differing value

Eugene R. Dykema

preferences can wander about and freely associate with each other through economic exchange without being affected by the values of others or the prevailing ethos. This is unrealistic. People not only bring values to the market; they also take values home—and to church, the village hall, and elsewhere. And the marketplace has a prevailing ethos; it has institutional, systemic characteristics much more complex and value-laden than Novak recognizes. This leads us to look more closely at the relationship between persons and structures.

Persons versus Structures

There has been much debate in Christian and other circles about the issue of the morality and the ethical responsibility of individuals versus those of institutions. Many see the latter as devoid of moral characteristics, forgetting, I think, that social institutions are the products of human action. In this sense they are products that function morally or immorally. The bishops' critics seem to be of two minds on this matter. On the one hand, they call for "practical institutional arrangements through which . . . valid principles can be routinely embodied in the laws and habits of everyday life." And they acknowledge that such values as "liberty and justice are achieved not solely in the heart, but also in institutions."[10] Brian Griffiths calls for "institutions in our society which can cope with the reality of a fallen world."[11] Yet, according to the Christian right, moral values such as those affecting the proper use of property or care for the poor appropriately enter the market only through the commitments of individuals. Apparently such values ought to remain individual and not institutional because they are considered inconsistent with the basic wealth-getting drive of the marketplace. So the truncated value-set of the market forces it to appeal to the moral-cultural system to motivate individuals to care for the poor even if their poverty is caused by the market system. While some of this stress on the values of individuals versus the values of institutions comes from a proper concern for pluralism, some of it reflects individualism and an inadequate notion of an autonomous market.

The bishops take a different tack. They call for the development of a common moral vision (pars. 23, 61, 83, 125, 153, 363), but they also see this vision as affecting structures. In response to world hunger, for example, they call for farmers to consider this issue as they make their individual choices, but they call for a systemic response to the problem at the same time (par. 228). This systemic response presumably follows upon the common moral vision. But what if a common moral vision is not achieved? When does some group's moral position form the basis for a social imperative? To maintain, as the critics of the bishops do, that the market is a neutral arena that ought to be open to all regardless of moral belief is to side-step the issue. The market is not value neutral. We should indeed avoid the presumption that Christian principles ought to be imposed on all people just because they are right and belong to the created order. And there is a proper role for economic freedom in the marketplace; however, it stops short of anarchy and injustice. The freedom of the marketplace is properly a constrained freedom, just as its efficiency is properly (as I will argue shortly) a constrained efficiency. The form of the constraints must be thought out in terms of the issues of pluralism and the rights of persons to individual freedom, but I see no basis for assuming that constraints are inconsistent with a proper social structure. For one thing, constraints are necessary in a fallen world to provide precisely what both the critics and the bishops want: a broad and just distribution of rights and opportunities. This leads us to the question, What constraints are appropriate in a market system?

A Market System

The bishops and their critics both celebrate elements of the market system. The latter, however, are relatively uncritical of the historical upheaval and the current costs that a market system has created. They attribute most of the monetary wealth of the West to the emergence of this system, forgetting other factors such as rich natural resources, military might, trickery, and "random" elements that have played a big part in creating affluent Western countries. They celebrate, without regret, the emergence of the deliberate, calculating, pragmatic spirit, and thus show implicit gratitude for the market system's throwing off the shackles of church and tradition, whose moral sensitivities they deem irrelevant to economics. They seldom see that an economic homelessness and a narrowness set in simultaneously. They celebrate monetary wealth and engage in creative redefinition of such sensitive concepts as self-interest and competition until they are quite compatible with the basic working of markets.

The bishops have different sensitivities. Grateful for the heritage of freedom of choice that a market system brought, committed to pluralism and a healthy work ethic, they nevertheless emphasize substantive rights to participation, rather than merely formal freedoms or the right by virtue of property ownership to exclude others from participation. And they believe, it seems to me, that the getting and spending of wealth may indeed lay waste other powers that they associate with human dignity. The bishops and their critics have different perceptions of the reward of engaging in economic activity. The critics see it largely as creation of monetary wealth; the bishops see it as well-being. Wealth is necessary to well-being, but it is clearly not sufficient.

Productivity, wealth creation, and efficiency are the chief claims to virtue of the market system. But the questions of whether wealth pays for all and whether pursuing it is an adequate and honorable goal are hotly debated. In modern economic terms, wealth gets its value from being desired by those willing and able to pay for it. The value of the artifacts of wealth is therefore philosophically subjective in origin (someone's valuing them is adequate proof of value, so long as the individual backs these preferences with the ability to pay) and monetary in definition. Maximizing wealth, thus defined, is not necessarily the most desirable or beneficial economic outcome. It does, however, make the calculus of wealth simpler because it reduces all value to dollar value. Broader notions of wealth[12] pose nasty problems of commensurability. In optimizing well-being, how can we compare monetary wealth to such "wealth" as good family life, social amenities, and the preservation of animal species?

These problems can't be resolved here, but a comment can be made about the framework of the discussion. We need to think about economic well-being in broader terms than we customarily do. We can begin by doubting that monetized wealth can capture what we are after. The critics of the pastoral letter border on making a fetish of wealth—they are simply far too convinced of its essential worthiness. For example, they tend to treat it, without qualification, as a necessary precursor to all other values. Want justice? Get wealth first. Want community? Get wealth first. In a material creation, material goods are necessary, but not in the open-ended, unqualified way so frequently suggested. We ought to seek, with justice, those things that are simultaneously good for our service to God, good for society, and good for the creation.

This simultaneity applies not only to the goals of economic life but to the economic process as well. What happens to us as we engage in economic activity? What are we taught? How are we formed? How do we treat our neighbor? What happens to our relationship to God? As we engage in market activity, we produce more than material goods. We also produce a worldview, a practical morality (even a practical theology), and an understanding of virtue. Here the pastoral letter is far richer than the views of the critics. The critics have carefully laundered two key concepts so that their view of what happens to people when they engage in market activity is far more pristine than is realistic.

Self-Interest and Competition

Christians have long puzzled over the problem of self-interest. It seems to be a given of human behavior to place self ahead of all others, even God. Christians recognize this as sin, and it makes them uncomfortable. But its very power and pervasiveness make self-interest alluring as a motivator to action. In more than just the economic sphere, we frequently presume that there is no sense in appealing to justice or morality. Only appeals to self-interest will be heard; only consideration of what's in it for me will move anyone to action. Caught in the tension between what they believe is right and what they think they see going on around them, Christians have settled for some uneasy compromises.[13]

Defenders of free markets commonly resolve this dilemma by defining self-interest in as innocuous a way as possible, by pulling the moral fangs of the serpent which calls us to violate the two great commandments of love for God above all and neighbor as self. In a market system, they explain, self-interest is at once unintentionally benevolent and otherwise benign. These proponents accept the notion that self-interest is the only path to an acceptable level of monetary wealth, that if self-interested economic activity is crippled, the rich and the poor alike will suffer the effects. They hold that it is the market that coordinates the pursuit of self-interest in such a way that monetary wealth is maximized. The faith that the needs of everyone, the poor included, will be met along the way is far more implicit and more weakly argued. Competition is the only necessary institutional restraining force. But is a sanitized self-interest restrained by competition both accurate and adequate?

Self-interested economic man, as Kenneth Boulding points out, rests improbably on the zero point of the scale between benevolence and malevolence.[14] Coordination of self-interest through markets may sound alarming to some, but it sounds far better than saying that markets coordinate hatred, racism, fetishism, and oppression. Of course, by this definition markets also coordinate the positives as well as negatives—love, esteem, fellowship, and benevolence—but economists from Adam Smith onward have been convinced that there is so little of this found in market behavior that we needn't talk much about it. When self-interest is broken down into these less neutral-sounding categories, another question becomes more evident: What conditions, including market conditions, tend to promote benevolent forms and discourage the malevolent? Those who would put no bounds on self-interest on the grounds that the market is properly a morally "open place"[15] would put no bounds on the effects of malevolence, either. As a culture we have decided that through our institutional structures we will reward self-interest regardless of its moral and practical inadequacies, and we have taken a laissez-faire stance toward alternative mores. Novak and others are far too close to this stance, it seems to me, while the bishops are striving for a different approach, one that reckons with the more fully moral character of economic actions and economic institutions.

Free marketers attempt the same strategy with competition as with self-interest: to render it harmless by definition. Their argument for competition is similar to their argument for self-interest: they tell us that competition is natural in one or both of two senses. One view is that it is natural for humans to be competitive, or at least to strive. The second holds that striving, coupled with the natural condition of scarcity, leads to the inevitability of competition. Further, they normally define competition merely as free entry and exit, thus differentiating it from rivalry—and arguably from the most common forms of competition in modern economics. In the process, competition is spared any of the hostile overtones of competitiveness that bring it too close to being antithetical to Christian values of community and fellowship.

This is too simple. Scarcity is frequently contrived, not natural. Even in the presence of scarcity, competition is not the only feasible response—sharing is an alternative. The critics, who pride themselves on realism, have taken a flight of fancy. Their notion of competition is far from the reality of winners and losers in economic activity. Competition is not always degrading or punishing, but it is frequently so, according to the testimonies of honest people in business. Public policy has long recognized the tendency for competition to get out of hand and the need to create other rules of the game. Such policies intervene in market institutions, but in the interest of preserving healthy economic activity, not destroying it.

The critics have done Christians a disservice with their whitewashed definitions of self-interest and competition. They have made both appear unproblematical morally and practically. In practice, people have discovered the opposite and have thus been confused because of the discrepancy between the idyllic picture of the free market and the forces that tug at them in the marketplace. Finding no place in the marketplace for many of the moral teachings of the Bible and the church, but told that Christians can celebrate the joys of wealth creation, they are tempted by a practical dualism in which they conform to the prevailing mores and perceived reward structure of the marketplace while maintaining a personal piety.

A New Ethic for the Marketplace

The resolution of this dilemma must be to reunite moral principle with economic practice in a richer and more honest way than has been done. In this effort, I think the bishops' pastoral letter is a step in the right direction. I would hope for a greater convergence between their perspective and the positions of Christians such as Novak and Griffiths. When Peter Berger struggled with the ethics of change brought on by economic development, he found too large a gap between his list of moral principles and his actual cases of social development. He concluded that something other was needed and labeled the people that would have to lead in this new direction as "pedantic utopians."[16] Perhaps we are still looking for them. The problems created by the existence of self-interest on the one hand or by the absence of competition on the other are significant. I'm not convinced that the bishops have adequately handled them. But the critics' defense of the market is too facile. Their reliance on "unintended consequences" does not constitute an adequate argument in favor of the market system, in part because intentions count and in part because consequences ought not to be measured solely in terms of monetary wealth. Markets cannot depend on altruism alone, but likewise they cannot depend, in their own sphere, on self-interest alone. We need to look to the building of a more self-sustaining ethic in the marketplace that interacts favorably with the moral-cultural sphere, sustaining it in the process rather than threatening its well-being while parasitically depending upon its values.

I have no complaint against the argument of Novak and others that the sphere of personal morality is crucial here and that this sphere must be nurtured by the church. I would make two points: the morality thus nurtured is not properly individualistic, and a communal ethos is needed as a complement to individual moral efforts. The first point implies that community has a claim on individual action—something normally denied in practice by free marketers and too seldom fully accepted by Christians. This demand and the notion of economic well-being broader than monetary wealth both ask for economic decision-making that is not guided by self-interested maximization of "wealth creation." Individuals will need a far richer framework of a type at least suggested by the pastoral letter. The second point implies that the individual may expect something from the community—namely, support for morally correct actions. This communal support includes the reward structure of the marketplace, which has both a private and a public dimension.

Private economic action supports a richer communal ethic when buyers and sellers alike consider dimensions other than price and individual "profit" maximization. For example, if we want someone to produce cars with an eye toward the value of good work, care for the environment, and the possibilities of future generations, then as car buyers we need to seek out such producers and be prepared, if necessary, to pay a higher cost for our cars. Although it complicates our lives somewhat, the principle holds for all market actions: buyers and sellers must reckon with the multifaceted conditions of production and consumption, each with an eye toward the responsibility of the other. With a richer notion of well-being goes a richer notion of responsible participation in economic activity.

But individual market decisions are not the only ones needed. There are the standard realms of market failure—public goods, common property resources, and so on, all of which are lumped into the term "externalities"—that I will not go into here except to suggest that these have not yet been given their due.[17] In addition, once we redefine "winning" as economic well-being instead of wealth and see "fair play" in light of the "simultaneity" of spheres, we must give new attention to the rules of the game. Two examples of such rules are the rights granted to private-property owners and the standards for a proper distribution of income. Briefly, both have been argued on the principle of efficiency in maximizing monetary wealth. With more concerns in the picture—for example, the right to participate in economic life and a preferential option for the poor—each may require a refined definition to modify the restrictive, exclusionary character of property rights and to insure that equity is treated as a precursor of efficiency.

It is clear that I find the framework provided by the bishops a more comfortable one than that put forward by the critics. No one should presume the creation of wealth to be unimportant or automatic. But our presumptions about the meaning of wealth and the means necessary to get it need re-examination. And if it comes to a choice between wealth creation and moral rectitude, the bishops strike me as hearing better the wisdom of Proverbs:

> Better a little with the fear of the Lord
> than great wealth with turmoil.
> Better a meal of vegetables where there is love
> than a fattened calf with hatred. (15:16-17)

5 | *The Bishops and Third World Poverty*

Mark R. Amstutz

When he was president of the World Bank, Robert McNamara coined the term "absolute poverty" to describe the condition of life found in many Third World nations in which people live beneath any reasonable level of decency. Estimates of the number of Third World people living in this condition range from 500 million to 1.3 billion.[1] This enormous level of poverty in Asian, African, and Latin American nations presents a major challenge to the church, particularly to the Christian community in the rich nations of Western Europe and North America.

In November 1986 the U.S. Catholic bishops issued the pastoral letter entitled *Economic Justice for All,* which offers one of the church's most serious attempts to respond to the problem of poverty in the United States and in the world by formulating public policy recommendations. While the letter is concerned chiefly with the U.S. economy, the bishops address the problem of justice and poverty in the world, recognizing that American Christians bear a moral responsibility for ameliorating the basic needs of the Third World poor.

Robert Bellah has observed that the issuing of the U.S. bishops' pastoral letters on the nuclear dilemma (*The Challenge of Peace*) and economic life represents a new paradigm for the church's public policy witness. Bellah suggests that from the early nineteenth century through the mid-twentieth century, the missionary enterprise was the major mode of witness of the American church. In this first phase churches contributed to foreign affairs indirectly by personally modeling social, political, and economic values common in America.

Mark R. Amstutz

According to Bellah, the pastoral letters on peacekeeping and on the U.S. economy are significant because they call attention to public and governmental responsibilities for domestic and international problems.[2]

The aim of this essay is to examine and assess the bishops' political economy of development, with a special focus on the dilemmas of Third World development. In carrying out this task, it is important to recognize that the pastoral letter is fundamentally a document on the U.S. economy, addressing only peripherally the problems of Third World poverty and the concomitant U.S. moral responsibilities for assisting those in absolute poverty. I believe that the biblical and moral arguments of the pastoral letter are sound and thoroughly consistent with the theological heritage of evangelicals, but that the social science analysis of the bishops is incomplete. While I applaud their moral vision of justice and commitment to the poor, as a social scientist I question the adequacy of the letter's analysis of Third World poverty and the implied policy prescriptions for alleviating it.

The Bishops on Third World Poverty

The bishops' assessment of Third World poverty is based on the biblical-moral framework developed in the first part of the pastoral letter. This framework is based on four key principles. First, the aim of national and international economic life is the affirmation of human dignity (pars. 25, 28). Second, because the worth of individuals is affirmed in part through work and adequate living conditions, all people have a claim to participation in the economic life of society and to a minimal standard of living (pars. 71, 74, 77). Third, the poor have a special claim on society. Indeed, the bishops write that the poor have the "single most urgent economic claim on the conscience of the nation" (par. 86). The priority of the poor is based on the biblical "preferential option for the poor" (par. 52) and moral obligations derived from community justice (pars. 70-71). Fourth, government has a major responsibility in ameliorating economic injustices. Since the major aims of government—including the protection and enhancement of human dignity—are moral (par. 122), the bishops argue that the government must play an indispensable role in directing national economic affairs and in promoting the economic well-being of peoples in impoverished foreign lands.

In the light of these principles, the bishops argue that the meeting of Third World basic needs must be the chief aim of U.S. foreign economic policy (pars. 258, 260). While the disparities of income among nations are troubling to the bishops, their major international concern is with the poverty, disease, and rampant malnutrition found in the poorest Third World nations.

The bishops address five major themes relevant to the poverty of the Third World: development assistance, trade, finance, foreign private investment, and the world food problem. The basic message of the bishops is that the U.S. government should increase its financial transfers to the Third World. Among other things, the letter recommends the following: increased bilateral and multilateral aid; a more equitable trading system; cancellation of foreign debts owed by the poorest nations, along with the creation of more effective international financial institutions in which developing nations have greater representation; increased foreign private investment by medium and small companies, especially through joint ventures; and the expansion of food aid, coupled with the development of long-term cooperative programs in agricultural production in food-deficient Third World nations.

In addition to recommending financial transfers, the bishops argue that the international economic order needs to be reformed in order to decrease egregious inequalities of income and to ease the plight of those in absolute poverty. The bishops assert that they "want a world that works fairly for all" (par. 258), and to strengthen international economic justice they recommend major reforms in international economic policies and structures. While they do not specify the types of changes that should be brought about, it is clear that the reforms would involve an increasing economic and political participation by the poor developing nations.

Assessing the Bishops' Message

It is important to recognize that the moral authority of the bishops decreases as they move from biblical and moral analyses to the assessment of economic life and ultimately to proposed policy recommendations. Although Christians need to agree on goals, it is also important to develop consensus on how to implement them. Thus, while the letter indicates that there is room in the church for diversity of opinion on how to protect the economic rights of people, it correctly asserts that "there can be no legitimate disagreement on the basic goals of economic justice" (par. 84).

As an evangelical, I applaud the letter's moral concern for peoples suffering from absolute poverty in the Third World. Evangelicals will heartily agree with the bishops' central concern for the poor, not only because it is consistent with evangelical teachings and

Mark R. Amstutz

missionary activities but most importantly because this is what the Scriptures teach. Evangelicals have, of course, been in the forefront of world evangelism, not only teaching about Christ's redemption but calling people to demonstrate divine love by caring for those in need. They have also been leaders in promoting social welfare. Throughout the world there are countless schools, hospitals, and universities established by evangelical missionary societies. In short, Christians everywhere can agree with the bishops' challenge to care for those in need.

I take issue with the bishops' analysis of Third World poverty not on moral or biblical grounds but on economic and political grounds. I question the adequacy of the bishops' emphasis on redistribution and transnational financial transfers as a means of alleviating absolute poverty. Fundamentally, a sound economic policy must maximize productivity (without which there can be no rise in living standards) and ensure that the benefits of community production are distributed fairly. It is not enough, however, to reform economic structures and to redistribute resources. The essential requirement is to produce—to add to the value of goods and services within a community. Given the rapidly expanding populations of developing nations, the only adequate long-term strategy for promoting human dignity must involve significant increases in economic productivity. What is lacking in the bishops' letter is a doctrine or strategy of job creation for developing nations. While articulating the ideal of economic justice is important, the major challenge is to define policies that are most likely to promote economic growth and thereby reduce the poverty of states.

What explains the bishops' emphasis on resource transfers and structural reforms of the world economy? Why do they place so much emphasis on aid, food transfers, and international finance, and neglect the topic of job creation? One possible explanation is that the brevity of the document did not allow for a discussion of private and public initiatives to create jobs. Another possible explanation is that, since the letter was concerned with the U.S. economy and its responsibilities to the poor, the chief aim was to articulate the moral responsibilities placed on the U.S. government and its citizens toward people in need. But neither of these theories is fully satisfactory. The most likely reason why the bishops' document focuses on domestic and international redistribution of resources is that the bishops' political economy assumes domestic and international structures to be the major impediment to economic justice. This conviction derives not from the Catholic concern with the common good but from a deficient political economy of development—a political economy that places more stress on sharing than creation, on redistribution than production.

Alternative Models of Development

In order to illuminate and assess the bishops' Third World political economy, I shall compare two alternative models or explanations of the wealth and poverty of nations. Both approaches are ideal types, representing two competing explanations of the unequal distribution in world income.

The *first* approach—*the structural thesis*—explains the poverty of the world as a consequence of unjust structures and exploitative economic policies. This approach has three distinctive features. First, it is based on the assumption that the basic condition of mankind is sufficiency, not poverty. According to the structural model, the increase in absolute poverty is a direct by-product of the expansion of modernity and more particularly of world capitalism. The expansion of international institutions of capitalism has resulted in significant disparities of income, with the wealth of the rich states gained at the expense of the developing nations. Evangelical philosopher Nicholas Wolterstorff, for example, has written that the poverty of the developing nations is a direct consequence of the expansion of Western capitalism. He writes that the mass poverty in the Third World is not a result of actions by "a few aberrant individuals" but a consequence of the unjust, exploitative international economic order.[3]

A second key element of the structural approach is its view of economic growth. According to the structural thesis, economics, like politics, is a zero-sum game, where the gain of one individual, group, or nation is made possible by the loss of another. Since the total value of economic wealth is fixed, the expansion of one group's income must inexorably lead to the decline of another group's income. Exploitation by the rich and the powerful peoples and nations is an inevitable consequence of wealth creation.

A third element of the thesis is that the international economic order is unjust, favoring the rich, powerful nations over those that are poor and weak. The gains from trade are not distributed fairly but tend to accrue disproportionately to the rich, industrial nations. Evangelical theologian Ronald Sider, for example, has expressed this conviction as follows:

> We are all implicated in structural evil. International trade patterns are unjust.... Every person in developed countries

> benefits from these structural injustices. Unless you have re-
> treated to some isolated valley and grow or make every-
> thing you use, you participate in unjust structures which
> contribute directly to the hunger of a billion malnourished
> neighbors.[4]

There can be little doubt that the disparities between the rich and the poor nations are excessive, but is it correct to assume that such economic inequalities are a result of the international economic structures and trade patterns? Or are the income gaps among states primarily the result of the different productive capacities of nations? The structural thesis assumes that the inequalities are chiefly the result of an unfair international economic order.

The *second* model of development is *the modernization thesis*. According to this view, the wealth and poverty of nations is the result of different productive capacities. The wealthy nations are those that have developed the most efficient production through the application of modern science and technology. Poor nations are those that have been the least successful in developing efficient production. To a significant degree, the essential features of this model can be expressed as direct opposites of the structural thesis.

First, the modernization approach assumes that the basic condition of life has been poverty, not plenty. According to this model, the major economic challenge is to increase economic production—the only source by which living standards can be increased within society. It is important to recognize that the rapid improvement in living standards in the past hundred years has been made possible primarily by increased economic production. While modern societies are beset with many social and economic problems derived from modernization, generally people are much better off today than they were at the turn of the century. What has made this international improvement in living standards possible for so many people? The answer is simple: increased economic output.

A second feature of the modernization thesis is that economic expansion is assumed to be a positive sum process—a means by which the increase in wealth by one person or state need not result in a decline in another's wealth. According to the modernization thesis, economic expansion can and will lead to significant disparities in income as it rewards groups, peoples, and nations that are most productive. But the rewards come not through exploitation or at the expense of someone else but as net additions to the value of national wealth. It is possible, therefore, to expand national wealth in some nations without bringing a net reduction in another nation's wealth. International economic exploitation is not an inevitable result of economic expansion and job creation.

Third, the modernization approach assumes that the international economic order is a relatively neutral system, rewarding the firms and nations that most efficiently apply the skills and tools of modernity to production. Under the existing economic order those who are most efficient in producing and marketing goods and services will benefit the most economically. Because the continuing economic well-being in society depends on continuing comparative efficiencies in production, the economic status of nations is not immutably fixed. Rather, it depends on the continuing ability of societies to adapt to the changing nature of the world economy. The rapid rise of Japan as a major industrial power, threatening firms in Western Europe and the United States, is the most graphic example of this.

The underlying premises of the bishops' political economy are based, to a significant degree, on the structural thesis. While the letter does not explicitly endorse this paradigm, the bishops assume that the international economic order and the policies of the rich, industrial states are the major causes of the egregious international economic inequalities. There is virtually no discussion of the role of individuals, groups, and Third World nations themselves in the promotion of economic growth.

My own reservations about the bishops' political economy derive to a large degree from my conviction that a *modified modernization model* can best explain the wealth and poverty of nations. To begin with, I believe that the basic explanation for the dramatic rise in living standards during this century is the increased economic potential of states. While domestic and international economic exploitation has surely contributed to inequalities in income within and between nations, the basic explanation for the radical economic disparities in our contemporary world lies in differing rates of economic production. Since I share with the modernization model the conviction that the living standards of most people throughout history have been characterized by poverty and primitive conditions, what needs to be explained is not the causes of poverty but the causes of wealth.[5]

It is important to stress, too, that the expansion of wealth (the reduction of poverty) is a positive-sum process. While the rich and powerful states have no doubt exploited poor states in the past, the notion that wealth in some nations is derived from their exploitation of poor nations is empirically unfounded. This may have been the case in the past, but it is surely not the case for modern wealth. Supporting my contention is *Toward the Future*, an alternative report on the U.S. economy prepared by a group of lay Catholic leaders and issued at the same time as the publication of the first draft of the pastoral letter. "We reject as false," notes this lay letter, "the proposition that the poverty of poor nations is caused by the wealth of richer nations."[6] Brian Griffiths, a British evangelical economist, has similarly noted that it is impossible to accept the thesis that the poverty of the Third World is the result of the prosperity of the First World. Modern wealth, he suggests, has not been gained through exploitation but has derived from increased efficiencies in production.[7]

Finally, while I believe that the international economic order is a relatively neutral system, rewarding those nations that are most productive, the modernization model is inadequate to respond to major human needs in the short run. Because the model is largely insensitive to differences in national economic outputs, it does not address the problem of short-term basic needs. It does not provide a means for assisting peoples and nations that have been unable or unwilling to use the rules and structures of the international economic order to national advantage. Thus there is no place in this model for affirmative-action programs and policies to promote social justice. While I believe that economic expansion can only be realized in the long run through policies that effectively adapt to the existing international economic order, some resource transfers from the rich nations to the poor nations will be necessary in order to alleviate absolute poverty. In addition, some reforms in the international economic order may contribute to the generation of job creation in the poor nations.

However, the redistribution of wealth is not an adequate long-term solution to the problem of world poverty. Brian Griffiths has written that "continued emphasis on redistribution can only exacerbate the world's economic problems."[8] There are two reasons why resource transfers are an inadequate long-term solution to the hunger problems of the Third World. First, transfers alone cannot meet the increasing needs of the growing populations of the Third World. Since the average annual population growth of the developing nations over the past decade has been in excess of 2.5 percent per year, simply maintaining living standards under such conditions of growth will be a formidable task. Moreover, the rapid migration of people from the countryside to the cities imposes enormous financial burdens on poor governments. In short, given the exponentially increasing needs in many Third World nations, the only effective strategy is to enhance job creation. It is not enough to give people bread and fish; our moral responsibility must involve teaching people how to fish and how to make bread.

A second reason for the inadequacy of financial and resource transfers is that human dignity depends partly on work. Human dignity is not realized by achieving a particular standard of living or by acquiring a particular level of wealth. Rather, human dignity, as the bishops rightly affirm (pars. 96-97), is inextricably related to human labor, since labor affirms self-worth and encourages self-realization. It is ironic that the bishops emphasize work and participation in the economic life of society but fail to set forth an economic strategy for job creation.

The Need for Job Creation

Since there can be no effective distribution without production, the failure to emphasize job creation and economic expansion is a major failing of the bishops' pastoral letter. To its credit, the lay Catholic study *Toward the Future* views job creation as a fundamental pillar of a just economic order. Given the importance of job creation to the amelioration of Third World poverty, I will sketch the biblical rationale for creation and some propositions about the process of economic growth.

One of the important biblical themes is the mandate to create. The human responsibility for managing and controlling the earth derives from the special place that God has entrusted to humans in his created order. In the encyclical *On Human Work*, Pope John Paul II has eloquently called attention to the creation mandate: "Man is the image of God partly through the mandate received from his Creator to subdue, to dominate, the earth. In carrying out this mandate, man, every human being, reflects the very action of the Creator of the universe."[9] Work is important because it allows people to express themselves in society and to develop and realize their individual potentialities. Even more significantly, work allows people to participate in the divine process of creation, a task for which they were in part created. As *Toward the Future* observes, "Creation is not finished. . . . Humans become co-creators through discovery and invention, following the clues left by God."[10]

Creating through work—participating in the economic life of society—is both a right and a moral responsibility. It is a right because human dignity depends in part on work. But it is also a responsibility because the need to work derives from the need to care materially for ourselves and for others. Theologically, this responsibility derives from the biblical command to be stewards of the gifts, talents, and resources entrusted to us. Because we are called to be co-creators with God, we have a responsibility to God to continue the process of creation.

How are jobs created? While the literature on economic development provides no simple or clear program for promoting employment, economists have associated economic growth in the West with two important principles. First, human resources are more significant than physical resources in explaining economic expansion. Second, the rise in economic output has been associated with a favorable environment—one conducive to invention, innovation, and investment. I do not believe that favorable human and cultural factors alone bring about economic expansion, but if they are not sufficient conditions for job creation, they are clearly necessary for it.

One of the most controversial notions in economics—one implied by these two principles—is that wealth creation is fundamentally rooted in noneconomic factors. Such a notion is controversial because the creation of wealth is often associated with the discovery, possession, and accumulation of tangible resources. But as P. T. Bauer has noted, economic achievement historically has depended chiefly on human capabilities and attitudes as well as on society's social and political climate. "Differences in these determinants," he writes, "largely explain differences in levels of economic achievement and rates of material progress."[11] Primary resources are, of course, important in production, but their possession does not assure economic growth. This is the reason why disparities in physical resources do not themselves explain the poverty or wealth of nations. Indeed, the focus on tangible resources is basically misconceived, since the creation of wealth has little to do with the possession of resources. As Max Singer and Paul Bracken have noted, the key to the creation of modern wealth is not things but ideas, techniques, information, and other intangibles that encourage higher productivity through better motivation, superior organization, and more efficient marketing.[12] The validity of this principle is corroborated by the modern economic history of countries such as Germany, Hong Kong, Japan, Singapore, Switzerland, and Taiwan—all of which have limited primary resources but have achieved impressive standards of living.

Human qualities are often neglected when considering Third World economic expansion. Roger Darling, a former official of the U.S. Agency for International Development, has observed that the equating of development with material resources is perhaps the most prevalent misconception about development.[13] This misconception is so widespread that the division of the world into rich and poor nations is based on readily quantifiable resources. But if human factors are the foundation of economic growth, economic assistance must emphasize such areas as education, skill development, and the creation of a cultural environment that facilitates rather than impedes economic growth.

The human qualities on which wealth creation rests do not appear in a vacuum. Rather, they are nourished by a culture that is conducive to economic enterprise. Michael Novak has written that the religious and cultural norms of society—what he calls the "moral-cultural system"—are the basic pillars of economic expansion, since the institutions of political economy originate from and are sustained by the cultural values of society.[14] Lawrence Harrison, another former official of the U.S. Agency for International Development, has also called attention to the importance of culture. According to him, disparities in levels of economic development can best be explained in terms of culture. He argues that the heart of the development process is human creativity. "What makes development happen," he writes, "is our ability to imagine, theorize, conceptualize, experiment, invent, articulate, organize, manage, solve problems and do a hundred other things with our minds and hands that contribute to the progress of the individual and of humankind."[15]

Novak illustrates the significance of culture by comparing the economic histories of Latin America and the United States. According to him, in the nineteenth century the levels of economic development were roughly the same in North and South America, but during the next one hundred years, the United States' economy developed rapidly while that of Latin America remained virtually static. The reason for the radically different rates in development, claims Novak, is that both regions had different cultural norms: "Latin Americans do not value the same moral qualities North Americans do. The two cultures see the world quite differently."[16]

Space does not permit an actual comparison and evaluation of cultures in terms of wealth creation. What is important to recognize is the major role that culture and institutions of political economy play in the process of economic expansion. While informed Christians will disagree on the particular cultural values and patterns that are most conducive to productivity and social justice, there can be little doubt of the importance of values and institutions in the creation of wealth. Thus, if the bishops are to help alleviate Third World poverty and serve as a catalyst for reform in U.S. international economic policy, they should, at minimum, take note of the decisive role that the cultural, political, and economic environment plays in job creation, recognizing that some cultures and some institutions of political economy are more supportive of innovation, investment, and efficient production than others.

Mark R. Amstutz

The Morality of Foreign Aid

In considering the role of foreign economic assistance, it is important to differentiate between humanitarian aid—designed to alleviate short-run human needs resulting from disasters, famine, or civil strife—and developmental aid, designed to develop the infrastructure necessary for economic expansion. There can be no doubt that the biblical model of the Good Samaritan places a direct moral responsibility on individuals and societies to respond to human suffering. People of goodwill bear a moral responsibility to care for those in need, whether they do so through public or private channels. And this is especially the case for Christians. As the pastoral letter notes, Christians bear a moral imperative to share food. "Relief and prevention of Third World hunger," the bishops state, "cannot be left to the arithmetic of the marketplace" (par. 28).

If there is a clear moral justification for humanitarian relief, is this also the case for developmental aid? Is there a moral responsibility to provide further loans to Third World nations and to provide debt relief to those unable to meet existing payments? Answers to questions such as these cannot be provided solely out of the Sermon on the Mount. Given the enormous material needs of the developing nations, it would be easy to advocate increases in economic assistance to all Third World nations. But since the aim of economic assistance is not to cleanse the conscience of rich peoples but to improve the standard of living for the poor, the level and type of developmental aid should be determined not by biblical and moral analysis alone but by ascertaining which policies and programs will most likely improve the living conditions of those suffering from absolute poverty. The challenge, therefore, is to devise a discriminating policy which ensures that those who are in greatest material need will be assisted the most.

If official economic assistance is to contribute more effectively to job creation, new directions in official aid policies will be needed. There are three modifications that would strengthen financial transfers. First, the United States government should improve accountability within its economic aid program. One of the major obstacles to promoting the well-being of Third World peoples is the enormous waste and mismanagement associated with Western economic assistance. For example, the total external public debt of non-oil developing nations exceeded 700 billion dollars in 1984. The annual debt service for such loans was nearly 110 billion dollars, with many nations spending more than 50 percent of their foreign exchange on loan interest. While some of the sources of the contemporary international debt crisis are external, Third World nations must also share the blame for the crisis because of misguided public policies and unwise investment of loans—actions that have resulted not only in wasted funds but in capital flight.[17]

The mismanagement of aid by donor nations pushing ill-designed projects and by recipient nations that politicize the distribution of aid is especially evident in Africa, a continent where more than 150 million people are currently on the verge of starvation. During the period from 1960 to 1983, for example, Africa's external debt increased nearly tenfold (from $5.7 billion to $51.3 billion), but instead of increasing the economic viability of the poor states, the loans helped nations to become even more dependent on the West. Moreover, during the 1970s the West provided over $22 billion to sub-Saharan Africa, the area most affected by starvation. With the growing hunger in central Africa in the early 1980s, the West increased its assistance to more than $7.7 billion annually. Yet such aid appears to have had little impact on the economic prospects of the poorest states.[18]

A second needed reform in the official U.S. aid program is the need to bypass Third World governments. Whether the aid is for developmental or humanitarian purposes, the poor peoples of the Third World are likely to receive the greatest benefit if the United States directs its resources through nongovernmental channels. Since many Third World regimes are corrupt, nondemocratic, and often dictatorial, foreign aid channeled through governments has simply strengthened the power of ruling elites, exacerbating corruption among government officials. Moreover, since government officials are usually involved in distributing economic aid and in defining the general distribution of public funds, misallocation of aid is widespread in the Third World. This is so because investment and allocation decisions are significantly influenced by political considerations. Finally, the transfer of aid has been detrimental to economic production because it has encouraged the centralization of economic decision-making. This is in direct opposition to the bishops' affirmation of the Catholic norm of "subsidiarity" (par. 124), which requires that government assume only those responsibilities that individuals and private groups cannot effectively carry out alone. In short, aid politicizes life, strengthens the power of central governments, and centralizes economic decision-making—developments which have helped to promote the very conditions and environment that are harmful to economic expansion.

Finally, the United States should emphasize nonresource transfers. To be sure, tangible resources are important in promoting job creation, especially in the strengthening of a nation's infrastructure. But if the most important determinants of wealth are human factors, as I have argued, it is doubtful that changes in the structural environment will lead to significant expansion. What Third World nations need is not only tangible resources but education, skill development, and the creation of modern values and attitudes relating to enterprise. While the U.S. government can contribute in this task, professional associations, churches, interest groups, and other nongovernmental institutions can play a vital role in promoting the attitudes, values, and cultural norms conducive to productive enterprise. Lay churchmen, for example, can contribute to Third World development by participating in indigenous business ventures, by helping to guide the educational process, and by modeling the virtues and habits that are central to economic efficiency. Mennonite communities in Paraguay and Belize, for example, have contributed to the economic potential of those states by modeling the personal values of persistence, thrift, planning, and so on. It is a pity that the bishops did not give a more prominent place to church institutions in modeling and promoting personal values, attitudes, and skills essential in productive enterprise.

We can agree with the bishops that the U.S. government bears a moral responsibility to help reduce Third World poverty. It is important to stress, however, that the moral responsibility is not to governments per se but to peoples suffering from poverty. Given the corruption in Third World governments, the mere transfer of financial resources from one nation to another is not an adequate policy. What is needed is a strategy for channeling resources efficiently in order to stimulate job creation. Since there can be no long-term reduction in absolute poverty without economic expansion, the major aim of any long-term official aid program must be the promotion of labor-intensive growth. This can be most effectively carried out when the United States provides economic assistance to important economic sectors in Third World nations while also promoting those values, aspirations, and practices that have facilitated job creation domestically.

Part 2 | *Jewish Perspectives on American Economic Life*

6 | *Jewish Perspectives on American Economic Life*

Even a passing acquaintance with Judaism reveals the profoundly ethical character of this religious tradition. Deeds of justice and loving-kindness form part and parcel of the central Jewish mandate to be holy—as God is holy—and thus to sanctify the world. In the face of today's severe economic problems and their dire human consequences, it may seem curious that Judaism has not issued a pronouncement on economic justice to equal the pastoral letter of the American Catholic bishops, *Economic Justice for All.*

There are a number of reasons to explain this fact. One lies in the fact that Christianity and traditional Judaism have markedly different modes of "doing ethics." From the Bible onward, ethics has been an intrinsic and essential aspect of Judaism. But it was not until the Middle Ages that books on Jewish ethics as such were written, and only in the modern period has "Jewish ethics" become a separate academic discipline. Unlike Christianity, which, being a faith-based tradition, systematically derives ethics from theology, Judaism moves from faith to law. Law—*halakhah*—organizes God's will for Jews. It articulates the commandments to be followed in acting toward God and human beings alike.

Halakhah itself is not systematized, however. When searching for teachings on an economic issue, for example, the traditional scholar must often choose from majority and minority opinions or from more or less well-known rabbinic interpreters, following traditional methods of selection.

Jewish communities were organized according to the teachings of *halakhah,* since the religious ideals of Judaism were codified into a system of explicit obligations regarding all facets of social and personal life. The economic order—including perspectives on private property, wealth and poverty, and fairness and honesty in business transactions—was extensively and precisely addressed through laws and practices derived from the Bible, the Talmud, Midrashic collections (case law), responsa (replies by rabbinic scholars to questions about Jewish law), and legal codes. Thus, in traditional, premodern Jewish societies, an authoritative religious tradition provided direction regarding every facet of life—including the economic—and exacted conformity through a variety of religiously grounded institutions.

With the onset of emancipation and the entry of Jews into Western societies—and hence into modernity—the ideological and institutional mechanisms of traditional Jewish life began to weaken and in some cases to disappear altogether. As Jews became influenced by alternative systems of thought and alternative lifestyles, *halakhah* no longer remained the sole authority governing Jewish consciousness and action. The impact of secularization and the pressures to conform to Western and frequently Christian ideals compromised the role of traditional Judaism in shaping Jews' commitments. Traditional Judaism itself underwent major changes. Reform Judaism questioned the binding nature of *halakhah* as it sought to make Judaism and modernity more compatible. Orthodox Judaism arose as a movement in defense of the tradition. Conservative Judaism and later Reconstructionism became additional branches of Judaism attempting to bridge the traditional and the modern.

The entry into the modern West represents a watershed in Jewish history, thought, and experience. The central status of *halakhah* in Jewish life became so impaired that today most Jews do not find it authoritative in their life choices. Thus we can no longer speak of *the* Jewish ethical perspective on any one issue. Jewish ethics is now radically pluralistic, revealing attachments to alternative Jewish religious movements and their interpretations of Judaism and Jewish ethics. It thus becomes difficult to make pronouncements on behalf of Judaism to which all Jews will assent. Jewish ethics also confronts the general problem of religious ethics in modernity: a secularism so profound that when it does not lead to total disconnection with the tradition, it results in the compartmentalization of religion and politics, the synagogue and the world.

The passage to modernity brought another challenge to Jewish ethics—namely, the confrontation with problems of the larger society. Prior to emancipation, European Jews were resident aliens of the nations in which they lived. They formed part of semi-autonomous Jewish communities that often had a measure of political and religious independence. As non-citizens, Jews were denied access to the larger political arena. So while *halakhah* organized premodern Jewish life and thought in a comprehensive manner, ritual and ethical obligations applied specifically to Jewish intra-communal life.

Since Jews were for many centuries a minority outside the power centers of society, they had to learn how to become power brokers themselves. Now that we as Jews have achieved significant financial and political security in America, our entry into public discussion on social issues is essential. We have at our disposal a religious tradition rich in prophetic mandates to reform and transform society, a tradition that fully codified into laws the biblical imperatives to care for the poor and the disenfranchised. We have participated in movements for social justice and social reform in proportionately greater numbers than members of virtually any other religious tradition. All too often, however, our participation has been uninformed, or certainly underinformed, by our religious tradition. Although we resonate profoundly with calls to end injustice, we are painfully impoverished by our illiteracy in Jewish ethics.

The impact of modernity on Jews has led to a tragic and artificial bifurcation between religion and ethics. The fact that these two realms were inseparably united in classical Judaism adds bitter irony to the current impasse. The Jewish world is currently inhabited by divided groups. At one extreme are the traditionally religious Jews whose concerns remain intra-communal and whose focus is ritual practice to the neglect of traditionally concomitant ethical action. At the other extreme we find Jews who have embraced the ethical pole of Judaism as they have dislodged it from its religious grounding. Both extremes are engaged in bad faith. The majority of Jews, one might guess, respond with admiration to religious-ethical documents like the Catholic bishops' letters on nuclear war and the economy, feeling disappointed and frustrated by their own religious community's failures to speak out publicly in a more assertive manner.

The essays in this section reveal the complexity of issues currently confronting Judaism and Jewish ethics. Byron Sherwin's discussion of classical sources in Jewish economic ethics differs substantially from Frida Kerner Furman's treatment of modern Jewish figures trying to construct a Jewish social ethics by connecting the prophetic tradition to their contemporary experience. While Sherwin works directly with rabbinic teachings on the economy, Furman explores a more general and prior concern: How have modern Jews living in the broader American society approached the question of social transformation from a Jewish but non-*halakhic* perspective? Arnold Wolf's identification of socialism with central biblical injunctions represents a modern attempt to link modernity with tradition, while Leonard Fein's reading of Jewish detachment from traditional religious imperatives leads him to search for a contemporary Jewish social ethic to which today's Jews will be receptive.

Sherwin and Wolf largely work out of a *halakhic* framework, but their respective readings of traditional texts differ. Their conclusions regarding the traditional view of the poor, for example, vary significantly. Furman and Fein address the obligations of post-*halakhic*, religiously liberal Jews to forge a new link between religion and ethics, between Jewish tradition and social change.

Even as we represent the fracture in Jewish thought and experience, our essays nonetheless exhibit points of contact as well. Most explicitly, the tone of each essay is Jewish, inasmuch as each reveals a moral passion ever present in Jewish life. The sources, although different from one essay to the next, are traditionally Jewish, though there would be disagreement about which sources are the more authentic and significant in Jewish economic ethics. All four of us, however, assume Judaism's legal history; *halakhah* is implicitly or explicitly addressed by all.

The distinctively Jewish element in our perspectives is not a religious confession, for Judaism is not a faith-based religion and lacks a hierarchical, doctrinal structure. Instead, it is the unique Jewish historical experience that binds us together. Jewish minority status, for example, from the development of classical Judaism to the present day in America, informs the ethical positions and concerns we discuss. In these discussions Jewish ethics represents the variously conceived ethics of the Jews across time and space.

7 | The U.S. Catholic Bishops' Pastoral Letter on the Economy and Jewish Tradition

Byron L. Sherwin

Once Rabbi Samson of Shepetivka went to see Rabbi Ezekiel Landau, the great sage and chief rabbi of Prague, to discuss matters of scholarship. The two rabbis never had met before. Rabbi Samson approached Rabbi Ezekiel in disguise, dressed as a beggar, asking for alms. Rabbi Ezekiel, who was a very busy man, treated Rabbi Samson—whom he thought to be an unlettered beggar—very rudely, whereupon Rabbi Samson said, "How can you, a sage and a religious leader, treat a poor person in this fashion? You should rise at my presence, and you should respond to my needs, for God's Presence stands at my side. As it is written: God stands at the right hand of the needy to save him from those who would condemn him" (Ps. 109:31).[1]

Unlike the insensitive religious leader portrayed in this story, the Catholic bishops of the United States have responded to the condition of the indigent, to the plight of the poor. Through the compilation, publication, and promulgation of their pastoral letter on the economy, they have risen in response to the needy. For their insight they are to be praised. For their courage they are to be blessed.

The pastoral letter is an attempt to articulate Catholic social teaching on economic justice as it relates to the U.S. economy. The purpose of this essay is to offer a response to that letter from the perspective of classical Jewish religious tradition. Part of such a response must be a query about the Christian and particularly the traditional Catholic authenticity of the bishops' pastoral letter. Those within the Christian community in general and the Catholic community in particular will have to respond to this query to their own satisfaction.

81

However, to the Jewish observer the pastoral letter does not seem to portray either an authentic Christian or a traditional Catholic position on economic justice.

From one perspective, this apparent lack of authenticity is unfortunate because it weakens the authority of the document and its teachings. From another perspective, however, this lack of authenticity is fortunate because it allows the pastoral letter to focus on the application of *current* Catholic moral teachings to current economic conditions. In so doing, the pastoral letter is able to avoid preoccupation with earlier Christian doctrines, such as the idealization of poverty, that would have weakened the moral thrust of the document on issues such as assistance to the poor and the unemployed.

One would expect such a document to cite classical Catholic teachings regarding economic justice in support of the positions stated therein. Nevertheless, the pastoral letter seems to jump from Scripture to the statements of popes and church councils of the past century to support its views. Indeed, the document unabashedly states, "This letter is based on a long tradition of Catholic social thought, rooted in the Bible, and developed over the past century" (par. 25). The teachings of the church fathers and the medieval Scholastics seem thereby to have been disenfranchised from this presentation of Catholic moral teaching.[2]

Catholics may maintain that the papal encyclicals of recent decades—upon which the pastoral letter so heavily relies—represent authentic Catholic teaching on *contemporary* moral issues as well as or even better than ancient and medieval Catholic texts. However, this view of traditional authenticity, in which modern texts can supersede in authority ancient and medieval texts, is foreign to traditional Jewish thought. Furthermore, Jews would find incredible the ascription of moral authority to papal encyclicals issued by pontiffs of questionable personal moral stature. For example, the failure of Pius XII to condemn the mass murder of European Jewry during the Holocaust and to intercede on their behalf, as well as his blatant support for Nazi Germany, particularly in the 1930s, severely calls into question the validity of any claims regarding his alleged moral authority or credibility.[3]

Not only are the teachings of key Catholic theologians from the end of the New Testament period to the nineteenth century neither dominantly present nor prominently represented, as one might expect, but the pastoral letter is singularly lax in confronting the meaning of relevant New Testament passages understood within the context of the times and place of their composition. Taken within their social, religious, and historical context, New Testament teachings regarding economic matters are distinct both from that which the pastoral letter would have us believe them to be as well as from the views of Judaism in late antiquity formulated in the Mishnaic text. Simply put, early rabbinic tradition attempted to develop detailed laws regarding economic justice that carry forward the application of the authoritative codes of Leviticus and Deuteronomy to a historical situation. However, the teachings of the Gospels and Paul's letters are eschatologically rather than historically focused. They are preoccupied with the imminently expected end of the ages rather than with contemporary sociohistorical conditions. They utilize Hebrew scriptural texts more for homiletical observations than for the formulation of a concrete rule-ethic regarding economic justice.[4] It is intriguing, therefore, that the bishops' pastoral letter retains the sermonic approach of the New Testament while it seems to adapt the sociohistorical awareness characteristic of Jewish religious literature.

Pastoral Suggestions versus Religious Law

In view of the homiletical nature of various New Testament texts that deal with treatment of the poor and needy, and considering the historical role of the Christian cleric as pastor, it is neither surprising nor inappropriate that the bishops decided to express their views in the form of a pastoral letter. Within the context of classical Jewish tradition, however, both the genre of the pastoral letter and the role of the rabbi as pastor are virtually unknown.[5] Authoritative Jewish teachings on issues of economic justice would be found not in pastoral letters nor in homilies but in Jewish legal texts, particularly responsa and legal codes. Thus, not only might the content of classical Jewish teachings on economic justice differ from that of Catholicism, but the process of arriving at those teachings as well as the form in which those teachings would be conveyed would also differ.

In Judaism, homiletics is suggestive and evocative, but only *halakhah*—religious law—is binding. Rabbinic homilies tell one how one might live; *halakhah* tells one how one is duty-bound to live. *Halakhah* in Judaism is "applied theology." Theology is the soul of Judaism; law is the body. Without theology, Judaism is a lifeless torso. Without law, Judaism is a vagabond spirit. Law is the vehicle by means of which faith may be translated into deed.

For the Jew the leap of action *is* a leap of faith. *Imitatio dei* in Judaism is not simply a theological category worthy of contemplation but a prescription for specific action. The Talmud puts it this way:

What means the text: "You shall walk after the Lord your God" (Deut. 8:6)? Is it then possible for a human being to walk after God, for has it not been said, "The Lord your God is a consuming fire" (Deut. 4:24)? But, the meaning is to follow the moral attributes of God. As He clothes the naked, tends to the ill, and comforts the bereaved, so you do likewise.[6]

In Christianity one aspires to discipleship, one is called to imitate the pattern of Jesus' life (pars. 45-47). In Judaism one is required to imitate God's acts of benevolence. Christianity rests content with vocation (par. 59); Judaism, however, requires *specific* action. For Judaism the human condition is too precarious, human needs too numerous, for one to await the call to action. Israel accepted the commandments of the Torah with the words "We shall do, and we shall hear" (Exod. 24:7). Doing precedes hearing; duty precedes vocation.

The bishops seem to have glossed over the distinctive nature of Jewish tradition in their attempt to extend the pastoral letter's messages to other faith traditions, and to Judaism in particular. The letter states, "We also claim the Hebrew Scriptures as common heritage with our Jewish brothers and sisters, and we join with them in the quest for an economic life worthy of the divine revelation we share" (par. 29). This statement is a natural extension of *Nostra Aetate*,[7] a noble gesture of friendship and goodwill toward the Jewish people. Nevertheless, the claim of a shared revelation and of a "common heritage" is problematic and requires clarification from a Jewish theological perspective.

Jewish theology is identical not with Hebrew Scriptures but with a tradition of rabbinic interpretation of Hebrew Scriptures. Abraham Joshua Heschel has summarized this Jewish theological position:

Judaism is based upon a minimum of revelation and a maximum of interpretation. . . . The prophets' inspirations and the sages' interpretations are equally important. There is a partnership of God and Israel in regard to both the world and the Torah: He created the world and we till the soil; He gave us the text and we refine and complete it. . . . The source of authority is not the word as given in the text but Israel's understanding of the text. . . . The word was given once; the effort to understand it must go on for ever. . . . To study, to examine, to explore the Torah is a form of worship, a supreme duty. For the Torah is an invitation to perceptivity, a call for continuous understanding.[8]

Just as Judaism is not Scripture but how Jewish tradition understands Scripture, so Catholicism is not Scripture but how Catholic tradition interprets Scripture. For Judaism and Catholicism the text of the Hebrew Scriptures is identical, but each gives that text a different meaning. There is a text in common, but, contrary to the pastoral letter, there is no "common heritage." The text is shared; the heritage differs. It is precisely this difference that makes Judaism and Catholicism distinct faith-traditions. Were the "heritage" identical, a Jewish response to the pastoral letter might be a photostat of rather than a counterpoint to Catholic social teaching on economic justice.

Because Judaism is equivalent not to Hebrew Scripture but to how Jewish tradition has interpreted Hebrew Scripture, terms in biblical Hebrew interpreted by the pastoral letter do not necessarily convey meanings identical to their interpretations in Jewish religious-legal literature. Indeed, certain terms that are crucial to the positions affirmed by the pastoral letter, such as "rights" (pars. 62, 80-85) and "conscience" (par. 360), have no real equivalents either in biblical Hebrew or in subsequent classical Jewish religious literature.[9] Thus, not only does the content of some of Catholic moral teaching on economic justice differ from that of classical Jewish tradition, but differences also obtain in the form, process, and language utilized in articulating views on economic justice.

Classical Judaism focuses on religious commandments (*mitzvot*) and prescribed duties (*halakhah*) as being essential to determining the behavior of the members of its faith community. The pastoral letter's appeal to conscience (par. 360) would have little meaning in a classical Jewish theological vocabulary. Rather, a prescription for specific required duties would be delineated. Furthermore, in Judaism duties related to areas such as commercial behavior and to the alleviation of the plight of the poor are considered to be valid in themselves. Duties are not perceived as being correlative to rights. One is obliged to perform righteous deeds simply because they are required by God, not because they are related to anyone's rights.

A Jewish Theology of Poverty

While some Jewish sources, like some Christian sources, extol poverty on the one hand while evoking the doctrine of divine retribution to explain the plight of the poor on the other hand, the pastoral letter's understanding of poverty as a calamity rather than a virtue, as a social misfortune rather than as a divine punishment, is correlative with the dominant position taken by classical Jewish sources.[10] In this regard a rabbinic statement affirms, "There is nothing in the world more grievous than poverty—the most terrible of sufferings. . . . Our teachers have said: If all troubles were assembled on one side and poverty on the other, poverty would outweigh them all."[11]

Despite its acute awareness of the tragedy of poverty, and despite its apparent replacement of an eschatological view regarding economic justice with a presentation and an analysis directed to the here and now, the pastoral letter nevertheless seems to cling to an ideal or messianic vision of economic justice. In this it represents a position that differs from that espoused by Judaism.

For the bishops, the "kingdom has been inaugurated among us" (par. 67). We live as "redeemed people" (par. 330). Although redemption is not complete, the "victory over sin and evil already has begun in the life and teachings of Jesus" (par. 41). For the rabbis, however, the kingdom is yet to come; at present, "the earth is given into the hand of the wicked" (Job 9:24). "In this world," a rabbinic statement claims, "war, suffering, the evil inclination, Satan and the angel of death hold sway."[12] Although God is an ally in the struggle against sin and evil, for Judaism divine redemption is an expectation rather than a fact. Human beings can engage in the battle, but only God can win the war. For Judaism that victory is yet to begin. We live in a "messy" age, not in a messianic age. As Abraham Heschel has put it, "At the end of days, evil will be conquered by the One; in historic times, evils must be conquered one by one."[13]

The pastoral letter's call for the eradication of poverty and for full employment (pars. 136-37, 151) is a messianic hope. By establishing such an elevated goal, only frustration and the neglect of more attainable goals can ensue. For example, while the pastoral letter calls for full employment as well as for the application of its message to the administration of the Catholic Church in the United States (pars. 347-58), it does not deal with personnel layoffs by Catholic dioceses throughout the United States. While it evokes many scriptural citations regarding care for the indigent, not once does it quote Deuteronomy 15:11: "For there will never cease to be needy ones in your land." Nor does it seem to grapple with the problem addressed by much of classical Jewish literature on economic justice—that is, how to relate virtually limitless needs to limited resources, and how specifically to set priorities for the use of those limited resources to respond to those seemingly limitless needs.

Unlike the pastoral letter, Jewish sources deal not only with the problem of relating limitless need to limited resources with specific reference to the poor, but they also devote considerable attention to two issues not substantially addressed by the pastoral letter. The first of these is the prevention of poverty, and the second is the situation of the individual who was once economically solvent but who is presently poor.[14]

Like Jewish religious literature, the pastoral letter deals with economic assistance to the poor. However, Jewish religious literature does not restrict its attention to therapeutic means of curing the malady of poverty. It also extensively concerns itself with the prevention of poverty. For Judaism, economic aid must be prophylactic as well as therapeutic. Detection of the early symptoms of unemployment and poverty and their treatment are viewed as necessary means to preventing the individual's fall into economic disadvantage, with its attending spiritual, psychological, and economic consequences. If the swelling of the ranks of the poor is prevented, communal funds for the support of the poor are not strained on a long-term basis. Short-term economic assistance to prevent poverty is more cost-effective than long-term payment of a dole. In addition, if concrete steps aimed at preventing poverty are taken, the dignity of the recipient is better upheld than if he or she were permitted to join the ranks of the indigent.

Commenting on "then you shall uphold him," a phrase in Leviticus 25:35 (a passage that deals with the person who falls into poverty), Rashi, the eleventh-century Jewish commentator, writes, "Do not let him come down until he falls completely, for then it will be difficult to raise him. Instead, uphold him at the time that he begins to fall. To what is this comparable? To a burden that rests on a donkey. While it is still on the donkey, one person can hold it and set it back in place, but if it fell to the ground even five people cannot set it back in its place."[15] In other words, prevention of poverty is part of the cure of poverty.

This approach regarding the potentially poor articulates a paradigmatically Jewish approach to issues of economic justice. Neither the poor nor the potentially poor are ever dealt with generically. Jewish sources never deal with "the poor" but always focus on the individual. Economic assistance is always determined by the particular needs and personality of the individual in need, not by a predetermined objectification of the needs of members of a socioeconomic group.[16] Judaism considers the objectification of individual need to be an immoral assault on individual human dignity. For example, commenting on Deuteronomy 15:8—"You must open your hand and lend him that which is sufficient for whatever he needs"— the Talmud states, "'For whatever he needs' [includes] even a horse to ride and a slave to run before him. It is related about Hillel the Elder that he bought for a certain poor man who had been born into a good family (but who now was poor) a horse to ride upon and a slave to run before him. On one occasion, he could not find a slave to run before him, so he himself ran before him for three miles."[17]

Elsewhere in rabbinic literature we find a commentary on Deuteronomy 15:11: "Open your hand to your brother." This commentary, later codified into law in the medieval Jewish legal codes, states, "To one for whom bread is suitable, give bread; for one who needs dough, give dough; for one who requires money, give money; for one who needs to be fed, feed him."[18]

In his twelfth-century code of Jewish law, the *Mishneh Torah*, Maimonides writes: "You are commanded to give the poor person according to what he lacks. If he has no clothing, he should be clothed. If he has no house furnishings, they should be brought for him."[19]

The emphasis upon the individual in Jewish sources on economic justice inevitably leads to a special concern not only for the individual who is poor but also for the individual who wasn't poor but became poor. One finds a particular sensitivity toward such an individual because the decline from economic solvency to economic indigency was perceived as a greater assault on the dignity of such an individual than poverty would be on one who always had been poor. The Palestinian Talmud states, "It has been taught that if a person [who was rich] has become poor and requires public assistance, if he had been used to vessels of gold [to eat and drink from], then give him vessels of gold; if of silver, then give him vessels of silver."[20]

In order to retain the dignity of the person in need, especially the formerly wealthy person, a loan was given rather than a dole. If the loan was not repaid, it was considered a gift. In this way the dignity of the recipient was maintained and a way in which he or she might reinstate economic self-sufficiency was provided. According to some Jewish sources, a loan to a poor individual established a business partnership between the giver and the recipient. If the recipient of the loan produced profit with the loan, he or she divided the profits with the giver. In this way a partnership of equals was established rather than the always-unequal relationship of donor and donee.[21]

In biblical economics the able-bodied poor were not unemployed. Rather, they were expected to work for their receipt of welfare. The economically solvent were required to set aside the crops from the corners of each field and to leave discarded gleanings for the poor. Correlatively, the able-bodied poor were required to work in the field in order to retrieve their entitlement (Lev. 19:9-10; Deut. 24:19-21). In this way no able-bodied person was unemployed. The poor were not disenfranchised from the dignity of honest labor.

The acquisition of wealth was not considered an improper endeavor by most classical Jewish religious sources. However, the jealous protection of wealth that prevented others from sharing in God's bounty, the wasting of resources required by others, and trade practices that eliminated fair competition were prohibited by Jewish legal and ethical tradition. Such behavior often was identified with the corrupt practices that had characterized the people of Sodom and Gomorrah.[22] Ultimately, the Jewish view regarding wealth rests upon the notion of stewardship. What we own, we owe. We serve as trustees for the property of God: "The earth is the Lord's and the fullness thereof" (Ps. 24:1); "Mine is the gold and the silver, says the Lord of Hosts" (Hag. 2:8). A midrash quotes God as saying, "Honor the Lord from whatever substance He has bestowed upon you. You are only My steward."[23]

The notion of the stewardship of wealth is discussed both in classical Jewish sources and in the pastoral letter (par. 27, PM; par. 34). A number of medieval Jewish texts consider a wealthy individual who does not help support the poor to be a thief. One text says, "God says to him [i.e., to the wealthy person]: I have supplied you with abundant wealth so that you may give to the needy to the extent of your means. Yet, you did not give. I shall punish you as if you have robbed those people and as if you have denied having in your possession something that I entrusted to you. The wealth I put into your hand for distribution to the poor, you appropriated for yourself."[24]

While the pastoral letter cautions against speaking too vocally regarding fraud in welfare payments (par. 194), Jewish law exhibits no such inhibitions. According to the notion of stewardship in Jewish law, the "welfare cheat," like the miser who refuses to help the poor, is also guilty of theft. As one blunt rabbinic text puts it, "Whoever takes a single coin from charity when he or she does not need it, shall not depart from this world until he or she needs it. He who binds rags around his eyes or loins and cries: Help the blind, help the afflicted, shall eventually be speaking the truth."[25]

The "welfare cheat" is condemned not only because he steals from God's bounty but because he robs the truly needy.

Justice and Loving-kindness

As was noted previously, the pastoral letter uses Hebrew terms to articulate a number of its views on economic justice. One such term is *tsedakah,* which it translates as "justice" and explains according to its own exegetical understanding. In fact, it describes "justice" in a variety of ways. Usually it is described as a value that includes love. Occasionally it is defined as a value that is distinct from charity. Sometimes it is described as a minimal societal requirement, and other times as a goal to be obtained (pars. 37-41, 68-77, 103-20).

In Jewish sources the view on the nature of *tsedakah* is far less ambiguous. In matters of economic justice, *tsedakah* refers to the minimal requirement placed upon each individual for care of the indigent. *Tsedakah* is not an aspiration but a legal requirement. Every person, including the poor, is required by Jewish law to fulfill this duty. The codes of Jewish law specify an absolute minimal contribution level, a median level, and an upper level in terms of specific amounts and percentages of income.[26] Maimonides and others also establish degrees of *tsedakah*, the lowest being that of the recalcitrant donor, and the highest being that of the donor who gives freely, who wishes to remain anonymous, and who provides the poor with an opportunity for self-support rather than just offering a dole.[27]

"Charity" and "philanthropy" are not *tsedakah*. Both of these terms denote a love of the giver for the recipient. *Tsedakah* refers to a duty to be performed whether or not one can or does love the recipient. Nevertheless, Judaism is not devoid of the concept of "charity"—that is, of helping another out of love. The Hebrew term for this, which does not appear in the pastoral letter, is *gemilut hasadim*, meaning "acts of loving-kindness." *Tsedakah* is the fulfillment of a duty, while *gemilut hasadim* is an expression of *imitatio dei*. *Tsedakah* articulates the Jewish understanding of justice and righteousness in action. *Gemilut hasadim* expresses the Jewish understanding of compassion and love in action. *Tsedakah* refers to actions directed only to the poor. *Gemilut hasadim* refers to any act of graciousness toward any of God's creatures. *Tsedakah* helps to insure the personhood of the recipient. *Gemilut hasadim* helps to insure the personhood of both the giver and the recipient.[28]

In Mark 10:25 Jesus is quoted as saying, "It is easier for a camel to go through the eye of a needle than for a rich man to enter the kingdom of God." However, the Talmud says, "In accordance with the camel is its burden."[29] For Jewish tradition, the wealthy have an opportunity not granted to others. Heaven can be theirs if they handle their wealth properly—not surrendering it but using it as faithful stewards for the sake of heaven.

Ultimately, economic justice, like charity, begins at home. Religious institutions and their leaders must realize that people who live behind stained-glass windows shouldn't throw stones. Religious leaders and the communities they guide must practice the economic justice they preach before they can expect their teachings to be taken seriously. Moral credibility can flow only from demonstrable moral action.

Since it was a vulnerable, isolated, and often outcast minority community for much of its history, the Jewish community developed an effective mechanism, through its ethical and legal tradition, for implementing its teachings on economic justice within its own parameters. The poor, the infirm, the orphan, the destitute widow, the undowered bride, the captive who needed to be ransomed, the traveler who required food and lodging—all were cared for by each Jewish community.[30] Already in the twelfth century Maimonides observed, "We never have seen nor heard of a Jewish community that does not have a charitable *(tsedakah)* fund."[31] When the first Jewish settlers in North America arrived at New Amsterdam in 1654, they were permitted to remain only on the condition that they care for their own indigent and infirm.[32]

The perspective of the Jewish legal and ethical tradition coupled with Jewish historical experience holds that each religious and ethnic community within the broader social sphere must take primary moral responsibility for the implementation of moral justice within the purview of its own particular constituency. In Jewish law there is "no agency for the performance of virtue." Neither the state nor other institutions or agencies can or should be expected to relieve religious communities of their obligation to care for their own. Were each community more aggressive in dealing with economic justice, in translating their teachings into action, particularly for their own constituents, addressing the physical and economic needs and not just the spiritual needs of its membership, particular religious visions of economic justice would be better served than they are at present.

The admonition of the biblical prophets and the prescriptions of Jewish law were aimed at producing individual actions and attitudes toward economic justice that, it was hoped, would coalesce to form a just society. Rather than change the system—whatever that might be—the initial goal was to sensitize the individual in such a manner as to precipitate the desired type of society in which economic justice would prevail. Furthermore, as was noted earlier, from the Bible onward, Jewish tradition has recognized that until the messianic advent, complete economic and social justice remains a hope rather than a reality. In an unredeemed and imperfect world, we can only treat the illness of economic injustice to the best of our ability, utilizing the resources at our command. A total cure is relegated to a future redeemed world. The focus in Jewish religious literature on stemming poverty with regard to specific individuals has been viewed as having more effective and immediate outcomes than concentrating on changing complex and often enormously formidable systemic causes of poverty and economic injustice.

In modern Jewish history, some Jews, impatient with waiting for the messianic advent, joined with revolutionary endeavors to address the systemic causes of economic injustice. For example, in the early twentieth century, many Jews saw communism as a vehicle for bringing about systemic changes and for realizing the messianic hope within a secular sociopolitical context. These hopes were never realized. It is a fact of history that neither Jews nor Judaism have fared well in countries that have embraced communism.

Without a doubt, Jews have been disproportionately represented among the avant-garde seeking to implement systemic socioeconomic and political change in Europe and in the United States. However, systemic social change historically has been more of a threat than a blessing to Jews and to Judaism. For example, full employment is desirable, but at what price? Systemic change in Nazi Germany and the Soviet Union brought about full employment but not economic justice.

Jewish religious literature and Jewish historical experience teach that it may be desirable to seek to improve rather than to perfect society. Scripture speaks about the pursuit of justice, and Jefferson speaks about the pursuit of happiness; neither speaks about attaining those goals. There is danger when reach exceeds grasp.

The obligation of Jews to seek the well-being *(shalom)* of the societies to which they belong flows from Jeremiah's observation (in 29:7) that "in the well-being *(shalom)* thereof [i.e., of lands where Jews reside], you shall have well-being *(shalom)*." Coupled with the imperative in Deuteronomy 16:20 to "pursue justice," Jeremiah's statement laid the groundwork for Jews to act in concert with others toward a just and moral society. Throughout rabbinic literature, the concepts of *mipnei darkhei shalom* (for the sake of the ways of peace) and *tikkun ha-olom* (the repair of the world) were employed to encourage Jews to join with others in accelerating movement toward a more just and moral society. All human beings are stewards of God's world. We all are partners in the attempt to reconcile human society with God's vision—"God saw that it was good" (Gen. 1:12).

8 | *The Bishops and the Poor: A Jewish Critique*

Arnold Jacob Wolf

The bishops' pastoral letter on the economy arouses the most diverse of reactions in an American Jew, at least in this one. I have deep respect for the seriousness with which the bishops have faced the fearful problems of inequality and injustice in our country. I admire their wish to connect with biblical and philosophic tradition in an effort to ground their political and economic policies in basic religious thought. I am grateful, too, for their policy proposals, which seem to me not only defensible but necessary as a minimum.

It is the mood of the pastoral that raises questions. Unlike a papal encyclical or a party program, the document is moderate, nuanced, and balanced with views from many perspectives. While this gives the work a scholarly, even dialectical character, it is by no means obviously the right tone for a statement on the hazardous state of the American economy. A sense of outrage at unemployment, racism, and huge gaps in wealth and income is muted by not-always-convincing statistics and by what seems undue qualification. In a laudable attempt to be both collegial and precise, the bishops have lost not only the once-common Catholic prophetic (or at least semi-prophetic) mode but even one of simple human indignation.

This style of thoughtful balancing of rights and thoughtful consideration of empirical research yields a result more appropriate to the academy than to the clergy. The bishops would like to be considered sophisticated in economic theory—and this at precisely the time when the entire discipline of economics is at hazard. Precisely at the time that economists have come to agree, for example, about the importance of "money," they no longer have any consensus about what "money" itself is. Overall, the discipline is without any consensus. The chaos and lack of conviction that mark departments of economics in major universities are not reflected in the bishops' rather touching concern for what professionals pretend to know. Why at this particular time is it so important for clergy to have their moral sensibilities refracted through alleged but fictitious economic expertise?

In sharp contrast to the somewhat pedestrian tone of the pastoral, biblical literature is far more apodictic and challenging. The Hebrew Bible is characterized by *halakhic*, legal formulations, especially in the Torah-Pentateuch, the most crucial element in Jewish Scripture.[1] I might also note that Jesus as he is portrayed in the Gospels did not adopt the rhetorical style or the philosophical assumptions of the Roman intelligentsia, nor quite that of the Pharisaic *havurah* (collegium) and academy. One should not expect the bishops, writing in our late-capitalist twentieth century, to imitate biblical models slavishly. Yet one feels a certain diminishing of self-confidence and an inappropriate regard for models quite distinct from those that created the Christian church in the beginning.

I believe that this temporizing—or, to put a more favorable face on the project, this balancing of ideas—reflects a deep ambivalence in the minds of the authors. One also expects inevitable compromises resulting from a committee working together to produce a consensual document. I have the distinct impression that the bishops are very unhappy in Ronald Reagan's America, that they believe not only that something is wrong in the system but that the system *itself* may be fatally flawed. I believe that the bishops, or some of them at least, nurture a nondoctrinaire socialism as a model for American political culture. I believe that many of them would like to be as outspoken and direct about poverty and injustice as they are, for example, about sexual morality and peace.

It is not mere fear of dissent that keeps them from a more faithfully biblical tone and doctrine. It is, curiously enough, their very humility and caution. They cannot and no longer want to order the laity to perform; they are no longer that certain of their own credentials. They are committed to a patient process of listening and sharing that would be revolutionary if adopted everywhere by a hierarchical church. Their heroes are not Innocent III and Gregory VII but rather Saint Francis and Mother Teresa. An outsider welcomes this new modesty and inhibition while at the same time worrying about its potentially paralyzing consequences. To be successors of the prophets is, of course, no longer to be prophets. Judaism teaches that the age of prophecy is over once and for all. But neither are the bishops called to become professors or technicians, moralizing only amid a thousand qualifications and preaching the gospel of Christ with elaborate footnotes.

No Temporizing: A Reading of the Torah

An uncompromising flat-out reading of the relevant passages from the Torah reveals a vigorous statement about the rights of the poor and the nature of the community. Exodus 21, perhaps the earliest formulation of the sabbatical and jubilee principle (a crucial part of the Book of the Covenant), specifies that slaves go free in each seventh year, a law that virtually eliminates the possibility of slavery in the strict sense. Beginning with Chapter 22, verse 24 (Hebrew original; cf. RSV, v. 25), the forgiveness of debts in the seventh year is specified, a law that virtually eliminates the possibility of a credit economy. "When [the debtor] cries out to me, I shall hear him, since I am merciful," says God, the Guarantor not of the creditor but of the rights of the poor.

The Sabbath is a sign of a covenant between God and the people. It is a gift of grace that is accepted not with acquiescent passivity but in the creative response of holy "rest." So, too, the sabbatical year is a sign that God is the one Creator and Owner of all and that his people may safely trust in the gifts of the earth that he has put into their hands. The holiness code in Leviticus 25 takes up this theme and renders it even more precise. "The land is to observe a sabbath to *Adonai*," a complete rest in which there is to be no sowing, pruning, or reaping. In the forty-ninth (or fiftieth) year all land reverts to its original owner, a law that precludes tenancy in the usual sense. "The land must not be sold beyond reclaim, for the land is mine; you are only strangers resident with me" (Lev. 25:23).

Leviticus further forbids the taking of interest, advance or accrued (Lev. 25:35ff.). There must be no ruler and ruled among the people of Israel, no oppressor and oppressed, no real masters or servants. The law is incredibly strict and perfectly clear! Under God, who is our one Master and Lord, all of us are merely but uniformly equal, and the Law must protect us against those economic and political forces which inexorably lead a society toward inequality.

What might well be the final version of these laws is found in Deuteronomy 15:

> Every seventh year you shall practice remission of debts. This shall be the nature of the remission: every creditor shall

remit the due that he claims from his neighbor; he shall not dun his neighbor or kinsman, for the remission proclaimed is of the Lord. You may dun the foreigner; but you must remit whatever is due you from your kinsmen.

There shall be no needy among you—since the Lord your God will bless you in the land which the Lord your God is giving you as a hereditary portion—if only you heed the Lord your God and take care to keep all this Instruction that I enjoin upon you this day. For the Lord your God will bless you as He has promised you: you will extend loans to many nations, but require none yourself; you will dominate many nations, but they will not dominate you.

If, however, there is a needy person among you, one of your kinsmen in any of your settlements in the land that the Lord your God is giving you, do not harden your heart and shut your hand against your needy kinsman. Rather, you must open your hand and lend him sufficient for whatever he needs.

Beware lest you harbor the base thought, "The seventh year, the year of remission, is approaching," so that you are mean to your needy kinsman and give him nothing. If he cries out to the Lord against you, you will incur guilt. Give to him readily and have no regrets when you do so, for in return the Lord your God will bless you in all your efforts and in all your undertakings. For there will never cease to be needy ones in your land, which is why I command you: open your hand to the poor and needy kinsmen in your land.

If a fellow Hebrew, man or woman, is sold to you, he shall serve you six years, and in the seventh year you shall set him free. When you set him free, do not let him go empty-handed: Furnish him out of the flock, threshing floor, and vat, with which the Lord your God has blessed you. Always remember that you were slaves in the land of Egypt and the Lord your God redeemed you; therefore I enjoin this commandment upon you today. (Deut. 15:1-15, New Jewish Publication Society of America translation)

The Bible seems to prohibit taking any interest from another member of the community, though it permits the accepting of interest from an outsider, Ezekiel's idiosyncratic dissent notwithstanding. The reason for this distinction is important: the community is a kind of family in which invidiousness and gradation are completely inappropriate, but the outside world is distinct, if not inimical. This state of "tribal brotherhood" may be compared directly with what Marx and Engels term "primitive communism." Of course, in a pre-industrial society no full socialization could be envisaged by Marx, but the sabbatical and jubilee year did cancel indebtedness and return all land to the original folk community; they mandated a kind of proto-socialism, a community that shared as much as possible.

The Rabbinic Vision of the Ideal Community

These biblical laws about lending, exploiting, and sharing are clear as crystal. In rabbinic explication they lose some of their pristine clarity, but they gain in richness of detail and situational positioning. I hold that they cannot be reduced merely to treatments of the specific problem of usury. Rather, they adumbrate a much more comprehensive view of society. Capitalism, of course, means more than speculative investment, and these laws forbid more than usurious use of money. They delineate an ideal community in which the concern of each is the concern of all, in which the convoked commonality takes precedence over the will to power of any individual. If this is not a kind of "socialism," what is it?

The Talmud prohibits all taking of monetary interest, no matter where it comes from.[2] Now, as we shall see, rabbis offered legal fictions that deflected this apodictic, utopian legislation, but the principle itself was never abrogated in all Jewish history. The community—indeed, in principle the entire world community—was to be as egalitarian as possible, and no person might legitimately take advantage of any other. The Talmud regards universal prohibition of interest as mere extrapolation from biblical standards. To be sure, there is no clear demarcation between "biblical" and "rabbinic" legislation, since everything is finally derived from the Torah-in-writing, and everything is also capable of elaborate interpretation in the Oral Torah at the hands of the sages.[3]

The rabbis also know the principle of "beyond the mere letter of the law," and, for them, it is a firm moral demand not to take interest or otherwise to oppress the poor, one of eleven fundamental values that are the essence of the Torah.[4] God himself gives without expectation of recompense; so must we, his children. We are even less than stewards of God's world. Essentially, we do not own it at all, even temporarily. We may be forced to bend our egalitarian principle in order to survive, and our survival is a very important commandment; we might be able to make a living only by doing what is impermissible, but violation remains impermissible. "One

97

who increases money-lending on interest is an idolator." It is the exception to the rule, the weakening of the equality principle, that is the basis for Jewish money-lending in the medieval and early modern world. The norm hides itself, but it never disappears completely.[5]

Hillel the Elder, the most decisive legalist of early rabbinic Judaism and the founder of a rabbinic dynasty, began the process of evasion in his famous *prozbol*,[6] a method of avoiding the law by submitting loans in advance for collection by the *bet din* (rabbinic court). But we must remember that the *prozbol* (notice the Greek term, since no Hebrew word was available for such a clear violation of essential Hebrew law) was to be valid only while the Jewish people were in exile, when the sabbatical legislation itself could not be properly observed. The *prozbol* was permitted *mipnai tikkun ha'olam*—that is to say, in order to keep the world in being. But Samuel, one of the greatest of Talmudic sages, permitted himself to say that if he could, he would nullify what Hillel had innovated 250 years earlier.[7]

The rabbis even forbade what they called "the dust of interest," any increment achieved by merely automatic development of financial values as well as by initial agreement.[8] They also forbade "evasive interest" (cover-up of usury), and accused those who dealt in interest of being thieves and murderers, vicious people who will have no share in the world to come. These quasi-violations of the principle may have been suggested by the *prozbol*, but they were never really allowed.

These legal formulations, however theoretical at various stages of Jewish history, imply that no one has a right to make money without working for it. Lending capital is not working, nor can interest be understood as compensation for releasing one's wealth for a period and thus be permitted. Money is not a commodity, from which it follows that "money never effects possession, never gives legitimate title." Rights are not guaranteed by apparent ownership. No one can claim to own something just because he "has" it. Coins are only as valuable as their simple physical reality; there can be no real depreciation by use of them. A profit is legitimate only when and if real risk has been shared. To sell money for more than it is worth is *ona'ah*, forbidden overcharge.[9]

Borrowing and lending money inexorably change relationships between people into master-slave relationships (Prov. 22:7). Proto-capitalism reduces human contact to mutual exploitation. It is not only the poor who are thus dehumanized, but the whole society that becomes contaminated by a cash nexus. The tribal family is reduced to a society of exploitation, even one of mutual exploitation. The weaker depends on the stronger and begs from him the use of his greater resources, by which the more powerful becomes even more powerful in accepting some recompense from the weaker.[10]

The *halakhic* mode is apodictic and meta-ethical. It makes specific demands upon specific individuals in specific situations. Rabbinic tradition builds on the biblical law at the same time that it renders that law more precise and more elaborate as well as more realistic. Economic issues, like all other human-social problems, are dealt with in legalizing formulations. Obviously I cannot summarize the whole of Jewish tradition here, but I understand this tradition to be moving normally in the direction of egalitarianism. Hillel might bypass the law against taking interest. Others might permit, even glorify, early "capitalism." But no one could ignore the basic, authentic, *halakhic* demands to take the poor more seriously than any other segment of society, to unite with their needs and their demands.

Jewish legalism cannot be identified *tout court* with utopian socialism, but I believe it moves closer and closer to that very ideal. By limiting the right of the powerful, by refusing to let privileged individuals manipulate society, by seeing political problems in social— not to say theological—terms, the rabbis serve the cause of equalization, equalization not only of opportunity but also of outcome. The law of Judaism is no (mere?) pastoral suggestion. It is the demand that God places upon every Jew, and to disobey it is to court retribution. The rich may not get richer, and the poor are not condemned to vain, unheard complaining. As Hermann Cohen always insisted, we see that neighbor whom we must love as ourselves pre-eminently in the poor. God has more than a preferential option for the poor.

The *Shulhan Aruch,* an authoritative code of the sixteenth century, is especially explicit about the dangers of interest.[11] The laws of interest are not found, as we might expect, in the book of civil law; they are found in the part of the code that deals with religious and moral duties, the central theme of which is to avoid heathenish behavior. This is both unexpected and theologically sound: owning property is theft unless it is also religiously validated. Even section 159, titled "It is permitted to lend to non-Jews on interest," in fact makes it almost impossible to do so. "The Talmud prohibits the lending to non-Jews except to preserve life, for which reason alone we now permit it." Moses Isserles, the crucial Ashkenazic commentator, adds an immediate qualification: "It is better to be rigorous about interest if at all feasible." He even insists that we may take no interest at all from a non-Jew, if only because the non-Jew may once have been a Jewish child stolen from his parents and raised by Gentiles.[12] If there is any reason to take non-Jewish interest, it is that Gentiles have persecuted us and driven us to defend ourselves in the only way we can.

In the twentieth century, Rabbi Israel Meir Ha-Kohen of Lithuania, called the *Hafets Hayim* and perhaps the most famous moral and legal authority of the early part of our century, devoted the greater part of a book, *The Love of Kindness,* to the evil of taking interest. To him biblical *hesed* means nothing more or less than lending money without gain; taking interest from Jew or Gentile decreases the amount of love in our God-given world.[13]

Halakhic Norms as a Model for Humanity

These are strong statements, and they are to be taken seriously. They are not pastoral suggestions; they are *halakhic* norms. Jews must do what they are commanded to do; they are not allowed to make the world less equal, or to exploit their neighbor in the interest of becoming more successful. The poor are not there for us to use but there for us to succor, to eliminate as an underclass. Methodologies may be debated. What is beyond debate is the straightforward law that obligates us to reduce inequities at our own expense, to do nothing that widens the gap between rich and poor. This is no mere "preferential option for the poor"; it is plain identification with them. We do not help the poor; we share their fate and are bound to change their status even at personal cost for the sake of our religious commitment. God commands us to divest ourselves of anything that makes us more able to exploit our fellow. The year of release is a profound symbol and a model for humanity as a whole.[14]

Martin Buber brilliantly formulated the modern import of these Jewish approaches to a better society in *Paths in Utopia,*[15] a book he wrote during the Holocaust of World War II, a time of the greatest possible threat to optimism or even to intellectual courage. In this book Buber traces the history of utopian socialism as a corrective to and a crucial modification of Soviet Marxism. Assuming that the future belongs to some version of socialist thinking, Buber insists that alternative scenarios are available that would have sharply differing consequences for modern societies. One he labels "Moscow" and the other, with some diffidence, "Jerusalem."

One version of socialism is the state socialism of a centralist polity—coercive, relentlessly collectivist, and regularly transgressing the bonds of personal freedom in the service of a totally regulated economy in which equality is only a pretense while power is decisive. Against this model Buber posits the "Jewish" alternative of a truly participatory democracy, a "community of communities" in which the political principle (the community's organization of force) would be subordinated in theory and in practice to a humane, human-scale social principle that is rigorously biblical. The community practices functional autonomy and mutual responsibility. It insures the "custody of true boundaries," the protection of individual rights, especially the rights of the underprivileged, because, above all, it is to be centered in a "religious" idea, one that conforms to a Jewish model of folk and law at least as much as to the Christian model of brotherhood and agapic love. This raises a question about the bishops' pastoral: Is an approach which seeks a political principle that would encompass all ideologies really preferable to one which fosters a communal ethos that is harder to define, let alone to defend, but, as Buber holds, would be more useful to the hazardous future of humankind, because it would delineate truly human situations?

I am not prepared to argue that Buber's model is the only one possible for Jews, but I do claim that, as in so many other cases, Buber has reached the heart of the Jewish message—in this case, our urge to equality. "Functional autonomy" in the context of "mutual responsibility" is precisely what Jewish social ethics is all about. A laissez-faire personalism is permitted only in the normative context of concern for all others in the community, especially for the disadvantaged. The bishops may be giving more than mere advice; they must consider their teaching, in some respect, moral principle as well as prudential judgment. But Buber, it seems to me, soars above them in messianic vision balanced by a careful rehearsal of the utopian moment in history. From the Bible to Buber (but also to the *Hafets Hayim* and the late codes of Jewish law, which are far more orthodox in provenience and in acceptance), there is an unmistakable desire to shake off the provisional and the unfair in human society and to substitute, first in theory and then in practice, what God not only wants but demands of us all.

If the bishops' pastoral is in any sense typical of Christian thinking about poverty and human dignity and if, similarly, my critique is in any sense an authentic Jewish response, then matters are quite different than customary comparisons of Christian and Jewish ethics suggest. Most students would probably say that Christian ethics is a utopian, messianic ethics of love and that Jewish ethical systems are both more realistic and willing to accept less of humankind. Still, from Deuteronomy to Marx, there has always been an element of the "excessive" about Jewish ethical principles, and the Roman Catholic Church, at least, has long learned to live comfortably with political and economic structures that are far from perfectionist, much less perfect.

I am urging that, contrary to received opinion, the Jewish moralist must want more than a "preference for the poor"— indeed, must press on in economic matters toward increasing equality of outcome as well as of worth among all human beings. The laws of the Sabbatical Year and Jubilee are good examples of the Jewish insistence that naked competition is equivalent to oppression and that society must continously regulate greed as well as what the rabbis called *ona'ah,* which I dare to translate "capitalism." The bishops have tried energetically to adapt and modify customary rhetorical and scholarly modes but have, I believe, surrendered the most important religious resource of all—the believer's attempt to see things from the perspective of God and of that unity of the human species which is projected by any authentic messianism. They have gained in clarity and nuance and perhaps also in the possibility of persuasion. But something precious has been lost that, one fears, will never be recovered in all the time to come.[16]

9 | *The Prophetic Tradition and Social Transformation*

Frida Kerner Furman

As a religiously liberal Jew, I appreciate the bishops' construction of the moral vision that informs their perspective on the American economy. For the bishops are interested not only in reaching their own religious constituencies but in making common cause and moving toward cultural consensus with other groups and individuals in the American polity. In regard to Jews, the bishops explicitly state, "We also claim the Hebrew Scriptures as common heritage with our Jewish brothers and sisters, and we join with them in the quest for an economic life worthy of the divine revelation we share" (par. 29). Despite differences in substance and experience between the two traditions—Catholic and Jewish—the bishops' marked appeal to the Hebrew prophets rings true to liberal Jews, certainly to this one. Liberal Jews would readily agree with the bishops that the "substance of prophetic faith is proclaimed by Micah: 'to do justice, and to love kindness, and to walk humbly with your God' (Mi. 6:8, RSV)" (par. 337). Many Jews would go so far as to say that this, in fact, is the substance of Judaism itself. These would be Jews deeply influenced by early Reform Judaism's accent on the ethical—especially the ethical as proclaimed by the Hebrew prophets—as the very core of Judaism.

In their efforts to generate public discourse on issues pertaining to the American economic order, the bishops succeed in constructing a bridge between the religious convictions and traditions of their own community and a pluralistic society that might not assent to their particularistic commitments. That bridge involves the use of

103

the prophets, who in person as well as in message model a profound sensitivity to injustice—a sensitivity that transcends significant differences as it links those sharing a common inheritance. The prophets thus offer Christians and Jews a basis for a common vision of social justice and a possibility for joint action in its achievement.

As the bishops use the prophets for this bridging role, so did modernizing Jews who began to find a place in Western European society late in the eighteenth century. They too were called upon to bridge the particular and the universal, the religious and the secular, the traditional and the modern. Not surprisingly, the prophetic message became a principal tool used by the early Reform movement to interpret the meaning of Judaism to a rapidly modernizing Jewish population. Conversely, the "prophetic" interpretation of Judaism— as a religion committed principally to universalistic ethical commands—allowed for Jewish access to a Christian world then deeply informed by the Enlightenment's universalistic and rationalistic convictions.

That interpretation of the prophetic tradition has left its mark. Among American Jews interested in formulating a Jewish social ethic, there has been a pervasive tendency to find the source for social transformation in the prophets. In this essay I will explore three interpretations of the prophetic tradition by Jews living in twentieth-century America. I will look at the ways in which Stephen S. Wise, Abraham Joshua Heschel, and Arthur Waskow use prophetic consciousness and mandates in linking Judaism to social demands. Given the absence in modern Judaism of a single, coherent perspective that encompasses all Jews, the manner in which each of these individuals defines Judaism and its moral imperatives varies according to historical context, personal background, and ideological orientation. But all three, like the bishops, are involved in the task of religious social ethics—that is, connecting religious vision and social dilemmas, theology and action.

Stephen S. Wise

I begin with Stephen S. Wise (1874-1949), a rabbi and major public figure in both Jewish and non-Jewish worlds in the first half of this century. From an early age, Wise was an activist on behalf of numerous progressive causes: labor unions, racial equality and civil rights, women's suffrage, and workers' rights, including the battle against child labor and economic discrimination. He worked actively against political corruption and economic exploitation, often at a high cost to his personal life.

Despite his many activities in the political arena, Wise's self-identity was always principally that of a rabbi. He repeatedly argued that there is no boundary between religion and politics, between the synagogue and the work of the world. He asserted, in fact, that "for me the supreme declaration of our Hebrew Bible was and remains: 'Justice, Justice shalt thou pursue'—whether it be easy or hard, whether it be justice to white or black, Jew or Christian."[1] It was this passion for justice that sent Wise in search of a specifically Jewish vision of social transformation.

Ordained in 1893, Wise soon joined the Reform movement and was deeply influenced by many of its assumptions. In locating the core of Judaism in prophetic Judaism, Wise was working out of a *particular* conception of Judaism, one reflecting Reform influences. Later in life, Wise was to wonder whether this conception was too narrow, since the Jewish tradition is much broader than the prophetic message alone. In his autobiography, entitled *Challenging Years*, he writes that he and the Free Synagogue, his New York congregation of forty-two years, had made a mistake in changing the Sabbath service to Sunday and in dispensing with the reading from the Torah Scroll: "What we sought was to substitute the living voice of the Hebrew Prophets for the little-understood reading of the Hebrew Pentateuchal or Torah Scroll. . . . Herein we erred, for . . . even the form of the Torah, the Scroll of the Law, had become too precious to the tradition of the synagogue to be lightly, indeed on any account, abolished."[2]

Wise and others of his day were deeply influenced by the Social Gospel movement of American Protestantism. This movement, which spanned the period from the 1880s to the beginning of World War I, linked the social message of Jesus to the thought of the Hebrew prophets. Wise cites his indebtedness to several Social Gospel writers in formulating his own connections between religion and social transformation. It is therefore not surprising that Wise's social agenda closely mirrored that of Social Gospel adherents in the face of rapid industrialization and its concomitant economic exploitation.

Progressivism, Americanism, and liberalism further served to fortify Wise's attachment to the prophetic tradition. The early part of the twentieth century was a time of optimism and belief in progress. Progressivism and its concerns with social welfare were crucial in formulating Wise's actions on behalf of social justice. Wise's devotion to American democracy and its ideals was no less influential in charting the course of his commitments. Here his passionate belief in the ethical teachings of the prophets merge with Jeffersonian conceptions of an egalitarian society. As his biographer suggests, Wise saw his Americanism and his Jewishness as mutually reinforcing: "It was his Americanism that led him to support throughout his life the liberal ideals of democracy *whose roots he found in the writings of the biblical prophets*" (emphasis added).[3] Similarly, Wise developed an ideological linkage between political liberalism and Judaism. He believed, for example, that liberalism is the religious expression of "the Jewish spiritual genius" and that the Jew "is a native and incurable liberal, as well as idealist, and liberalism [is] a part, a very considerable part, of [the Jew's] political faith."[4]

Consistent with the Reform emphasis on the ethical basis of Judaism, Wise focused on the ethical content of the prophetic message and left the *religious* nature of the prophet's calling relatively unaddressed. An activist by temperament rather than a thinker or scholar, Wise did not locate his ethics in deep theological grounding. He simply viewed human beings as partners with God, doing God's work on earth, fulfilling the prophet's command to pursue justice. It seems to me that Wise's view of justice—his concern with human rights, for example—emerged as much from the shaping context of early twentieth-century America as from the voices of the Hebrew prophets, was as much a result of historical circumstances as a result of religious necessity. Religious liberals of the period, whether Jewish or Christian, often fused their religious ideals with the moral imperatives of the moment. The Hebrew prophets surely appeared to provide to Wise and to others a fitting model for the expression of moral indignation against the widespread instances of social exploitation and oppression in their day.

While he was unquestionably rooted in the Jewish religious and cultural tradition, Wise had strong universalistic proclivities—that is, leanings toward values transcending the particularism of Jews and Judaism. Indeed, at times his use of the prophetic message as his central ethical thrust reveals this universalistic sensibility seeking Jewish legitimation. The various strands of thought and social movements that influenced him during his life repeatedly led him in search of a religiously valid source. In locating this source in the prophets, he succeeded in finding a Jewish but also an inclusive ground from which he could appeal to Jew and Christian, white or black, religious or secularist alike. His success and popularity as both a religious leader and a civic leader across religious and racial lines testify to his success as a cultural broker, as a builder of consensus that transcends deeply entrenched differences by finding common ground—one shaped by a shared heritage. In fact, Wise did mediate between and among communities, using the prophets to justify moral passion on behalf of political aims. As John Haynes Holmes put it, "Here was the paradox of the Jew become the universal man. Wise was a Jew who was more than a Jew. This was the secret of his greatness as a prophet and a statesman. Rabbi Wise loved Israel as his own, and then found in Israel mankind."[5]

Abraham Joshua Heschel

Like Stephen Wise, Abraham Joshua Heschel (1907-1972) was a rabbi intensely attuned to the Hebrew prophets. Born in Poland, he emigrated to the United States during World War II. Heschel was fundamentally a scholar, steeped in both Jewish learning and the Western philosophical tradition. Unlike Wise, Heschel became a social activist late in life. In the early 1960s, while preparing the English edition of his influential work entitled *The Prophets,* Heschel acknowledged this late change: "I've written a book on the prophets, a rather large book. I spent many years. And, really, this book changed my life. Because early in my life, my great love was for learning, studying. And the place where I preferred to live was my study and books and writing and thinking. I've learned from the prophets that I have to be involved in the affairs of man, in the affairs of suffering man."[6]

Heschel's involvements in social action included the civil rights movement, ecumenism, the antiwar movement of the Vietnam era, and opposition to ageism. In many circles Heschel himself came to be characterized as a prophetic figure; Reinhold Niebuhr, for example, described him as "the most authentic prophet of religious life in our culture."[7]

Heschel develops his understanding of the Hebrew prophets and the significance of their message for the condition of the world in *The Prophets.* His profoundly theological probing of the character of the prophet and of prophetic consciousness carries us far beyond Wise's efforts. Heschel identifies the prophet as a figure who stands between God and humanity: "The prophet's eye is directed to the contemporary scene; the society and its conduct are the main theme of his speeches. Yet his ear is inclined to God. He is a person struck by the glory and presence of God, overpowered by the hand of God. Yet his true greatness is his ability to hold God and man in a single thought."[8] In brief, prophets are profoundly theocentric figures, and so is their message, for the main task of prophets is "to bring the world into divine focus." Through the prophets' words, "*the invisible God becomes audible.*"[9]

Through their pronouncements the prophets reveal God's care and will for humanity, but never God's essence, for the latter is not available to them or to any human beings. And in prophetic consciousness, God's will always means a call for human beings to repent, to change their ways, and to act on behalf of justice. For the prophet, this call to justice is not simply a principle or norm but a command. What most people may judge to be a social injustice the prophet judges a desecration.

The call to justice is such a pervasive aspect of prophetic discourse that Heschel is compelled to ask, "Why should a worldly virtue like justice be so important to the Holy One of Israel?" He concludes that justice is not a human value or a cultural convention but a "transcendent demand, freighted with divine concern . . . a divine need. . . . It is not one of His ways, but in all His ways." Justice, then, is a presupposition of biblical faith, "not an added attribute to His essence, but given with the very thought of God. It is inherent in His essence and identified with His ways."[10]

Heschel cites Isaiah 5:16: "But the Lord of hosts shall be exalted in justice, The Holy One of Israel sanctified in righteousness." Then he asks, "Why should His justice be the supreme manifestation of God? Is not wisdom or omnipotence a mode of manifestation more magnificent and more indicative of what we associate with the divine?" Heschel's response provides an entree into his concept of divine pathos. He argues that the "preoccupation with justice, the passion with which the prophets condemn injustice, is rooted in their sympathy with divine pathos. The chief characteristic of prophetic thought is the primacy of God's involvement in history."[11]

The prophets' understanding of justice is not based on an abstract idea. Rather, prophets are proclaimers of God's pathos: they speak for the God of justice, for God's concern for justice. The God of Israel is a God who cares for his creation, who is involved in history because of concern for humanity. The prophets proclaim God's intimate relatedness to humanity. They report their knowledge of God not by virtue of superior intellect or illumination but through their receptivity to the word of God and to the presence of God.

When referring to God, the basic biblical category is action. God chooses to become involved in the human drama, and in so doing he elicits a human response. As God acts in the ways of justice, so must human beings act too. For Heschel this is the meaning of the *imago Dei* of Genesis 1:26-27:[12] "The idea of man having been created in the image of God was interpreted, it seems, not as *an analogy of being* but as *an analogy of doing.* Man is called upon to act in the likeness of God. 'As he is merciful be thou merciful.'"[13]

Divine pathos suggests that while God initiates contact with humanity and engages in human history, God *needs* human beings as co-actors in the life of the world. Human beings are commanded to act justly as partners with God in the business of the world. Such obligations are imperative not only in the great events of human history but also in the routines of everyday life. The prophets demonstrate that point in the importance they attribute to the "trivialities" of human affairs:

> The prophet's field of concern is not the mysteries of heaven, but the affairs of the market place; not the spiritual realities of the Beyond, but the life of the people; not the glories of eternity, but the blights of society. He addresses himself to those who trample upon the needy and destroy the poor of the land; who increase the price of the grain, use dishonest scales, and sell the refuse of the corn. (Amos 8:4-6)[14]

Like Wise, Heschel located the imperative of social justice in the Hebrew prophets. Unlike Wise, however, Heschel arrived at this perspective through a prolonged study of prophetic consciousness, which he found to be fundamentally informed by religious experience. Heschel's understanding of justice is grounded in his view of a God of justice, who, through the prophets, informs humanity of his will, his actions, his vulnerability, and his need of human help in completing the work of creation. In this way Heschel's treatment of the prophets considerably expands that of Wise by making the prophetic experience, reality, and message quite explicit.

While Heschel's interpretation of God's pathos and its concomitant call for human action provides a religious orientation to sociopolitical life, his discussion remains at a certain level of abstraction, short of a full-fledged social ethic. Although Heschel invokes the prophets in connection with problems of racial equality, peace, and ageism, his use of the prophets remains at an evocative, inspirational, spiritual level. Heschel's treatment reveals a fundamentally accurate understanding of the power and the limits of the prophetic message. The prophets sensitize us to identify evil—or, conversely, good—in our midst. Yet we may have to turn elsewhere to find principles that will justify our specific social policy positions and decisions.

Arthur Waskow and the Movement for Jewish Renewal

No figure of Wise's or Heschel's stature or public influence whose social ethics is infused with a powerful prophetic consciousness has emerged in the 1980s from the center of the Jewish community. As in American society at large, elements of the Jewish community have turned toward social and political conservatism. Instead, the prophetic voice is being heard from the margins of the established Jewish community, as part of what some have called the movement for Jewish renewal.

Loosely conceived, that movement includes the rise of *havurot* (fellowship groups) in the early 1970s as a reaction to the perceived alienating and hierarchical nature of large synagogues. These groups, now existing both inside and outside synagogue structures, have contested some major features of Jewish religious life and have attempted, through joint study and celebration, to internalize some central values of Jewish tradition. In some cases serious thought has been given to the application of Jewish values to the *havurah's* social and political action in the community. Those *havurot* committed to an agenda of social transformation could be seen as middle-class Jewish analogues to Latin American base communities.

The movement for Jewish renewal also includes New Jewish Agenda, an organization founded in 1980 that is committed to progressive political action from a Jewish perspective. Its national platform states, "Many of us base our convictions on the Jewish religious concept of *tikkun olam* (the just ordering of human society and the world) and the prophetic tradition of social justice. . . . New Jewish Agenda's national platform upholds progressive Jewish values and affirms that the goals of peace and justice are attainable."[15] Specific commitments of the New Jewish Agenda include the complete equality of women and men; struggle against racism and militarism; affirmative action and the defense of civil liberties for all; support for the labor movement, economic justice, and environmental concerns; and work for a comprehensive peace agreement between Palestinians and Jews in the Middle East.[16]

Many of these goals are shared by *Tikkun,* a progressive journal founded in 1986. Its name refers to the Jewish obligation to mend and transform the world. "TIKKUN MAGAZINE hopes to provide a voice for those who still dare to hope," its editors assert, "for those who are not embarrassed to dream, for those Jews and non-Jews alike who are still moved by the radical spirit of the Prophets and who insist on keeping their message alive. . . . The utopian demand for transformation is something we proudly identify with—it remains a central ingredient in Jewish vision."[17]

Arthur Waskow has been an architect and frequent spokesperson for the movement for Jewish renewal. A member of New Jewish Agenda and of the editorial board of *Tikkun,* he was an early activist in the *havurah* movement as well. Waskow's writing provides a helpful example of the way that the prophetic voice is being used by some contemporary Jews. We must therefore consider him an important representative of one strand of contemporary American Jewry and its attempts to link Judaism to social transformation.

Waskow was deeply involved in leftist politics during the 1960s. During an eventful Passover in 1968, he "crossed the frontier from being a committed Jewish radical, to being a committed radical Jew."[18] This transition was effected through the use of *midrash*, an ancient Jewish interpretative method for connecting ancient texts to contemporary reality. Waskow felt he undertood the real meaning of the political events taking place that spring in Washington, D.C., once he saw them through the prism of the Hebrew Bible. Since then he has consistently returned to the Torah narratives and the prophets in an effort to link Jewish tradition and experience to the social, political, and economic problems of the larger world.

Waskow's writing is evocative and explorative. Autobiography blends with social and political analysis; *midrash* co-exists with anecdotal recollections. While he may as readily appeal to a biblical narrative as to a prophet's pronouncements regarding, say, economic justice, he is nonetheless working out of what the Catholic theologian Rosemary Radford Ruether calls the "prophetic principle." Ruether argues that this principle, emerging from the biblical prophetic tradition, at heart advocates the liberation of the oppressed and the critique of dominant systems of power and their power-holders. Prophetic consciousness thus calls for liberation from bondage and for the acknowledgment of an underlying equality among human beings, dictating a position against hierarchies.[19]

Invoking the Exodus as the history of a "band of runaway slaves," Waskow commits himself to liberation—political, economic, and cultural. A recurrent reference to Egypt's Pharaoh bespeaks his opposition to all forms of repressive, idolatrous power. The law of the Jubilee Year (Lev. 25) becomes for Waskow a major principle of distributive justice, calling as it does for the utter leveling of economic differences in the face of God's ultimate ownership of the land. For Waskow the Jubilee has critical implications for our time:

> The Torah's definition of economic justice is that once every generation, every face-to-face community . . . in a society must attain equal ownership and control of the crucial means of production. If that doesn't happen once a generation, you don't have economic justice. The tradition doesn't require continuous equality from moment to moment, month to month, year to year. What it does require is that we be willing to transform the society, to start over.[20]

The task of sociopolitical transformation is critical for Waskow. He symbolizes such transformation by reference to the Lurianic mystical notion of *tikkun:* divine sparks of holiness were once scattered throughout the world and now need to be regathered through the work of repair and transformation. Heschel's understanding that the God of pathos needs human beings finds congruence here, as does the traditional Jewish idea that it is through human effort that God's creation is completed. For Waskow the prophets' call for justice is a central part of the process of *tikkun: wholeness and justice go hand in hand.*

The key to achieving social transformation is to fuse those elements of Jewish consciousness that have become fractured with the advent of modernism. Waskow calls for the linking of those aspects of Jewish experience that have become disjoined: the spiritual and the material, the religious and the secular, the particularistic and the universalistic, the religious and the political, the traditional and the modern. Waskow's approach to social transformation is a synthesis of Wise and Heschel. He recognizes the moral imperatives emerging from a modern, secularized culture, as Wise did, and the necessity for Jews to work with others in bringing about a more just society. But Waskow is also aware, as Heschel was, that a connection to religious values and resources is essential if the Jew is to remain a Jew and to live an authentic Jewish existence.

One of Waskow's favorite images for bringing about renewal—and hence sociopolitical transformation—is that of wrestling. As Jacob wrestled with the angel on the eventful night that forged his identity as Israel, contemporary Jews must wrestle with the Torah—with the textual corpus of Judaism—in constructing an identity that is authentic and complete.

Waskow's analysis of the bifurcation of Torah and politics in the world of American Jewish organizations is a perceptive one. Premodern Jews had little hand in determining political and economic policies for themselves, let alone for the societies of which they were a part. Questions of war and peace, the use of natural resources, and the choice of private or public investment of capital were not part of their experience for two thousand years. In the last few generations, organizations with political influence have been developed in the Jewish community: witness the American Jewish Committee, the American Jewish Congress, the Anti-Defamation League, and the American Israel Public Affairs Committee. Yet these organizations "have operated without regard to Torah when they were deciding what Jewish interests were. . . . No one hurried to fill these institutions with Jewish content. That, like the other aspects of the regathering of the sparks, has been an effort of the movement for Jewish renewal."[21]

Here Waskow's agenda is parallel to the bishops' attempt to provide a moral vision, based on Catholic teaching, for the economic order. Recognizing the shortcomings of existing modern political ideologies, Waskow intends to explore the Torah, the wisdom of the Jewish past—not to control current societal decisions but to inform them profoundly: "It is out of an authentic encounter between our different selves (postmodern Jews and Torah) that renewed truth will emerge. . . . Torah carries teachings that are crucial if humankind is to survive its present profound crisis and to transform the world rather than destroy it."[22]

For Waskow the call to renew Jewish identity through a wrestling with Jewish sources is not a call to retreat into Jewish insularity. Rather than turning either inward, forgetting the world for the sake of a rich Jewish life, or outward, stripping ourselves of our Jewishness in order to improve the world, we must bridge particularity and universality, Waskow insists: "Our task is to see *within* our own particular path the Rainbow of universal truth, and . . . weave new Jewish cloth from those strands of universal modern thought that will blend with the strands of our ancient wisdom, and then go actively to the other peoples to encourage them to weave their own new clothing—so as to warm us all."[23]

Justice and Wholeness

None of these figures whom we have examined deals with the problem of economic justice in a systematic or comprehensive manner. All three, I believe, are involved in finding a Jewish perspective from which to address issues of social transformation as diverse as racial and gender equality, the labor movement, war and peace, and Jewish-Arab tensions. That all three turn to the prophetic faith of the Bible is significant.

I believe the use of the prophetic tradition in part attests to its classic nature. After more than 2,500 years, the prophets' pronouncements still tap our moral sensibilities—those of Jews and Christians alike—and sometimes stir us to action. This is all the more true in America, given the religious roots of this country and the continuing expression of a civil religion grounded in the Bible.

The pluralism of American culture does not automatically lead to a value consensus on matters of great social importance such as economic justice. What our complex society needs are moral sensibilities inclusive in nature—powerful enough to give ethical direction but not so narrow in their focus that one or another group feels excluded. The prophetic message has continuing transformative possibilities for American culture. We have seen this in the early religious liberalism of Wise but also in the postmodern thought of Waskow.

Within the American Jewish community, the prophetic tradition has played an important role. Many Jews have become wholly acculturated to American society; others have retained their attachment to Jewish culture while eschewing a religious identification. For this population of non-*halakhic* Jews, an inclusive, nonparticularistic message of social justice—such as the prophets'—may be more appealing and more familiar than principles drawn from classical or rabbinic Judaism, which may not resonate with their experience and may in fact prove to be alienating. For those affiliated with the liberal branches of Judaism, prophetic Judaism may form part and parcel of their ideology, readily identified as an essential element of Judaism. In these cases the prophets are used to inspire commitment to social transformation. All too often, however, the prophetic message is truncated when it is torn from its religious grounding and presented solely as ethical mandates. The prophets were "incurably religious," standing, as they did, between God and humanity. Thus Heschel's work offers a necessary corrective to the nonreligious appropriation of their pronouncements.

What we have seen in this discussion is that the bishops' use of the prophetic tradition in developing their moral vision finds parallels in attempts by modern Jews to establish a link between religion and social transformation. Wise, Heschel, and Waskow alike ground their concerns with issues of social justice in the biblical prophets. All three, I believe, find that the prophets provide insights universal enough to transcend Jewish particularity and to allow for engagement with others in the struggle for social justice in America. Here too there is confluence with the bishops' intentions. The bishops might lend an ear, however, to the broader conception of the prophetic principle articulated by Waskow. For Waskow *tikkun* suggests bringing justice and wholeness not only to the public square but to the fractured elements of contemporary Jewish life and experience. For different reasons and through different dynamics, today's Catholic world is also fragmented, also in need of *tikkun*. If Waskow is correct, social transformation must go hand in hand with gathering the sparks of holiness within our separate communities.

10 | *Bishops, Rabbis, and Prophets*

Leonard Fein

No Jew who is fluent in the Jewish tradition can fail to be struck by the consonance between the themes and language of the U.S. bishops' pastoral on the economy, *Economic Justice for All*, and the relevant texts of the Jewish tradition. In significant degree, the consonance is explicit: the bishops specifically rest much of their case on biblical writings and paradigms. But even where they move beyond the classic texts to "the reasoned analysis of human experience by contemporary men and women" (par. 28), their form of expression will strike resonant chords for the informed Jewish reader. The pastoral is addressed principally to Catholics, but the bishops plainly had in mind that it would be read with interest by others, and wisely framed their arguments in language that would be accessible to all Americans, especially to those who share in what has come to be known as the Judeo-Christian tradition.

Still, and for all its catholicity, the pastoral remains—as it should—a *Catholic* document, resting heavily on the specific imagery and metaphor of Catholic doctrine. From the opening of its covering letter—"Brothers and Sisters in Christ: We are believers called to follow our Lord Jesus Christ and proclaim his Gospel in the midst of a complex and powerful economy"—to the references in its last paragraph to Mary and Jesus, its appeal is to a particular community of faith.

One understands the belief, habits, and strategies that give rise to such an appeal. In theory, the prospects for what the bishops call "conversion" (and Jews would call *t'shuvah*) are thereby enhanced; people are most likely to be moved if we speak to them in their own language. But can we confidently assume that American Catholics (or, as I will soon ask, American Jews) still have their own language? In fact, the bishops do not make that assumption: While they argue valiantly that Christians' attitudes toward the economic realm cannot be sundered from Christian faith, they complain of "a tragic separation between faith and everyday life" (par. 5, PM). That is why they seek to make the relationship between the two explicit.

In order to succeed, they must repair the disjunction between the implications of faith and the exigencies of politics, between God's kingdom and Caesar's. That disjunction may or may not be thought "tragic"; it is by now part of the conventional understanding. We cannot assume that members of faith communities take for granted that the injunctions of their faith have compelling implications for their economic attitudes and behaviors.

Having long since lost the habit of connecting the two realms, most of us turn to religious sources (if at all) principally for sermonic themes or for general ethical insight, typically vague, even banal. If we are interested in matters economic, we are considerably more likely to turn to the econometrician than to the prophet. We do not turn to our priests and rabbis, the dead or the living, to learn what rate of unemployment or what pattern of income distribution is or ought to be acceptable in a modern industrial economy.

My purpose in this essay is to explore the compartmentalization of religion, the disjunction between ethics and interests, between the language of faith and the language of politics, as it affects America's Jews. What problems arise if one seeks to compose an appeal for economic justice that is addressed to Jews? In what language might such an appeal be written, and how persuasive might it be? How, in brief, shall we come to Jews qua Jews with a plea for economic justice?

Citation and Counter-Citation

One strategy might be (and often is) to cite "the Jewish view" on economic justice, arguing either from our classic texts or from our historic tradition, seeking to prove that Judaism "requires" this or that set of economic arrangements. Setting aside the problem that we are, by and large, ignorant of Jewish sources, which renders our texts inaccessible to most of us, we encounter here two problems.

The *first* is that our textual sources, as Harold Schulweis has observed, reflect an "absence of structured ethical theory . . . [a] casual and unsystematic form of ethics."[1] Moreover, again and again

116

we learn from modern scholarship that the nature of the rulings of the rabbis was shaped, as must be obvious, not only by the received tradition but also by the social, political, and economic circumstances of the time. Therefore, if one seeks to extrapolate from the wisdom of eighth-century rabbis some principles that will help guide us through, say, the thicket of economic justice (to say nothing of the jungle of genetic engineering), one ought not be surprised if the effort proves of little value, or if it produces conflicting principles. In the standard Orthodox view, *all* knowledge is implicit in the texts; a trained scholar can search out the applicable principle, arguing either directly or through analogy. But most contemporary Jews would say that such a view quite literally does not stand to reason. More precisely, to Reason.

The ambiguity of the texts is one reason that articles and symposia on "the Jewish view" of this or that are rarely persuasive. Most often the writers of such articles and the speakers at such symposia have gone to the sources to find support for their own prior dispositions. And virtually no matter what those dispositions are, they will find the support they seek. The same tradition informs us, for example, that on the one hand "every man will be held accountable before God for all the permitted things he beheld in life and did not enjoy" and, on the other hand, that "this is the way of Torah: a morsel of bread with salt must thou eat, and water by measure must thou drink, thou must sleep upon the ground and live a life of anguish the while thou toilest in the Torah."[2]

These days we confront a *second* problem as we turn to the classic texts to make the case for economic justice. There has lately been mounted an energetic and explicit attack against the relevance of the prophets. Irving Kristol and other Jewish neoconservatives argue vehemently that American Jews are too mesmerized by ethical concerns, that in the name of such concerns they engage in self-defeating behavior, neglect Jewish interests. Substantively, the neoconservatives call for a return to the rabbinic tradition, which emphasized stability, and a reduced emphasis on the prophetic tradition, which was concerned with justice.

Kristol's well-known line, "A neoconservative is a liberal who's been mugged by reality," suggests the general stereotype: liberals are mushy and vague; conservatives are tough and precise. Above all, liberals are dreamy, while conservatives are practical. The antagonism between the prophetic and the rabbinic traditions is, as Kristol says, "absolutely crucial to an understanding of the relationship between any religion and the real world—the real world of politics, the real world of social life."[3]

Amen. But it is also absolutely crucial to understand that the central reason we remember the prophets as keenly as we do is precisely that they stood at the intersection of the world of religion and "the real world"—the real world of politics, the real world of society—and did not flinch; their power derives from the fact that they brought the two worlds into intimate conversation. It is simply not the case that the prophets were victims of unanchored fervor, that they were escapists who responded to human misery by preaching of good (and just, and peaceful, and make-believe) times to come, realism be damned. That is not how they saw themselves, and that is not how they were heard.

It is easy to be misled into a mistaken view of the prophets. Their poetry was so powerful, their depiction of the future so compelling, that we are caught up in the imagery; what they say speaks so movingly to us that it seems timeless.

But the prophets were not speaking for the ages: they spoke for their times, their place. In the context of those times, that place, their words were chosen for immediate political effect. So, as David Biale observes,

> Prophets such as Isaiah and Jeremiah were neither pacifists nor apolitical moralists. . . . In one of the most famous passages in Jeremiah, the prophet writes to those in exile: "Build houses, settle down . . . , work for the good of the country to which I have exiled you; pray to the Lord on its behalf, since on its welfare yours depends." Far from advocating a withdrawal from politics, Jeremiah was suggesting the very kind of political activism that several generations later led to the successful return from Babylonia, a return predicated on the political successes of the Jews in the Persian court.[4]

Whether the substantive teachings of the prophets be thought wise or foolish, they were political teachings, not sentimental moralizings. Obviously, that is not to say that those teaching were without moral content. On the contrary: what the prophets understood was that the welfare of their society, in the most pragmatic terms, could not be separated from the moral quality of that society. Their analyses took account of both muscles and morals. So, for example, Isaiah 32:17: "The work of righteousness shall be peace, and the effect of righteousness, calm and confidence forever." Here we have a specific endorsement of the view that stability depends on justice, a view explicitly rejected by Kristol, who holds that stability is the precursor of and precondition for justice.

Choosing a Text

One can play an endless game of citation here, bringing this text or that to bear, and then its equally auspicious contradiction. There was Hillel and there was Shammai, there were the Pharisees and there were the Sadducees, there is rabbinic Judaism and there is prophetic Judaism—the sources are confoundingly rich. Sometimes it seems as if Jewish life is an ongoing search for the finally unanswerable citation. Is the difference between an emphasis on justice and an emphasis on stability merely a reflection of the inherent ambiguity of the texts? Is there no way to choose authoritatively between the two views?

There is none. There is only how a community of Jews, bounded by space and by time but not fettered by either, come to understand who and why they are. And from that understanding, what their interests are.

Most of America's Jews have chosen certain citations as normative, and their choices have been profoundly influenced by their experience of modernity in America. It does not much matter, except to the student, that Rabbi Akiba's "Thou shalt love thy neighbor as thyself" almost surely originally referred exclusively to "thy Jewish neighbor," as did the passage from Leviticus (19:18) he was citing. What matters is how we have chosen to understand the words, not how Akiba meant them. For our effort has been and must be to reach into our own souls, not into the minds of those who came before. And the way we have chosen to understand the words of Rabbi Akiba is that they apply to all the children of God.

Of course there are sources that point us in the direction of political quietism as powerfully as Isaiah points us toward activism. But if we spend our time trading sources, the argument will never be resolved. The search for the right source is a futile and mistaken search, for the question is not which source is the weightier, nor is it which is the more authentic; all, accurately cited, are authentic, even in the face of their contradictions and sometime ambiguities. The search is for a way to choose among them.

We are that way. Our search is not for sources to cite but for midrash to write. We pick up those threads of the tradition that seem to us most suited for this time, this place, this people. Inevitably, the way we choose to understand Akiba's words derives from the way in which we understand ourselves. *We* are the text; America, in the closing decades of the twentieth century, is the texture.

"Prophecy," writes Michael Walzer, "is a special kind of talking, not so much an educated as an inspired and a poetic version of

119

what must have been at least sometimes, among some significant part of the prophet's audience, ordinary discourse. . . . Prophecy aims to arouse remembrance, recognition, indignation, repentance." And "the power of a prophet like Amos derives from his ability to say what oppression means, how it is experienced, in this time and place, and to explain how it is connected with other features of a shared social life."[5] Or, as I suggested earlier, if you seek to move people through language, you must speak a language they understand. The God-talk of the prophets is the language that American Jews have traditionally shared; it remains at least rudimentarily accessible to them. That talk, as expressed in the language of a living community, is the bridge between ethics and interests.

I believe that Judaism in our time, as in the time of Amos and Isaiah, can come again to be on the side of indignation, and hence also of political activism. The moment we take seriously the religious injunction to heed the needs of the stranger, we enter the political realm. As Michael Ignatieff has pointed out, "The moral relations that exist between my income and the needs of strangers at my door pass through the arteries of the state."[6] Hence politics.

It is no accident that American Jews have "rediscovered" the prophets, restored them to a centrality they did not have during the whole of the time the rabbinic tradition dominated the Jewish understanding. Since the Enlightenment, Jews—not less than others— have been required to develop a new language in which to talk about God and godliness. That is a process which remains very far from completion, which accounts for the persistence of the compartmentalization of religion that I mentioned earlier. To the degree to which Jews have been able to meet the challenge, they have done so by reviewing their own sources and selecting from among those the threads that would weave most comfortably, most naturally, into the American fabric. Those threads, by and large, are found in the prophets. For it was the prophets who most explicitly addressed the contemporary dilemma of America's Jews—how to be a *part of* the larger community and *apart from* it simultaneously. The rabbis were concerned with a very different set of problems. In the centuries during which they wrote, Jews were not invited to be "a part of." It is the prophets who inspire us to insist on both the particularity of Jewish peoplehood and the universality of Jewish ethical insight.

Hillel the Elder asked rhetorically, "If I am not for myself, who will be for me?" and "If I am only for myself, what am I?" These two questions frame the tension between particularism and universalism. But the universalism that Hillel himself intended by his second question almost surely did not extend beyond the impenetrable walls of the Jewish community. Today we have come to understand that second question far more expansively; in effect, we have read Hillel's question with Jonah's eyes. And we are coming, ever so slowly, to understand that what is expected of us is to live where the two questions meet, there where particularism (read: stability, interests) and universalism (read: justice, ethics) intersect. From the prophets we learn how to bridge the gap, to restore the religious connection, to revive the understanding that ethics and politics are not separate.

Although the tension between the two traditions continues, most American Jews have quite decisively preferred the prophetic to the rabbinic tradition. They have perceived, it would seem, that the prophetic insights accord more naturally both with American themes and with their own situation in America. If the history of a community is part of its "text," as I believe it is and must be, then we have at least a rough method for choosing among competing citations.

From Citation to Action

In October 1986 a new Jewish organization came into being. Called "Mazon: A Jewish Response to Hunger" (*mazon* means "sustenance"), it was the product of a startling statistic and a disarmingly simple idea. In the aggregate, American Jews spend many hundreds of millions of dollars each year on catered celebrations. (The original estimate, in the $500,000,000 range, was based on weddings and bar and bat mitzvah celebrations alone.) Some of these are celebrations of *Goodbye, Columbus* proportions; most are considerably more modest. For years rabbis have railed against excessive consumption; for years, at virtually every level of income, people have been seized by a "can you top this?" fever.

What would be the response if celebrants were encouraged to add voluntarily a three percent surcharge to the cost of such functions, thereby creating a fund with which to make war against hunger?

Out of the statistic and the idea, the organization, a grassroots effort, came into being. In its first year, it raised $163,000; in its second year, now entering its final quarter, it will have raised between five and six hundred thousand dollars. Sometime toward the end of its third year, it will reach the million-dollar-a-year level, reflecting as many as 50,000 individual contributions.

What can we learn from the Mazon experience?

We learn first that there are people in substantial numbers who continue to care. Indeed, up to half the contributions Mazon re-

Leonard Fein

ceives are accompanied by letters expressing the donors' thanks. And we learn that very many people can be reached through the traditional appeal that our bread is to be shared with those in need. Mazon quite specifically avoids asking people to sacrifice for the sake of the poor; its appeal emphasizes instead that the joy of the celebrants is enhanced if their celebration includes this act of kindness toward the stranger. More specifically, Mazon makes its argument in classic language: At the Passover seder, we say, holding up the *matzah*, "This is the bread of affliction; let all who are hungry enter and eat." Citing the verse, Mazon asks whether we can expect the hungry to hear the invitation if we do not seek them out. Citing Isaiah 58—"Is this the fast I have chosen?"—Mazon, through congregational rabbis, asks that on Yom Kippur we turn toward those whose fast will not conclude at day's end, whose fast is not the holy fast of repentance but the scandalous fast of utter poverty.

The language resonates, and the number of contributions grows apace. At one time we left corners of our fields to be gleaned by the poor. At one time, in Eastern Europe, it was routine to invite the beggars to join in our wedding celebrations. Today, far from the fields and afraid of the beggars, we employ a new device.

Perhaps, then, things are not so bleak; apparently people may still be moved by the language of kindness. Mazon speaks to people in a language they understand. It speaks to Jews as Jews.

But why should Jews, *as Jews*, become involved in helping to feed the hungry, who are overwhelmingly non-Jews? If, as we would hope of a religious folk, Jews care about human pain and suffering, why should they not send their contributions directly to Oxfam or to any of the myriad other organizations that fight the good fight?

Here we return to the prophets and to that tension between particularism and universalism that characterizes creative Jewish life. In order for the language of faith to be understood and to elicit a response, there must be a community of faith. In order to repair the breach between "faith" and "everyday life," we must act in the world of everyday life from within the world of faith—or, as I would prefer, the world of faithfulness. In order to preserve that particularity which sustains a faithful community, we must discard the concept of "Jews as Jews." That concept immediately reflects the problem of compartmentalization, for it suggests that sometimes we act as Jews and other times we do not. Religion becomes an object, an activity, rather than a way of life. In a world fully informed by faith, Jews (and, mutatis mutandis, others) cannot but act as Jews; that is who and what they are.

122

What rescues that emphasis on particularism from becoming a narcissistic preoccupation with self-interest is precisely the prophetic tradition. We are anchored by our language—and liberated by it. We nurture both the particular structure and the universal ideology that is the prophetic mandate and, if we so will it, legacy.

The Function of Community

Comes the question: Can we move from the language of kindness to the language of justice? Can we move from philanthropic sensibility to political commitment?

In the context of a serious inquiry into the possibility of economic justice, into the religious mandate for economic justice, Mazon remains a device with important and instructive limitations. First, we learn, as we come closer to the facts of hunger (especially in the United States), that hunger is not so much a tragedy as it is a scandal (there being, in fact, enough food for all). And because that is so, the problem of hunger is not a problem that can readily be solved by charity. Hunger exists not because food is lacking but because the will to justice is lacking. There is, then, empirical confirmation for the ethical insight of the bishops, who say in *Economic Justice for All* that "the guaranteeing of basic justice for all is not an optional expression of largess but an inescapable duty for the whole of mankind" (par. 120).

Why then introduce, even so briefly, the story of a new way to encourage kindness?

Because, as the pastoral letter itself acknowledges, the work of justice—the more so if it is to be on a scale that warrants calling it "a new American experiment" (par. 95)—requires as its first step "the development of a new cultural consensus" (par. 83). Over and over again the bishops place the call for justice in the context of community. And, indeed, it is difficult to imagine any serious move toward economic justice, however defined, save as it arises out of a sure sense of community.

The story of Mazon comes to teach how the latent sense of community can be energized—how, that is, Jews can be joined with other Jews in the work of repair and redemption, and how a largely affluent Jewish community can be joined to the communities of largely non-Jewish poor people in an extended family of humankind.

The interplay between the efforts of private citizens, through their diverse associations, and the polity, through the government, is a subject of enormous complexity. In Catholic teaching it falls within the framework of the "principle of subsidiarity," and, as the bishops wryly observe in a footnote, "the meaning of this principle is not always accurately understood" (par. 99, n. 53). In the Jewish tradition the matter is still more complex, since the classic texts—that is, rabbinic literature—all assumed a fundamental estrangement between the Jewish community and the polity. "The laws of the kingdom are the laws"; Jews did not presume to propose public policy for the states in which they dwelt. Instead, they made "communal" policy for what were, in very large measure, self-governing communities. There was a radical disjunction between society (read: community) and state, rather than the intricate network indicated by the principle of subsidiarity. Clearly, that has changed here in America. Nevertheless, the Jewish experience does not give rise to the concern with subsidiarity to which the Catholic experience points. Generally, Jews have been more concerned with methods of education than with modes of organization and allocation. Specifically, we have learned that ethics are most effectively learned inductively. One learns responsibility for the family of humankind through experiencing responsibility in the smaller family of the group, then the people. We learn responsibility for the stranger by being reminded that we were once strangers.

In our time God's call must rise through the sounds of the cash registers and the lottery wheels, the self-help hucksters and the religious quacks, the jukeboxes and the Jacuzzis, through the sounds of silence and the sounds of indifference. It is not enough to "prove" that the authentic textual mandate is to clothe the naked and feed the hungry; the proof may be convincing, but it must be heard in order for it to convince. God asks, always, "Where are you?" But the question is not in the wind and not in the earthquake and not in the fire; it is in the still small voice. The claims of justice do not thunder; they whisper, and will not be heard above the bedlam. Here and there, from the pulpit and the polling booth, there will be an answering "Here I am." One person and then another will understand life as a response. But most—Jews, Catholics, others—will savor their daily cake, and put a penny in the alms box now and then to clean up the scattered crumbs of guilt.

Unless we build the needed communities that are tuned to the call, each in its own language. And then the bridges that connect politics to ethics and charity and justice.

Justice

On one reading, Mazon provides its participants cheap grace, a relief from the anxieties of lavish spending on self. On a more subtle second reading, Mazon begins the work of building community. It joins Jews to one another through language and through works; it joins those who have to those who want through acts of kindness. But it does not yet directly respond to the question of justice, which remains a far more complex and disturbing question. Indeed, it might be argued (in fact, it has been) that by focusing citizens' attention on voluntary charitable efforts, we relieve the polity of the burden for policy reform; that by emphasizing kindness, we run the risk of postponing justice, of depressing the necessary sense of urgency that justice requires.

Mazon is therefore only a step. It moves us from indifference to charity, but the question is whether we can then be moved from charity to advocacy—and then more, for advocacy of the rights of the poor is not yet justice. Suppose that we manage to build a more solid floor beneath the poor, that no one any longer wanders the streets hungry and homeless. Shall we then be satisfied that the claims of justice have been adequately addressed?

The bishops assert that "Catholic social teaching does not require absolute equality in the distribution of income and wealth," and then go on to describe the moral principles according to which unequal distribution should be evaluated. In the light of those principles, they find that "the disparities of income and wealth in the United States [are] unacceptable," and that "justice requires that all members of our society work for economic, political and social reforms that will decrease these inequities" (par. 185).

This is an explicit rejection of the conservative view that great disparities of income are acceptable so long as the people on the bottom are not "too badly" off. It is an endorsement of the view that great disparities are in and of themselves unacceptable. That view, which can be defended on the basis of both ethics and interests, requires more than its assertion to persuade. It is a view that I share, but it can scarcely be thought self-evident in a market-oriented America. Indeed, its implications would likely be thought quite revolutionary. For how might such a view be implemented?

The latest report from the United States Census Bureau[7] informs us that since 1970, the disparity between the most affluent and the poorest Americans has grown. Specifically, the most affluent fifth of all American households now receive 46.1 percent of all income (compared to 43.3 percent in 1970), while the share received by the poorest fifth is 3.8 percent (down from 4.1 percent). And income, of course, is only one source of wealth; we may safely assume that the data on wealth would reveal a dramatically higher disparity.

The belief that glaring disparity is unacceptable is built into various government programs for the redistribution of income—

most notably, the progressive income tax and the various welfare programs that are intended to provide support for the poor. But these are both indirect and inadequate ways for dealing with glaring disparities. Might those concerned with economic justice not seek to attack the problem more directly? Suppose, for example, that our society were simply to come to a decision that disparities above a certain multiple are unacceptable. For example, suppose we were to decide that the richest fifth of all Americans should not have more than X times the wealth (or income—for purposes of this example, it does not matter whether "richest" means highest income or greatest wealth) of the lowest fifth. Today, in the aggregate, the richest fifth earns roughly twelve times what the poorest fifth earns. (There are far more sophisticated indexes of inequality that might be used, but this gross measure will here suffice.) Plainly, the society could decide that it is unjust for the highest fifth to earn more than, say, ten times the lowest fifth, and tax policy could be adjusted accordingly. The interesting benefit of so direct an approach is that if the highest fifth wants to increase its income, it must first see to it that the income of the lowest fifth is increased. Social solidarity is thereby made manifest: a larger community is encouraged, but not at the expense of the smaller. Pluralism—the American expression of subsidiarity— is thereby sustained.

My point here is not that this example or some variant of it is the preferred expression of economic justice—although it has the virtue of a specificity that the pastoral letter avoids. My point is that a serious concern for economic justice will take us into a debate this nation has energetically evaded through most of its history. That, I presume, is what the bishops mean when they call for "a new American experiment," analogous to the political experiment that issued in our nation's Constitution. Anything less than a new way of thinking through our goals is merely tinkering.

Our ability to stimulate such a debate depends, it seems to me, on our success at restoring the nexus between prophecy and pragmatism that was so badly disturbed, if not yet destroyed, by the success of secularism. And that, in turn, depends on our ability to restore the power of faith communities. For their insistent effort at both these restorations, all who are devoted to justice are indebted to the bishops.

Part 3 | *Mainline Protestant Perspectives on American Economic Life*

11 | *Mainline Protestant Perspectives on American Economic Life*

Two of the traditions represented in this volume—Roman Catholicism and Judaism—have little difficulty saying quite precisely who belongs within their communities. This is less true of the two branches of Protestantism included here. Exactly who are "mainline Protestant Christians" and "evangelical Protestant Christians"? While it is best to let the parties concerned determine for themselves what such labels mean and whether or not to take them on, we do need briefly to characterize mainline Protestants in order to locate the following contributions within the religious and cultural landscape of the United States. It should first be noted that the term "mainline" is rather imprecise in its meaning and its application, that many prefer other terms such as "old line" or "established," that others avoid such categorizing altogether, and finally that the label is used here only to describe and not to praise those who bear it or to criticize those who do not.

It is a simple matter to name the major mainline Protestant denominations. These include those denominations of the four authors in this section—Lutheran, Episcopal, United Church of Christ, and Presbyterian. Such a list should certainly also include the United Methodist Church. Beyond these, disagreement increases, since certain other communions share some of the distinguishing characteristics of the mainline groups while lacking others.

It is not so simple to say precisely what makes these denominations mainline. "Mainline" is sometimes taken to mean a central core or tradition defined in part by departures from it occurring on both sides. Filling in this meaning of "mainline" historically would engage us in the seemingly interminable ebb and flow of the battles between fundamentalism and modernism, conservatism and liberalism, old-school and new-school theologies, and their disputes over who best represents the Protestant tradition. Fortunately, it is sufficient for our purposes simply to note that mainline Protestants may be located religiously and theologically in terms of two central convictions that have their grounding in the origins of Protestantism. As distinguished from Roman Catholicism on the one hand and the Anabaptist traditions on the other hand, Protestantism in its formation in the sixteenth and seventeenth centuries sought a reformation of Christian faith by returning to Scripture, with its emphasis on God's grace as the source of Christian formation, while maintaining that the church was responsible for supporting the magistrates in the preservation and nurture of the common good. Mainline Protestants sought both the reform of Roman Catholicism and the support of the work of the magistrates. For these reasons, mainline Protestantism is described historically as the Magisterial Reformation, in contrast to the Radical Reformation of the Anabaptists, who rejected the power of the magistrates and sought a nonviolent community of discipleship.

The meaning of "mainline" may then be construed as reformed by virtue of the power of God revealed and effected in Scripture, and as magisterial in terms of responsibility for the world at large. The mainline denominations may therefore be distinguished by their struggle to maintain an appropriate balance between particularity and universalism, a struggle to hold to the historic Christian tradition while addressing the modern world in all its complexity as revealed by various contemporary empirical and scientific methods of investigation and analysis.

In trying to address a complex world from a complex tradition, mainline Protestants arrive at complexity squared and so find themselves unable in good conscience to offer simple, all-inclusive answers to worldly problems. This dilemma, a distinguishing characteristic of mainline denominations, is not strikingly evident in the current volume, since all the religious traditions represented here recognize the inherent complexity of the current economic situation and of matters of economic equity and justice. Were our focus on abortion or homosexuality, this mainline Protestant dilemma would be more evident, since in such matters where the moral and policy options are fewer and more sharply defined, some evangelical Protestant and Roman Catholic communions find a quite direct line from Scripture and Christian tradition to the answer to the contemporary problem.

A second significant dimension of the term "mainline" as applied to these denominations is revealed by the origin of the term itself as a socio-economic designation. When the Pennsylvania Railroad bought land in the 1860s and 1870s to straighten out its track from Philadelphia to Pittsburgh and then sold unneeded land along the right of way to developers and individual purchasers, it created ideal conditions for the emergence of affluent suburbs with ready access to the city for well-to-do business and professional people wishing to live outside the burgeoning cities. "Mainline" then became the designation for those well-off and well-placed families who were major beneficiaries of and major powers in the social, economic, and political structures of major cities.[1] Even a cursory look at the socio-economic, professional, and political profile of the mainline denominations reveals that this dimension of mainline also applies here. Mainline Protestants are, on the average, comfortably above the national median in terms of income, formal education, and professional status. This, of course, may relate to an additional element in the mainline label—the fact that virtually all the mainline denominations were on the scene early in American history, and thus their members were generally at an advantage over latecomers in ascending to positions of power and privilege.

The authors of both denominational statements underlying Paul Camenisch's essay recognize that their members' being overwhelmingly among the conspicuous beneficiaries of current economic arrangements potentially jeopardizes their interpretation of and recommended solutions to the economic problems addressed. Furthermore, as would be expected, some observers will see the already-noted failure of mainline denominations to offer clear and decisive moral guidance in this case as more than the result of a complex tradition meeting a complex world. They will see it as a failure of nerve, a selling out to the prevailing culture, which many see as dominated by a mainline/WASP establishment.

This possibility of too comfortable a fit between the church as represented in the mainline denominations and the prevailing culture, especially its economic structures and policies, emerges in the following essays in the concerns about seeing the church as the soul of the nation, about the church's becoming encultured and letting the prophetic challenge to the culture atrophy. Interestingly, these authors and other commentators suggest that the Roman Catholic Church, in its increasingly secure place in middle-class America, faces these very same perils, although sometimes for reasons and out of a heritage different from those of many Protestant groups.

What major dimensions of mainline Protestant thought and

belief are reflected in the following essays? First is the conviction that we engage the world and its problems on the basis of as clear an understanding of their complexities as we can attain through whatever ways of knowing are available to us. This concern is seen most clearly in Rebecca Blank's discussion of the various types of poverty and in her insistence that to be helpful and fair, specific responses must be tailored to each type, an analysis she believes the bishops largely neglected. Camenisch's pursuit of the proper meaning and implications of corporate agency, especially as applied to business corporations in relation to the issue of economic justice, also reflects this concern.

A second characteristic of mainline Protestantism has been its concern with the issues of sin and power and their interconnections, with the temptations power presents to fallen human beings. This concern keeps alive in mainliners an element of the Radical Reformation and serves as a perennial check on any inclinations they might have to uncritically endorse existing regimes and arrangements. These concerns echo through Camenisch's attempt to portray the reality of corporate power more adequately than he sees done in either the bishops' letter or mainline Protestant documents. But it is the very foundation for Larry Rasmussen's charges that the Catholic bishops failed to confront the issues of structural power in the current American and world economies, and that they therefore rely unrealistically on moral discourse to bring about change.

These concerns about the uses and abuses of power and about attending to this complex world as it really is generate the imperative that we do sufficient research and analysis to assure that any power the church and Christians in their various roles have is wielded responsibly.

Third, the most persistent and characteristic theme of mainline Protestantism—namely, the necessity and sufficiency of God's grace—is most evident in Timothy Sedgwick's essay. He is concerned that the power and role of God's grace in transforming us and our society not be obscured by our efforts to achieve some moral ideal of economic justice. His hope is that we can sustain this awareness of God's grace-ful presence, especially in the poor, without cutting the nerve to responsible moral action—moral action which now, however, will be more modest in its claims and more realistic in its expectations. These themes are also at work as the other three authors struggle with issues of economic justice not as a matter of the Christian's own salvation but as a matter of obedience to the will of God and of service to the neighbor.

A final characteristic of mainline Protestantism is its rejection of an authoritative teaching hierarchy that can speak for the entire church, and its consequent refusal to require unanimity in matters of faith and morals. This trait is more illustrated than discussed here, for none of the four authors offers a single answer for all Protestants or even for his or her specific community. Furthermore, the documents Camenisch analyzes are committee products developed by a variety of people, both lay and clerical, and offered as study documents rather than as authoritative pronouncements.

The traits mentioned here exhaust neither the meaning of mainline Protestantism nor its influence on the following essays. Nor are any of those traits found exclusively in mainline Protestantism. Nevertheless, it is when mainline Protestantism has been most insistently and creatively faithful to these key commitments that it has been clearest about its own identity and has made its richest contributions to the life and thought of its co-religionists.

12 | *The Morality of Power and the Power of Morality*

Larry Rasmussen

The kudos for the pastoral letter on the economy are well deserved. The bishops have shown how a major religious body can go public with the gospel in a pluralistic society, and how it can do so in ways that both form Christian conscience and inform a complex public debate. Many a Protestant body has aspired to do this, with considerably less success.

There is a serious flaw in the pastoral, however. It is not in the formulation of the Christian moral vision for economic life. The bishops have, with much sophistication, specified moral principles and priorities that work effectively in the policy sections of the letter. Tl e strong use of Scripture and its interplay with other sources is particularly impressive in its contribution to the moral vision. Nor is the flaw in the factual analysis of selected issues and problems. One of the strengths of this pastoral is the careful and clear portrayal of concrete economic realities. Roman Catholic social teaching is not the flaw, either. As a body of material it has much to say about economic life. It surpasses anything Protestant and Orthodox communions presently offer.

What then is the flaw? It is the inadequate treatment of economic power in the United States and the morality of that power. Furthermore, the bishops unduly rely upon the power of morality—that is, upon moral suasion—to reach their goal of the new American experiment in economic democracy. The pastoral is "softly utopian," to use Reinhold Niebuhr's language. It underestimates the power of social sin to frustrate desired progress at the same time that

134

it overestimates the power of evangelical and educative means to effect the common good.

Economic Power Obscured

Yet what can this accusation mean, since the bishops clearly recognize power in economic life? They know that nothing good happens apart from power. They recall that the many achievements of the U.S. economy have come via "a creative struggle" among many players sometimes at odds with one another (par. 8). They also know that harsh realities result from the maldistribution and misuse of power. Some of these are "massive and ugly" economic failures (par. 3); the bishops forthrightly call them a moral and social scandal (par. 16). Furthermore, the bishops are emphatic that human dignity requires the empowerment of people who presently hold too little sway in economic life. Justice is participation, they insist, and that requires power, not charity (par. 78).

So it may seem curious to claim that the bishops treat power ineffectually and neglect the Christian teaching on sin. But take a closer look. The subsection called "Overcoming Marginalization and Powerlessness" begins as follows:

> These fundamental duties [to establish economic justice] can be summarized this way: *Basic justice demands the establishment of minimum levels of participation in the life of the human community for all persons.* The ultimate injustice is for a person or a group to be actively treated or passively abandoned as if they were non-members of the human race. . . . This can take many forms, all of which can be described as varieties of marginalization or exclusion from social life. (par. 77; bishops' emphasis)

The paragraph goes on to say that marginalization can and does take both political and economic forms, and that the key to a saving participation is attaining power. The comment is made that even "whole nations are prevented from fully participating in the international economic order because they lack the power to change their disadvantaged position" (par. 77).

Next the bishops identify the source of exclusion and powerlessness. Their designation of it is somewhat strange, since they characteristically name all other economic actors. "These [exclusionary] patterns . . . are created by free human beings. In this sense they can be called forms of social sin" (par. 77).

Who are these "free human beings"? They are never iden-

tified *in ways that display the causal sources of powerlessness and injustice.*
They are not named *in ways that show how the unjust patterns arise.*
Maldistributed power exercised by "free human beings" participat-
ing in "social sin" is hardly a concrete and adequate designation!

What we do know is that these economic actors will not be
excluded from crucial participation in the new experiment in
economic democracy. The whole tenor of the pastoral is "economic
justice for all" through participation by all. The bishops take pains to
underscore this by saying that the stated "option for the poor" is "not
an adversarial slogan that pits one group or class against another"
(par. 88). The presence of the poor is necessary; they must be brought
on board to join others in creating more just, less exclusionary patterns.

But just here something appears that is as striking as the abstract designation of certain critical economic agents as "free human
beings." It is the way in which the experience of the poor is described
by the bishops. They focus upon the negative *impact* of economic conditions. They ably describe, to give a few examples, the offense and
suffering of poverty and unemployment, the debilitation of welfare
dependency, and the burdens of crushing debt. Initially this kind of
treatment may not seem surprising, since viewing the economy from
the experience of its victims is the proper moral course for concerned
bishops. Yet it is striking when we realize the bishops' account does
not include a presentation of the institutionalized dynamics that
generate the very results they lament. What command the bishops'
attention are *outcomes* rather than *structural causes.*

Something elemental is missing here. There is, to be sure, an
occasional hint (par. 103) and call (par. 127) for a social-institutional
analysis of economic power in the U.S. economy. Yet the actual power
dynamics themselves are left untouched. Posing this omission as a
question, we cannot help but ask, Why are the economic evils that
the bishops so ably point out not connected at a structural level to
the concrete functioning of the economy?[1]

The answer has several facets, many of which can be seen
in the bishops' method. The bishops pursue policy deliberation by
moving between two poles. Early on they formulate their moral vision and norms on the basis of Scripture and Catholic social teaching. Then they describe economic realities. With a view to the latter
and from the perspective of the former, they go on to suggest policy
lines and steps toward economic democracy.

This method obscures two matters. It doesn't ask what
generates specific economic results, and it doesn't tell us what picture
of society the bishops hold. The latter is always crucial, since it medi-

ates the interplay of moral perspectives and economic realities and fundamentally affects both the bishops' perception and their goals. What they see and what they don't, as well as where they hope the economy will go, is largely a function of the bishops' picture of society.

The bishops would not deny that structural dynamics and an operative picture of society are present and important. Their method does not raise these to a conscious level, however. This leaves the concrete workings of economic power unarticulated.

A better method might well begin where the bishops do, with economic experience, especially that of the poor. It would then trace consequences back through the institutional matrix of U.S. and global capitalism. Scripture and the tradition of Catholic social teaching would not be engaged, in semidetached fashion, at the outset of the exploration, as is the case in the letter. They would be encountered *en route*, in the midst of social analysis, and would empower reflection for guides to action and recommended policy.

A better method would also clarify the bishops' own social theory. We need to know what it is, just as we need to know the outcome of its unstated use. Here in fact is the heart of the bishops' inadequate treatment of power.

The Common Flaw of Communalism and Liberalism

The bishops' social theory attempts a potentially creative and highly problematic marriage—Catholic communalism and Anglo-American liberalism, with the addition of partial influences from liberation theology. The first two, I contend, mask the darker side of economic power, and the last-mentioned is not called upon to illumine it. We must therefore look at communalism and liberalism.

The trademark of Catholic communalism is its organic conception of society. All groups belong to a single social "body." Each group has its contribution, and each merits attention to its needs for the sake of the whole. The decisive moral notion for communalism is that of the common good, attained when all parts, classes, and services contribute to an architectonic whole. There is a profound sense of social relatedness and social participation here. It has usually been expressed hierarchically and has frequently ratified static arrangements, most often in a marriage of organicism and patriarchalism. The U.S. bishops have inherited this, and they carry it in their Catholic bones. They have also sought a more dynamic and egalitarian expression of communalism and, under the influence of the American experience, have moved a considerable distance from the "classic" Catholic expression in feudalism.

Larry Rasmussen

This organic image of society assumes a deep *social unity* and *social harmony*. When these are not present—and they never are, fully—the common good is jeopardized, and measures must be taken to restore and secure this unity and harmony. This requires coercive power, which is sanctioned. More importantly for our purposes, people's *perception* of society under the influence of the organic metaphor usually overlooks *structured social conflict* and exaggerates the *harmonies of group interests* in society. Those who occupy economically and politically privileged ranks are highly prone to this perception. Invariably they overstate the degree of social well-being present in the society, and when conflict does occur, they react to it as an alien intrusion which threatens the entire organism. The language of communalism is thus typically that of moral and social consensus or the quest for it; the reality always involves layers of coercion, much of it subtle. Power is always active, of course. But its activity is obscured by language, perception, and the guiding image of society itself.

Anglo-American liberalism holds a very different image of society—society as contract. The basic unit of human reality is the individual, existing prior to and independent of any social arrangement. Against Catholic communalism's assumption that social relatedness and social unity are intrinsically present, liberalism posits them as the outcome of free choice guided by independent self-interest. This notion of society correlated splendidly with the rise of a money economy and the active emergence of the spirit of capitalism. The growth of the bourgeoisie and the social developments accompanying the Industrial Revolution in fact shattered the social organism of the feudal world.[2]

Yet the important note is not simply the powerful historical intrusion of liberalism into traditional forms of communalism, a process that continues. It is the many-sided observation that Anglo-American liberalism rests in an atomistic/contractarian picture of society while Catholic communalism holds an organic/functional one; that the logic of each is very different; that the bishops overestimate the powers of communalism to transform liberalism; and that the dynamics of power are obscured in both.

We must say more about liberalism. As a social theory, it discloses the actual operations of economic power even less than communalism. It differentiates the political sphere sharply from the economic one, granting the power of the franchise to the former and the power of the market to the latter. The measure of political justice is gauged by guaranteeing the presence of liberty and equality before the law, principles of procedural justice, and participatory democracy

138

as the exercise of citizens' rights to vote, speak freely, and associate by choice. None of these principles, it should be noted, measures the people's *economic* well-being. The division of labor in liberalism's social theory assigns that to the workings of an unfettered market, with its dynamic opportunities, its incentives for an entrepreneurial spirit, its consumer sovereignty, and its blessings for the tenacious and lucky. It should be mentioned that none of these entails the kind of *economic rights* the bishops seek. Such rights would not emerge from the social theory itself, at least not apart from its major reform. Noteworthy, however, is this: the bishops' new American experiment in economic democracy *hinges on precisely this reform*. We cannot avoid the judgment that either the bishops fail to see how opposed American economic liberalism is on theoretical grounds to any such reform from within, or they assume that communalism has a kind of hold on this society that cultural analysis hardly supports.

This judgment proceeds from the logic of liberal theory itself, with its distinctive trait that the dynamics of wealth and the control of productive resources—that is, economic power—is purposely separated from political power. This does not yet say what the *factual* realities of economic power are, however. Those reinforce mightily the judgment about the bishops.

Great concentrations of economic power have grown up within the frame of political democracy in the United States. The phrase "the American success story" commonly refers to minimally restrained economic activity and high economic growth. In any event, economic power presently has enormous influence in the corridors of political power and as an integral part of democratic processes. This is true from the financing of elections, to the lobbying for and drafting of laws, to the intricate relations with foreign powers (including trade and aid), to the massive amounts of public spending itself. Political and economic power go hand in hand in extraordinarily complex ways. While Reinhold Niebuhr's early conclusion about their relationship would later be qualified to allow variance in the sources of dominating power, his position retains a lasting significance.

> Economic [power], rather than . . . political and military, has become the significant coercive force of modern society. Either it defies the authority of the state or it bends the institutions of the state to its own purposes. Political power has been made responsible, but economic power has become irresponsible in society. The net result is that political power has been made more responsible to economic power.[3]

Niebuhr was also aware that the most pervasive, effective, and common uses of power are covert. They are subtly socialized and institutionalized, part of the routine fabric of daily life. He also knew that most citizens in a democracy are unaware of the degree of coercion present. And in the instance of economic power, the coercive influences are partially masked because of the very notion of society most citizens have internalized. That notion says that democratic arrangements allow the people to check the concentrations of economic power by way of legislative and administrative process; formal democratic arrangements provide the framework to render economic power accountable. But in a society where vast economic and political power interlock and move together, sometimes side by side, sometimes apart, the formal political arrangements (representation, an elected president, rule by law) can hardly be said to provide accountability for concentrated economic power. The global ways of competitive transnational corporations, including large commercial banks, the massive economic role of the military, the work of multilateral finance institutions and of large domestic corporations, the semipublic, semisecret world of arms trade, and the far-reaching effects of personal wealth concentrated in relatively few hands all severely qualify any conviction that economic power is democratically accountable.

In short, economic power ranges far beyond market exchange. It massively shapes social arrangements and political decisions. In his book entitled *Spheres of Justice,* Michael Walzer poses the kind of question and draws the kind of conclusion that can be applied widely, far beyond the particular examples he cites:

> Might not the enormous capital investment represented by plants, furnaces, machines, and assembly lines be better regarded as a political than an economic good? To say this doesn't mean that it can't be shared among individuals in a variety of ways, but only that it shouldn't carry the conventional entailments of ownership. Beyond a certain scale, the means of production are not properly called commodities, any more than the irrigation system of the ancient Egyptians, the roads of the Romans or the Incas, the cathedrals of medieval Europe, or the weapons of a modern army are called commodities, for they generate a kind of power that lifts them out of the economic sphere.[4]

Unrealistic Expectations for Moral Suasion

How do the bishops themselves judge economic power account-able? The pastoral seems to invest its hopes in an alliance of democratic process and the power of communal morality (the key notions of "the common good" and a "shared moral vision"). This alliance could be plausibly effective, *if* such notions were deeply in-ternalized in the culture and formed core sections of society's col-lective character and behavior. This seems to be the aim and hope of Catholic social teaching, but it is not a reality for American society in any near term. The sense of the common good is extremely thin among us and has been from early on. The key economic principle of liberalism itself claims that private vice makes public virtue and that the public domain exists for the protection and enhancement of the private. The very idea of "public" is understood as the aggregate of private pursuits, or as what is necessary to secure them. Most Americans think that "the good life" happens in the private domain. There is thus little reason to consciously cultivate civic existence among us, much less order our economic lives by "the common good" in accord with a "shared moral vision." This anticommunal-ism runs deep: Alexis de Tocqueville observed more than 150 years ago that "in democratic societies, each citizen is habitually busy with the contemplation of a very petty object, which is himself."[5] Recall-ing Niebuhr, we must conclude that the bishops are "softly utopian" if they place hopes for economic reform and accountability in the al-liance of formal democratic arrangements and the power of com-munal morality.

The triumph of economic individualism is only part of the reason to doubt communalism's reform of liberalism. There is another, closely related matter. The bishops' goal—economic democracy—is the classic vocation of socialism. Economic democ-racy has some strong affinity with major themes in Catholic social teaching, and the bishops have good reasons of faith to pursue it without actually calling it socialism or adopting present socialist models. But the culture and ideology of U.S. political democracy op-pose it deeply. The bishops make a very serious error in judgment if they assume that economic democracy is the natural extension of political democracy in this society. Existing concentrations of eco-nomic power will vigorously oppose the dispersion of economic power that the "new experiment" clearly calls for. Furthermore, such resistance not only has present power on its side; it has all the artillery of democracy as understood in the liberal creed. It can mount a con-siderable battle on culturally familiar ideological grounds and thereby avoid the appearance of being simply intransigent power. It can resist in the very name of that which "made this country great."

What shall we conclude overall? There is a potent convergence that reveals the pastoral's inadequacy on the critical issue of power. The convergence is sufficient to frustrate the bishops' own goal of a new American vocation in economic life. Catholic communalism exaggerates harmonies of group interest and overlooks structural social conflict as it desires to get everybody on board, dialoguing together for economic democracy and the common good. This downplays economic conflict, and in practice, though not by stated moral norms, it quietly favors those who already wield the weightiest economic influence. Anglo-American liberalism masks, distorts, or benignly neglects the concrete, systemic functioning of economic power and its penetration of democratic political life. Liberalism will not provide a framework of accountability for existing economic power; indeed, its traditions and ideology will fight the strong sense of public welfare and the social cultivation of the common good that the bishops' model of moral consensus both assumes and depends on heavily. In short, the "normative [social] gaze"[6] of the bishops reinforces the same inattention to structural economic power we witnessed in their method of deliberation itself.

What their soft utopianism means, in the end, is that the bishops' moral vision and their strategic endeavor are effectively on different tracks. Such will be the case until structural economic power is faced, probed, and illumined, and strategies of accountability are pursued.

Radical Faith and Public Witness

The bishops extended an invitation to constructive as well as critical response. It would be less than gracious to finish with critical remarks alone. What follows is an effort to sketch a different stance for the church, one more conscious of power realities. It is necessarily modest, not so much because of the limitations of space but because of the sheer dimensions and complexity of what the bishops have taken on in the pastoral. The picture of church presented here is not alien to the pastoral, however. There are already points of contact between the two views. This view is offered as one more response in the important debate the bishops have begun.

Both on theological grounds—the understanding of church—and on strategic ones—achieving the new American experiment in economic democracy—it is doubtful the bishops should favor a church/world model that prefers partnership with power.

Theologically this partnership compromises what is in fact a radical faith, as glimpsed with compelling clarity in Jesus and in the perpetual intrusions of the reign of God into history. The ecclesial vocation of being a pilgrim people in someone else's land and living a visibly different way of life is seriously muted, and sometimes abandoned, when the partnership with power is chosen and an intrinsically radical faith is adapted to it.[7]

From a strategic point of view, the new economic experiment needs a consensus about moral goals and all hands on deck— and I doubt if either of these is attainable—far less than it needs tangible examples of what economic life in accord with the bishops' vision could and might look like. In a time of uncertain exploration and transformation in economic life, the most helpful directions are provided by "demonstration projects" that incarnate a moral vision. Concrete public witness, rather than efforts at moral consensus and reformist measures within established systems, is the more catalytic service.

What collective endeavors, briefly, would characterize such witness? Two parabolic actions are vital: unrelenting criticism and pioneering creativity.

Catholic author Monika Hellwig writes that Jesus lived "as though God now reigned and none else had any power in the world."[8] So did—and so does—the Jesus community (on its better days!). Living as though God reigns and none else has power means in part a thorough critique of "this present age" (to borrow Saint Paul's phrase). It is a public stance that relativizes all other authorities. It peels away the commanding presence and moral legitimation from present cultural patterns and social forms, including economic ones. The prevailing family patterns, economic arrangements, community polity, and, not least, the standard ordering of ideas itself (ideology)—all are moved from the status of practical necessity to that of possibility. They are human constructs that are subject to change. They may be provisionally valid, but they are only that. No particular arrangements are indispensable. The forms for governance, economic provision, and family and community life are as open-ended as the imaginations and the resources of those struggling to live "as though God now reigned and none else had any power."

This means an exercise of unrelenting criticism on the part of a community living by the reign of God. It is a feisty freedom, refusing to take the standard formulation of issues as given and venturing to speak truth to power as best as that truth can be discerned. Moreover, as the bishops themselves note, such critique is launched from a highly particular point of view—namely, one that focuses on the impact upon the poor. It is a stance of criticism that combines "the view from below" (Dietrich Bonhoeffer) and the surging hope for a different future formed in anticipation of the reign of God.

There are openings for this posture in the pastoral letter, and the bishops have shown much courage in speaking truth to power. Yet their mode of moral consensus and their efforts to ground policy in a shared moral vision take the edge off more radical critique of economic realities and temper the ethics of the reign of God so as to make them amenable to pragmatic reform in a pluralist setting. It would be better to begin by distinguishing even more sharply the perspective, identity, and action of the faith community from "the American way of life," and then to call the wider society of which we are part to live by *its own* proclaimed values (e.g., freedom and equality). There is nothing wrong with pagan American values, provided they are good ones. But they should not be confused with Jewish and Christian efforts to reflect the dreams of God for the world, even when there is convergence. A slight shift in the pastoral would mean, on the one hand, a more independent stance for social critique by the faith community and, on the other hand, a sharp appeal to "Caesar's" *own* best values as the measure for judging Caesar's own policies.

Yet unrelenting criticism has little integrity apart from the second public task: pioneering creativity. Radical critique must be coupled with the power of an incarnation. Nothing is real until it is local and visible. For Judaism and Christianity, the form is concrete community reflective of the way of God for Israel and all creation.

The point is the bishops' own: the church itself is compelled to institutionalize in its own life the economic life it envisions in the pastoral. The church itself is the first arena for the social ethic it claims and proclaims. That means a stance of experimentation and some bold moves in economic life—especially those moves, like the ones Jesus made, that strike down the barriers between groups who are at odds with one another or who benignly neglect one another; it means finding new ways for their life together as those who share the same loaf and drink from a common cup. The faith community is to be an anticipatory community of inclusive membership and social exploration. Several examples of religious communities transforming economic life come to mind: Koinonia Farms in Georgia, the Alternative Investments Program of the Interfaith Center for Corporate Responsibility, the Ecumenical Development Cooperative Society, and Jubilee Housing of the Church of the Saviour in Washington, D.C., together with the housing ministries of the nearby Community of Hope and the Sojourners community. A full list would be a very long one. Yet it would be populated by little-known efforts, since the experiments tend to be local and small-scale, with limited visibility in the society at large and even in the churches themselves.

As mentioned, the pastoral already has openings for a distinctive stance of radical criticism and pioneering creativity in economic life. The need is to strengthen them. Radical criticism would better expose and illumine the world of economic power. Pioneering experimentation would help shape Christian imagination and markedly aid public policy by demonstrating concrete possibilities. Both the wider world and the integrity of the faith itself would be served.

13 | *Graceless Poverty and the Poverty of Grace*

Timothy F. Sedgwick

A prophetic voice within Christianity has continued to criticize both particular practices and the individualism of American culture. From racism and the abuses of labor to imperialism in foreign affairs, both Protestant and Roman Catholic churches have exercised judgment as the conscience of the nation. The Roman Catholic pastoral letter on the economy, *Economic Justice for All,* clearly stands in this prophetic tradition within Christianity as it holds up a vision of national life that is in marked contrast to the pervasive individualism of our culture. But despite its critical stance and constructive vision, the letter fails to comprehend adequately the contemporary crisis and therefore the task of the church. The problem, moreover, is not fundamentally a strategic failure in terms of what is to be done but a more damaging failure that derives from the theology at the center of the pastoral.

Why do we work for a just community, and especially why do we have "a special obligation to the poor and vulnerable" (par. 16, PM)? The bishops' answer to the question is a form of moral idealism. Christian faith is understood as a moral ideal, as an ideal state of affairs revealed and effected in Jesus Christ. Thus the call of the Christian life is to share in this ideal and to work toward its accomplishment in the world. Meaning and purpose are achieved by virtue of the realization of the ideal. Christian faith, therefore, holds the promise that the ideal is not in vain, that in the end the ideal will be accomplished.

The problem with such moral idealism is that it is patently false historically. From Ecclesiastes and Job to the Holocaust and world famines, the weak and innocent suffer unjustly. At the heart of Christian faith is the cross, a clear revelation of unjust suffering. To hold optimistically to the realization of a common vision of life lived together where the interests of particular individuals and communities are sacrificed in order to achieve a broader, more inclusive common life is naive. Theologically such optimism misunderstands how God is present to humanity and thus how conversion and reconciliation are inextricably tied to the embrace of the stranger, the poor, and the alien.

Those in need are not objects of charity whom we serve so that we may reach God. Such attempts turn the grace of God into a matter of moral achievement. Rather, the poor are strangers among us who invite us to go beyond ourselves by challenging our complacent security, preoccupations, defensiveness, and self-righteousness. As strangers they reveal God's presence beyond our grasp and control. In this way the poor effect our conversion, the enlargement of the soul until we are reconciled with creation. Here is the experience of grace: the sheer gratuitousness of life itself, of life's fecundity and radiance, such that we cannot help but give thanks and praise for all that is and, in turn, care for and nurture life about us.

For too long, Protestants have caricatured Roman Catholic thought as failing to grasp the radicalness of grace by focusing narrowly on morality as the means of grace. In turn, the Roman Catholic caricature has been that Protestant thought has cut the cord between grace and morality, resulting in a situation ethic that fails to provide guidance as it spiritualizes Christian faith.[1] In truth, Protestantism has had a moralism of its own, while Roman Catholic thought has also spiritualized faith. But the caricatures have expressed the dangers in Roman Catholic and Protestant thought, dangers present in both the Roman Catholic pastoral study on the economy and my criticisms. Any theological assessment of the pastoral on the economy, especially that of a Protestant, must explore these issues. I hope that I can suggest, as an Anglican middle way *(via media)* between Rome and the churches of the Reformation, a theological foundation that grasps the radicalness of grace as it is inextricably tied to the moral life.

Graceless Poverty in the Pastoral

In the tradition of Roman Catholic social thought, the pastoral on the economy "insists that human dignity, realized in community with others and with the whole of God's creation, is the norm against which every social institution must be measured" (par. 25). The confidence in the ability to realize this vision is expressed in the pastoral in the positive relation of redemption and creation, and between God's reign and human history. The optimistic, integral relationship is expressed in the understanding of humans as "co-creators" with God (pars. 32, 36). In light of the image of co-creators, work is exalted as the essential means of participation in the created order and as the primary end of humanity. "The human dignity of all is realized when people gain the power to work together to improve their lives, strengthen their families and contribute to society" (par. 91).

This understanding of redemption as participation in the creative activity of God is drawn from and warranted by appeal to the creation of humanity in the image of God and the consequent call of humanity to assume dominion over creation. As stewards, men and women "justly consider that by their labor they are unfolding the Creator's work" (par. 32). The covenant between God and God's people, which was made explicit in the great legal codes, gives form to the meaning of participation. Specifically, the sense of participation in creation requires the acknowledgment of the dignity of all human people and thereby the inclusion of all in the human community.

The prophetic tradition highlights the core of this biblical vision by condemning the violation of the conditions necessary for such dignity, most especially by the treatment "of the powerless of society, most often described as the widow, the orphan, the poor and the stranger (non-Israelite) in the land" (par. 38). Jesus confirms and renews what is here revealed. Salvation is found in discipleship, in "imitating the pattern of Jesus' life by openness to God's will in the service of others" (par. 47).

This theological vision is attractive because of its organic, teleological character. As Jesus Christ both reveals and enables participation in the ends of life, so the church carries that work forward in the world. The church is to human life in general and to the social order in particular what the soul is to the body. The formation of one body, of a body politic, depends upon the ensouling of the body with a common mind and spirit. Such is the task of the church. The "church is thus primarily a communion of people bonded by the Spirit, sustaining one another in love and acting as a sign or sacrament in the world" (par. 339). The problem with the pastoral is the inadequacy of its confident and optimistic understanding of a culture that is related to Christian faith as means are related to ends. This in turn reflects a more fundamental problem with the understanding of the relation between redemption and creation.

The Most Rev. Rembert G. Weakland, the archbishop of Milwaukee and the chairman of the committee that drafted *Economic Justice for All,* has acknowledged this inadequacy in the pastoral letter on the economy and in Roman Catholic social thought in general. After criticizing those who would separate religion from political, social, and economic issues, Weakland asks "how the church should function within our pluralistic democratic structures and be truly a leaven and a sacrament to the world." Weakland claims that the "integralism" of the past, for which a single set of teachings alone is true and, therefore, binding so that Catholic "doctrine alone should dominate in political affairs," is impossible and unacceptable. This he claims in sharp contrast to many Catholics—for example, those seeking to legislate against abortion or those seeking to deny civil rights to homosexuals.[2] An integralism is impossible, he argues, because the meaning of religious ideals for the political, social, and economic worlds is not self-evident. Any "neat deductive kind of moral process is idealistic and does not correspond to life's experiences." This means that the "most difficult question posed to the church today by the American political processes is precisely that of compromise" as this arises from the acknowledgment that "in a real world the ideal is never fully obtainable."[3]

But there is a matter even more fundamental than the question of compromise. The fact that the ideal is never fully obtainable raises the question about the theological vision and understanding that animates Catholic thought in the first place. The assumption of the pastoral is that human beings are in control and that by goodwill and cooperation they can "tend and till" the garden for the good of all. Despite acknowledging the tension in Genesis 1–11 between the goodness and the perversity in humanity (par. 33), the bishops do not develop the extent and significance of the Fall. Such creation theology, argues David Hollenbach, "runs the risk of arrogantly inflating the signficance of what we humans can do and who we humans really are."[4] Specifically, if the ideal cannot be realized in history, then redemption as participation in the creative activity of God is called into question. Why, to ask the question again, do we work for a just community, and especially why do we have "a special obligation to the poor and vulnerable"?

If the ideal cannot be realized, then creation remains fallen, unredeemed—unless, of course, it is saved by a supernatural end beyond history itself. The pastoral itself makes no strong appeal to a supernatural, suprahistorical end (although see par. 53 with its discussion of the "tension between promise and fulfillment"). Salvation appears within the pastoral fundamentally as a historical reality, and it is precisely this apparent rejection of salvation outside of history

Timothy F. Sedgwick

that animates and impassions the pastoral's call for action. However, apart from such a supernatural end, the moral idealism of the pastoral falls back upon an optimistic liberalism that is unwarranted. The impasse here is theological. What is needed is a rethinking of why Christians have a special obligation to the poor and vulnerable and how this is related to reconciliation and salvation. Especially important is a grasp of the radical character of Christian conversion and the experience of grace as this is related to the embrace of the poor and alien.

On the Poverty of Grace

Despite the dominant organic vision in the pastoral in which Christian faith is understood in terms of a moral idealism realized in the world, an alternative vision of Christian faith and the radical character of Christian conversion was suggested in the second draft of the pastoral and included in its final form. The bishops recognized that the embrace of the poor and the outcast is not simply an act of mercy on the part of the beneficent. Rather, God is with us (Emmanuel) "in those most in need; to reject them is to reject God made manifest in history" (par. 44). "Most radically, [the example of Jesus] calls for an emptying of self, both individually and corporately, that allows the church to experience the power of God in the midst of poverty and powerlessness" (par. 52). "Christian communities that commit themselves to solidarity with those suffering and to confrontation with those attitudes and ways of acting which institutionalize injustice will themselves experience the power and presence of Christ. They will embody in their lives the values of the new creation while they labor under the old" (par. 55). These three inclusions in the pastoral are the extent of the development of the relationship between conversion and the embrace of the poor. Nevertheless, they suggest a vision that is at odds with the dominant moral idealism of the pastoral.

To embrace and serve the poor and alien—the hungry and the thirsty, the stranger and the naked, the sick and the imprisoned (Matt. 25:34-36)—is not a matter of social salvation, of eliminating hunger and, more fundamentally, the lack of power that marginalizes and alienates individuals from the broader community, as desirable as such success might be. To serve the poor and powerless is, rather, to recognize that in them God is encountered and to acknowledge that they are blessed because they have a privileged opportunity to know God. This requires careful explanation in order to avoid the romanticizing of poverty. In Scripture—from the Exodus and the prophets to Jesus' ministry proclaimed in the Magnificat (Luke 1:46-

55)—material poverty is scandalous because it degrades the spirit by binding it to the concern for survival. Preoccupied with their own survival, the poor lack the resources necessary to participate in society or more generally in creation itself. What is ironic, however, is that throughout Scripture the poor and powerless are also blessed. According to the Beatitudes (Luke 6:20-26; Matt. 5:3-10), the poor shall inherit God's kingdom. The Psalms, holding out the hope of restitution, cry out for the poor and persecuted while they also proclaim the righteousness and blessing of the poor. Unable to depend upon themselves or anyone else, the dispossessed throw themselves upon God.

As Matthew emphasizes, what is blessed in Scripture is not material poverty itself but a spiritual poverty, the emptying and abandoning of the self before God in open trust. But as Luke makes clear, such spiritual poverty can never be separated from possessions and the use of material goods. What we own and what is at our disposal expresses our spirit. Such material things are essential matters of faith because they are the resources for our participation in community and creation as a whole. Moral judgments regarding material possessions are, moreover, complicated because what is necessary for participation in a community varies with the extent of its technological development. But whether the community is formed in a nomadic society or in a technological, information-intensive society, material goods present the problems of lust, envy, gluttony, and greed, and dealing with them justly requires a spiritual poverty, a larger purpose that is willing to give all things away. This evidences that the embrace of the poor can never be a matter of charity for the sake of remedying material poverty.

Fundamentally, the Christian life is not a matter of moral ideals working themselves out in history or reaching fulfillment beyond history. Rather, at the heart of Christian faith is the experience of grace, of the gratuitousness of life itself. Luther expressed this in terms of justification by grace, while Calvin expressed this by centering faith in the sovereignty of God. Knowing that "we are not our own," the Christian is called to give thanks and praise for what is—in Christian terms, for the goodness of creation. The movement from sin to righteousness is the movement of the soul from a preoccupation with itself—from self-absorption, self-defense, and self-righteousness—to the acceptance of grace and thereby the embrace of creation. Conversion and redemption are nothing other than the enlargement of the soul.

Central to this movement of reconciliation is the acceptance of the stranger, who most dramatically meets us in the many faces of the poor. We are born into a world of relations that draw us from the embrace of the womb. We are confronted from the beginning of life itself by the otherness of unknown worlds. Either we consent and are drawn forward into the life of the family, the community, and the world at large, or else we seek to secure an abiding protection from the world until our life confines itself to a narrow, private enclave. To acknowledge our utter dependence and correspondingly to accept and trust God's world beyond us is the first movement of conversion and reconciliation.

The movement of redemption, however, cannot be spiritualized as if the experience of grace were the end of life itself. The experience of grace, of the essential gratuitousness of life, is not experienced apart from our lives in time and space. The experience of grace confronts us with a radical decision—either to accept this God and embrace and care for creation or to seek self-sufficiency. There are no alternatives. Either the movement of faith from the experience of grace to trust in God and reconciliation with creation is enlarged and deepened in the embrace of the world, or else it is disregarded and lost altogether. As Christians we proclaim that Jesus reveals in his own life, death, and resurrection this fundamental movement of faith and effects that faith in us. It is in this sense that he announces and effects the reign of God.[5]

The stranger stands at the center of this movement of conversion and reconciliation because the stranger is the other who calls us beyond ourselves.[6] Because we share a common humanity, such care is not a narrow matter of charity, of seeking to fulfill specific needs. To care for and embrace the other must always be to empower the other to participate equally and fully in the community and in the care and embrace of the world. It is as much a mistake to think of the stranger, the poor and outcast, narrowly, as means to redemption, as it is an illusion to think that we can effect social salvation. Rather, the embrace of the stranger is impelled by the experience of grace. The embrace of the stranger arises from and deepens the poverty of the spirit, of emptying the self in trust and openness to God.

The Identity of Poverty in the Church

This shift in perspective from poverty as a problem to be solved to the poverty of grace may appear insignificant, especially given the pastoral's acknowledgment that God is encountered in the embrace of the poor. However, only a theology of grace arising from this understanding of conversion and hospitality provides an adequate ground for the Christian life, in contrast to appeals to moral idealism in either historical or supernatural form. To understand the embrace of the poor and powerless in terms of the movement and expression of faith is to ground the Christian life in the experience of grace itself, in the sheer gratuitousness of being itself. Reconciliation and redemption are given absolutely—instead of being dependent upon their realization in history or beyond history—even while they must be continually appropriated in faith, hope, and love.

This shift—beginning the movement of Christian faith in the experience of grace as it leads inevitably to the embrace of the stranger and those in need—effects a significant difference in understanding the church and its mission. The mission of the church is not dependent upon the realization of a moral ideal but is accomplished in proclaiming the story of Jesus Christ because this is the story of God that effects reconciliation. But since grace is not a once-and-for-all experience but always demands acceptance and appropriation, the telling of the story can never be separated from living that story in the world so that faith is witnessed and deepened and in this way proclaimed and effected in the world. Such is the mission of the church. In proclaiming Christ to the world, the church effects the reconciliation begun in Jesus Christ—or, in the language of sacramental theology, the church is the sacrament of Christ in the world.

This change in perspective restores the primary mission of the church as proclamation, to witness to the reconciliation with God testified to and effected by Jesus Christ. As Jesus' life, ministry, death, and resurrection make clear, God's reign and our reconciliation with God are not the result of human labor. Jesus had no social program to build the kingdom; rather, his mission was to announce the kingdom of God and thus call for the conversion of heart and mind so that men and women would acknowledge their true identity and live in the kingdom. For the church this same witness is effected by the telling and celebration of the story of Jesus Christ. What is said and what is done mutually interpret each other. In this way the church witnesses to what our life with God is meant to be.

The restoration of the primary identity of the church as evangel does not separate proclamation and service or evangelism and social action. Rather, this understanding reveals the foundation of Christian identity and action and thereby the central issue for the church in accomplishing its mission in the world. Specifically, the church must first of all bear witness to the truth about God and our relation to God. Central to this truth is the embrace of the poor, the sick, the enemy, and the alien. Again, here in the embrace of the stranger is the presence of God and the movement of grace. Accordingly, the first question that the church must ask is how the embrace of the stranger—what I have called the poverty of grace—is witnessed and effected within the community of faith itself. This must be the first question because only where the church has established its own distinctive identity can it accomplish its mission of evangelism. Only where the church has established its own identity distinct from that of the culture can it provide a witness that calls the world to conversion and reconciliation.

Finally, this sacramental understanding of the church as the sign of what the world is meant to be does not negate the concern to contribute to the formation of public policy for the sake of the common good. As citizens with a vision of what human life is meant to be, all Christians are called to strive for justice, to provide a prophetic challenge to the nation, to offer prudent counsel, and to exercise political power to make necessary changes. What is most admirable about the pastoral is its clear statement of the requirements of economic justice, especially as this is expressed in the specific issues of employment, poverty, food, and agriculture, and the relation of the economy of the United States to those of the developing nations. However, it should be reiterated that only when the church forms its own life distinct from the culture can it witness and form the identity of individual Christians sufficiently so that they may provide prophetic witness and prudent action as citizens of the world.

Central to any such description of the identity of the community of faith grounded in the poverty of grace will be what Dietrich Bonhoeffer called arcane disciplines or what may be called domestic rituals. Only through the discipline of daily life can Christian faith be fully witnessed and deepened in our lives. Traditionally this has included prayer, almsgiving, and fasting. Such daily disciplines are not private but essentially corporate in character. They form the community of faith by displacing self-absorption and self-concern with openness and trust in the other and, correspondingly, instilling hospitality and care toward the stranger.[7] On the basis of such identity and discipline, it is possible to describe public responsibilities and actions—what traditionally were called corporal acts of mercy—without separating the concern for justice in the world from the primary task of the church: to witness to God's reign through the telling of the Christian story and the formation of a people, the church, as the sacrament of Christ in the world.

Such attention to the formation of the church—and particularly to its distinctive, prophetic identity—is missing from the pastoral. The moral idealism of the pastoral focuses the identity of the church on the realization of the moral ideals in the world. This requires optimism and limits the pastoral's prophetic criticisms. An illustration will make the point. John Paul II offered a strident criticism of individualistic, hedonistic consumerism in the United States. He specifically called the American people to break with the "frenzy of consumerism" and adopt a "simple way of living."[8] But, in contrast to such a prophetic cry, the pastoral assumes that "new forms of cooperation and partnership" and "a renewed commitment by all to the common good" (par. 296) can move the nation toward the Christian moral vision in which all participate in the work of the human community. In fact, the bishops assume that one can achieve both economic justice and the aspirations of the American middle class for a more prosperous life.

To bear witness to the poverty of grace, the church in the United States must be a prophetic sign to the culture by the life it lives. To be sure, the pastoral concludes that "all the moral principles that govern the just operation of any economic endeavor apply to the church and its agencies and institutions; indeed the church should be exemplary" (par. 347). It then addresses issues of "wages and salaries, rights of employees, investments and property, works of charity, and working for economic justice" (par. 350). But the pastoral fails to provide prophetic criticism of itself and, in turn, devotes insufficient attention to how the church must form its own life in order to nurture and proclaim a distinctively Christian identity. Lacking is a description of the Christian community as a prophetic and sacramental community necessary to insure that the tension between church and society—and so between redemption and creation—remains. This is essential if the radical and transformative character of grace is to be proclaimed and not assimilated and domesticated into a moral ideal. Protestant protest still awaits incarnation within the sacramental substance of the community of faith.

14 | *Poverty and Policy: The Many Faces of the Poor*

Rebecca M. Blank

The issue of poverty serves as a central organizing focus for *Economic Justice for All*, the letter of the Catholic bishops on economic issues. In the letter the existence of widespread and acute poverty is used as a primary example of how inadequately current social and economic structures reflect the Christian vision of community. "The poor" are used throughout the document as a theological symbol, representing the brothers and sisters to whom we have unfilled responsibilities. In Chapter Three various policies designed to alleviate poverty are discussed at length.

Yet, to formulate effective solutions to poverty, one must understand *why* people are poor. There are currently a wide variety of views about the causes and conditions of poverty. And when we begin to look closely at those who are poor, a very diverse group emerges. These differences are not clearly distinguished in the bishops' letter. The document speaks often of "the poor," creating a cohesive image of a single population. While this adds to the symbolic power of the bishops' concern with poverty, it is less useful from a policy perspective.

This chapter is designed to analyze "the poor" more closely. In the first section I will present a variety of different images of the poor, based upon different views of how poverty is created and perpetuated. I will also discuss some of the evidence regarding the demographic diversity of those who are currently poor. In the second part of this chapter I will discuss the policy problems that arise because of the wide differences in opinion regarding the nature of poverty. In the last section I will present guidelines for setting priorities among the multitude of policy proposals.

Images of the Poor

The poor, particularly in the United States, are a diverse group and do not easily fit any single stereotype. Thus, the picture of an impoverished elderly women conjures up one set of responses, while the picture of a middle-aged homeless man sleeping in a doorway brings forth another response. Let me distinguish six commonly used images of poverty, and indicate which populations they most accurately characterize.

Image 1: *The poor are those who cannot work.* In biblical references, these are "the fatherless, and the widow" (Deut. 24:19)—those who have lost their (male) household head and thus lack economic protection and support. In our modern age, these are the vulnerable individuals who have little or no earning ability, including the elderly, the disabled, and children. There is little attempt to attach moral blame to the plight of this group. They are poor because of life circumstances over which they have no control.

How many of the poor in the United States does this picture accurately describe? At a minimum estimate, close to half. The sum of all poor children under the age of fifteen plus all those poor individuals over the age of fifteen who are not working and indicate that the reason is either "retirement" or "ill and/or disabled" amounts to 48.6 percent of all poor individuals.[1]

Image 2: *The poor are those who lack the productive resources to earn adequate income.* The working poor—those who work full-time all year and yet remain below the poverty level—fall into this category. In the United States these may be low-skilled or poorly educated individuals—those who are physically able and willing to work, but who lack the training and resources that would enable them to find a job that lets them escape poverty. Alternatively, the problem may be not lack of training on the part of workers but lack of investment in jobs, so that only low-wage, low-productivity jobs are available. This is the dominant form of poverty in many Third World countries, where families in subsistence-level agricultural communities lack the tools, the land, and the skills to produce any more than just enough to survive until the next harvest.

Image 3: *The poor are those who are systematically excluded from productive employment.* This group may have all the productive resources necessary to participate fully in society but be unemployed or unable to find full-time work. Clearly, this may be due to labor

157

market discrimination aimed at ethnic and minority groups, women, and older workers who are able and willing to work. Alternatively, individuals may also be excluded from full participation in the labor market because of recession or lack of adequate jobs in the macro-economy. The increase in unemployment and underemployment that occurs during hard economic times raises the poverty rate, since people who are willing and able to hold full-time jobs are unable to find work. Of course, systematic exclusion over time from education, job training, and experience will soon push many of these people into the previous category, so that even when jobs become available, they will lack the skills necessary to earn an adequate income.

We can estimate the size of these last two groups among the poor by counting those poor individuals who are not working but are looking for work (the unemployed), plus those who are working less than full-time but seeking more work (the underemployed), plus those who work full-time, year-round, but still earn less than the poverty line. This equals 20 percent of all poor individuals.

All three of the images just described provide an essentially economic explanation for poverty: the poor are those who cannot find a job that will pay a high enough wage, either because of their own personal lack of earning ability or because of an imperfectly functioning labor market. These images clearly reflect the experience of many who are poor. However, many Americans believe that poverty is grounded in attitudinal and behavioral problems and in-volves more than just a lack of economic resources. The next three images of poverty, which grow out of this perspective, are frequently more controversial, and create much more hesitation and confusion over the appropriate policy response.

Image 4: *The poor are those who choose not to participate.* This is the image of the "lazy poor" or the "undeserving poor." The bishops allude only briefly to this concept (pars. 193-94); nevertheless, it has been a very strong and persistent element in the public response to poverty in the United States. The suspicion that the poor may not be deserving of special aid but must take personal responsibility for their poverty has clear roots in the Protestant culture of this country. Dis-cussing the way in which our Calvinist and Puritan forebears created a climate in which the spirit of capitalism could flourish, Max Weber notes,

> In conformity with the Old Testament and in analogy to the ethical valuation of good works, asceticism looked upon the pursuit of wealth as an end in itself as highly reprehensible; but the attainment of it as a fruit of labor in a calling was a

sign of God's blessing. And even more important: the religious valuation of restless, continuous, systematic work in a worldly calling, as the highest means to asceticism, and at the same time the surest and most evident proof of rebirth and genuine faith.[2]

While few of our churches any longer explicitly preach that economic success is a sign of righteousness, the belief lingers that those who don't succeed economically are just not trying hard enough. George Gilder clearly states this belief in his widely read book *Wealth and Poverty:* "The only dependable route from poverty is always work, family and faith. The first principle is that in order to move up, the poor must not only work, they must work harder than the classes above them. Every previous generation of the lower class has made such efforts. But the current poor, white even more than black, refuse to work hard."[3]

Calculating any overall estimate of those who are poor because they are not working hard enough is virtually impossible. For instance, it is particularly difficult to classify the extent to which women who head households with children might be expected to work. As previously noted, children, the elderly, and the disabled comprise about 50 percent of all poor, and another 20 percent are actually seeking more work than they can currently find or are already working full-time. The remaining 30 percent of the poor are composed of students (6.5 percent), as well as people who are not working and indicate that the reason is "keeping house" (12.1 percent) or "other reasons" (1.3 percent). The remainder of the poor are those who work part-time but do not seek further work (11.5 percent). This last group includes women who can work only part-time because of their need to care for children, as well as a significant number of elderly and partly disabled individuals who would find full-time work a serious burden. Thus, while there are surely some among the poor who, by more diligent efforts, could escape poverty, this is clearly a relatively small percentage of all poor individuals.

Among those whose attitudes and behavior prevent them from escaping poverty, there are two specific groups that are often spoken of and deserve separate mention:

Image 5: *The poor are those whose despair and hopelessness prevent them from seeing or taking advantage of economic opportunities.* A long-term lack of opportunity and hope may ultimately lead individuals to give up any attempt to seek something better. This model is often used to describe those in isolated rural areas such as Appalachia as well as those in isolated urban-ghetto areas. This view of the poor often leads to a strong concern about "dependency." Even if better economic opportunities arise, the poor, blinded by despair, may be unable to perceive them or take advantage of them.

Image 6: *The poor are a hostile subculture that engages in a set of socially destructive behaviors, explicitly avoiding legitimate work.* This image is peopled with "welfare cheats," drug addicts who steal to support their habit, alcoholic "bums," or women who have children so they can receive welfare and avoid work. This group is often assumed to emerge in an urban subculture, where highly concentrated and segregated poor populations tolerate or even encourage behavior that denies the legitimacy of the majority culture's accepted social norms, encouraging people to "rip off" the system. Increasing discussion of "the underclass" in policy literature in recent years often focuses on this group.

Estimates of the size of these last two populations are impossible to establish because the defining characteristics are often hard to measure. Recent studies indicate that in 1980 only about 1 percent of the population lived in "underclass areas"—defined as areas that simultaneously exhibited unusually high rates of female headship, high-school dropouts, welfare usage, and unemployment.[4] And clearly not all of these residents were poor.

Each of the images described is a partial answer to the question "Who are the poor and why are they poor?" And there are surely individuals who fit into each category. It should be clear that the poor are a very heterogeneous population. The problems and causes of poverty vary from group to group—from the elderly, to women with children, to two-parent families where the husband works full-time, to homeless individuals. It is not clearly useful to think of "the poor" as anything other than an aggregate label for a very diverse population. But it is also true that the dominant images of poverty that many of us hold may not correlate well with the descriptive statistics on the poor population. The emphasis in this country on encouraging the poor to work harder ignores evidence that the vast majority of the poor either cannot participate in the labor market, are already looking for more work and not finding it, or are already working full-time.

Defining Strategies to Deal with Poverty

Disagreements over how we as a society should respond to the problem of poverty are typically disagreements over which of these images most aptly characterizes the majority of the poor, or disagreements about how we should differentiate between poor individuals from different categories. We run few programs in this country to which all poor have equal access, largely because we want to distinguish between the groups described in the previous section.

Numerous policy dilemmas are created when the poor are no longer viewed as a homogeneous population. Let me note just two, which relate to issues raised by the bishops.

First, there is a conflict between the social-contract approach to the poor and the minimum-rights approach, both of which are supported by the bishops at different points in their letter. The theory of a two-way social contract claims that on the one hand society has a responsibility to assure economic survival to each individual, while on the other hand, the individual has a responsibility to work and contribute to society. As the bishops put it, "Social justice implies that persons have an obligation to be active and productive participants in the life of society and that society has a duty to enable them to participate in this way" (par. 71). However, the bishops never actually come to grips with a crucial question: "Does the social obligation still exist when the individual violates his or her side of the contract?" The response in this country has been largely to say no. For instance, we run almost no support programs for non-elderly men, no matter what their economic circumstances. If one takes the two-way contract seriously, it can provide a justification for limiting social programs to those who are either physically unable to work (and thus exempted from the contract), or those who prove they are willing to fulfill some work requirement (e.g., the stipulation through "workfare" mandates that women who are able to work must put in a specified number of hours on an assigned job in order to receive welfare).

As a result, the social-contract approach can directly conflict with an alternative approach calling for minimum economic rights, which the bishops also support. They call for minimum guarantees of basic economic support to all poor individuals. Discussing the conditions necessary for community life, the bishops claim, "These conditions include the rights to fulfillment of material needs. . . . [These rights] are not created by society. Indeed, society has a duty to secure and protect them" (par. 79). It is not at all clear whether these minimum economic rights supercede or are subordinate to the two-way social contract.

A second policy dilemma, associated with the existence of multiple images of poverty, is the question of how we should respond to households that contain individuals who fall into different categories. The best example of this is the impoverished two-parent family with children. While the children clearly cannot work and bear no responsibility for their poverty, their parents, especially the father, may be viewed as "less deserving." This problem has kept the United States from providing major support programs to two-parent households. In 1986 only twenty-six states allowed two-parent households to receive Aid to Families with Dependent Children (AFDC), the primary form of welfare support.

AFDC funding for female-headed households with children, the traditional recipient group, is increasingly confronting the same issue. As large numbers of women from all income strata work, even when small children are present in the household, it becomes unacceptable for society to support women on the AFDC program without also encouraging them to work. Otherwise, the mother is not fulfilling her side of the social contract. But how does society enforce this? Excluding the mother from assistance also excludes her children. The original design of the AFDC program, which was to pay only child support and provide no money for the adult householder, is necessarily unenforceable; money spent for general household maintenance benefits both the children and the mother. These difficulties in directing antipoverty programs to the appropriate subset of the poor are a source of ongoing policy debate in this country.

The bishops are careful to indicate in their letter that they make no direct link between the theological arguments that indicate Christians have a moral obligation to respond to the needs of the poor and any particular policy that purports to alleviate poverty. In introducing Chapter Three, where they discuss specific economic issues and policies, they note, "We emphasize that these are illustrative topics intended to exemplify the interaction of moral values and economic issues in our day. . . . This document is not a technical blueprint for economic reform" (par. 133). It is not possible to determine through intensive biblical-theological study which anti-poverty policy will be most effective in our modern society. However, the bishops do present a set of policy options (primarily government programs) for consideration. But because the document does not distinguish well between different theories of who the poor are and why they are poor, the bishops' policy discussion becomes a checklist of possible approaches without a clear sense of priorities. In a world of limited budgets and resources, one must choose wisely among programs. While government intervention is but one way of dealing with poverty, in a complex society like ours it is the most indispensable way of expressing society's commitment as a whole to meeting the needs of each of its members. It is useful to look at a range of government anti-poverty proposals, many of them mentioned in the bishops' letter, and characterize their attractiveness in light of the differing images of poverty presented in this chapter.

Some form of a guaranteed minimum income to all low-income households is a frequently proposed scheme. The most commonly discussed form of this is a negative income tax, in which households below some income level would receive money from the government, while households above this level would pay the standard tax rates. This policy is typically supported by those who either see the majority of the poor as economically unfortunate through no fault of their own, or feel that the social obligation to provide a minimum floor of support for all citizens exists outside of any answering obligation on the part of the poor. This is a scheme that treats all poor as similar and deals with poverty as a purely economic phenomenon: the problem is that some people do not have enough money; therefore, as a society we must assure that these households have more resources.

Although we do not call it a guaranteed minimum income, we do provide this type of support to the elderly and to the disabled who are eligible for the Supplementary Security Income (SSI) program, which guarantees minimum income levels to the elderly and the handicapped for whom Social Security is not available or not adequate. The monetary support levels of this program are low, but they are uniform and nationally applied levels available to all eligible citizens throughout the country.[5] Single-parent households with children also receive some income guarantees through the AFDC program. But the provisions of this program are set at the state level, and they vary widely. In 1987 the median state guaranteed a maximum AFDC benefit payment to a mother with two children that was only $14 higher than the SSI benefit payment for a single individual. Thus, despite very high poverty rates among women with children, we are clearly much less willing to provide programs to this group of the poor than to their elderly parents or grandparents.

An alternative to guaranteeing cash income is to guarantee only certain goods such as food and shelter (referred to as "in-kind" services). This approach would be consistent with a belief that society has an obligation to provide individuals with certain basic services, but either should not provide anything beyond this or should not trust the poor to use a general monetary grant for these purposes. The one in-kind form of assistance we in the United States make available to all households below a certain income level, regardless of their composition or situation, is food stamps. In 1986 the average benefits paid per person through food stamps were around $45 per month, or about fifty cents per meal. In other words, we do guarantee some level of food to all, but we are unwilling to provide any additional support, except to those specific groups that we judge as "more deserving." Other countries provide greater in-kind services, guaranteeing housing and health care to all low-income households. (About 17 percent of the population in the United States had no health-insurance coverage in 1980.)

Those who view the poor as predominantly composed of people who either have not received enough education and job training or who are systematically excluded from the labor market look less favorably upon general income or in-kind support programs, preferring programs that involve job creation, job placement, and job training. This might mean programs that provide incentives for private-sector companies to employ and train less-skilled workers (such as the current Job Training Partnership Act), or it might involve the creation of additional public-service jobs when private-sector jobs are not available. Programs involving affirmative action and equal employment opportunity may also be part of this strategy, as are efforts to make more and better jobs available to low-wage and unemployed workers.

There is currently a great deal of interest in "workfare" programs—that is, programs attached to AFDC that provide AFDC participants with job training and placement. The validity of the two-way social contract in such programs is the current focus of much debate, since some states are implementing mandatory work programs for AFDC mothers deemed able to work, while other states are committed to keeping this a voluntary aspect of the AFDC program.

Clearly, the supporters of job training and employment programs may be concerned about the lack of skills among the poor population, about the poor's potential exclusion from labor markets, or about a lack of work incentives among the poor. Those who are convinced that the poor lack the motivation to work care more about making such work programs mandatory in exchange for other social services. Those who believe that the poor want to work more, but have been kept back by forces outside their control, believe that mandatory programs simply create an unnecessarily punitive environment for people who already want jobs.

Finally, individuals who believe that poverty reflects broader attitudinal and culturally embedded problems and who worry about dependency and hostility among the poor are often interested in programs that enforce behavioral standards. We run a variety of programs aimed explicitly at removing individuals from potentially harmful environments and retraining them in disciplined, alternative settings. A classic example of such a program is the Job Corps, which removes teenagers from their home neighborhood and places them in highly disciplined educational environments, encouraging basic educational skills as well as providing structured vocational training and work experience. In a somewhat different manner, the Head Start program puts preschool children into structured learning environments, hoping to give them remedial help that will enable them to perform better when they enter grade school. These programs are explicitly aimed at modifying the environment and thus changing attitudes and behavior. They focus not on the economic aspects of poverty but on deeper underlying problems that must be addressed before the poverty can be alleviated.

In the United States we have consistently insisted on making distinctions in our treatment of the poor. To some groups we are relatively generous. Our willingness to assist the elderly has dramatically decreased poverty rates among those over sixty-five. Once almost twice as likely to be poor than the average American, the elderly are now less likely to be poor than the average person—largely because of the increase in support programs for elderly households. We are less willing to assist other populations. Currently children are more likely to be living in poor households than any other demographic group in society. While we may not want to punish children for the lack of economic resources among their parents, we clearly are not willing to give significant subsidies to adults just to alleviate poverty among children. The increasing number of American women in the work force is creating discussion of the need to demand work from able-bodied AFDC recipients. And we completely refuse to help single individuals in their prime years. At least one of the reasons why we have been so slow in responding to the growing crisis of homeless individuals on the streets of our central cities is that this population is largely composed of single men between the ages of twenty and forty-five, a group that we have always resisted supporting.

How Do We Choose?

As Christians struggling to find ways to fulfill our ethical responsibility to be engaged in the problems of the poor, we must seek out the appropriate mix of responses that will most effectively deal with poverty. I have argued that we must think of the poor as a diverse population with diverse needs. This means that no single program will provide "the solution" to poverty. Thus the question "What should we do?" requires a sophisticated answer. Let me propose several standards to guide action.

Rebecca M. Blank

First, to provide the motivation for action, it is important to continually remind ourselves of the unacceptability of current poverty levels. We are challenged to speak with and for the poor, to name their needs to our fellow Christians and to our larger society. A crucial aspect of this challenge is to enable the poor to speak for themselves, particularly encouraging their increased participation and involvement in the political process. Effective implementation of this concern involves exercising the "fundamental option for the poor" called for by the bishops—that is, the "obligation to evaluate social and economic activity from the viewpoint of the poor and the powerless" (par. 87). The question "What will this mean for the poor?" should be asked whenever policy is being set. However, the challenge goes beyond simply raising a concern about poverty, to educating others to the causes and consequences of poverty. It needs to be more widely recognized that half of the poor in this country fit into our first category, those who *cannot* work, and that a significant number of others are working full-time, year-round, and are still poor. The stereotype of the poor as "less industrious," while perhaps accurate for some subset of the poor, is inaccurate for the vast majority of the poor. It is our responsibility to work on changing and challenging the images of poverty that many use to inaccurately characterize large numbers of poor households.

Second, as Christians we are called to respond generously and nonjudgmentally to the poor, even to those who may be less industrious or more hostile. The two-way contract of which the bishops speak is an ideal model of how one would like society to work. But even when individuals willfully violate their responsibility to be productive members of society, Christian teaching must lead us to recognize an ethical obligation to reach out to them. The minimum economic rights of each human being must take precedence over the two-way social contract. We may choose not to provide monetary guarantees, but a guarantee of food, shelter, and medical care to all human beings is a recognition of the value of individual human lives that transcends any judgment of appropriate or inappropriate behavior. Priority should be given to these programs over all others.

Third, the diversity among the poor population means that it may be entirely appropriate to have different programs for different groups. On the one hand, acceptance of minimum economic rights typically translates into large-scale programs available to all poor individuals. On the other hand, the diversity of the poor population indicates that the causes of poverty differ between different groups, and effective policy should target different programs for each group. For instance, it is almost surely desirable to primarily provide programs that offer labor-market skills and job placement for poor, non-elderly men, just as it is equally desirable to primarily offer income-support programs to elderly men. The important question is which set of services should be guaranteed to all, and which should be more selectively targeted.

Acceptance of minimum economic rights indicates that some services are so important that they should be provided uniformly to all poor individuals. However, beyond assuring food, housing, and health care, I believe that it is useful to run distinct and targeted programs. I would seriously question the usefulness of a guaranteed minimum income for all poor individuals; instead I would recommend providing a combination of education, job creation and job placement, and child care for employable groups in the population, providing long-term general income support to nonemployable groups only. In these targeted programs I would recommend enforcing some form of a social contract (if jobs are available, individuals should be expected to work), always with the assumption that certain basic minimum guarantees are in place.

Fourth, the difference between the long-term and the short-term needs of many groups in the poor population must be kept in mind. At the moment, many households are simply without the means to support themselves adequately. Either the adults in the household are without the skills to find employment to support their family, or no job is currently available, or child care is not available. In the short run, these households need basic minimum guarantees of food and shelter, but they also need income support. However, in the long term, the better answer must be to find a way for these households to leave poverty, to find a way toward adequate employment and self-support. There is a great deal of concern that income-support programs which solve the short-term problem create disincentives for poor households to seek employment, and thus do nothing to provide a long-term solution to poverty. However, programs to address these long-term needs typically run into two problems.

First, they are much more difficult to run effectively than are general income-support programs, since they require the joint implementation of a host of services. A truly effective program aimed at improving the employment opportunities for the poor must at minimum include components that provide additional education, job-skill training, job placement, child care, and job creation in areas where jobs are scarce. A number of newly emerging programs for AFDC women are trying to provide such a coordinated set of programs. Early results from these programs indicate that, despite the

Rebecca M. Blank

difficulties in establishing them, they can be successful at reducing welfare usage and increasing household income.⁶

Second, such a combination of programs is very expensive to run. Job training and job creation can be particularly costly programs, especially if the target population is a group without high-school degrees and with little previous work experience. If these programs are effective, much of this money will ultimately be repaid through decreased welfare payments, increased tax payments, and increased productivity. But few states and almost no localities have the budget resources to afford the costs of establishing such programs. Thus there is a serious need for increased federal resources aimed at addressing long-term issues of poverty and administered through states and localities to establish coordinated employment-oriented programs aimed at women and men who can work.

Dealing with the problems of poverty in this country requires a commitment to struggle openly with difficult policy decisions. We must be willing to deal with the complexity of this issue, to seek out and support those policymakers who resist monocausal reasoning and single-program answers. This necessarily means involving ourselves in a process of long-term struggle and change, which will require patience and commitment. Effective programs are not easy to design, and they are even harder to implement within the complex political process that determines policy in this country.

The bishops' letter provides a solid theological argument why Christians should be concerned with economic reality. But I have suggested that we must add analysis of the causes and conditions of poverty before we can move from principle to policy. Only by confronting stereotypes that treat "the poor" as a homogeneous group can we begin to recognize the differing human needs of low-income households. Effective social responses that reflect our religious convictions must deal in a sophisticated manner with the diversity of problems faced by our brothers and sisters who are poor.

15 | *The Churches and the Corporations*

Paul F. Camenisch

The emergence of the corporation as one of the most powerful, pervasive, and effective institutions in the modern world underscores the need to address the relationship between corporations and the political and social order.

United Church of Christ, "Christian Faith and Economic Life"

One of the most vexing problems is that of reconciling the transnational corporations' profit orientation with the common good that they, along with governments and their multinational agencies, are supposed to serve.

National Conference of Catholic Bishops, *Economic Justice for All*

The Problem

"Then the Judge will say to those at the left, 'Depart from me, into eternal punishment. For . . . I was homeless because you allowed multinational corporations to appropriate the land on which I was living.' . . .

"Then the Judge will say to those at the right side, 'Come, O blessed, inherit the future prepared for you from the foundation of the world. For . . . I was homeless and you required the corporation which seized my land to return it.'"[1]

Modern readers will likely have several problems with this updated version of Jesus' parable of the last judgment because of the way it conflicts with our prevailing thought patterns. But I will focus

169

on a problem that is quite current and congruent with contemporary thought. It has to do with the parable's portrayal of corporations. Corporations are here represented as forces doing things that sometimes harm people. But the corporations as such are not held accountable for what they do: they are not made to answer to the judge, nor are they punished or rewarded by the judge. They are not treated as morally responsible. Instead, responsibility for what the corporations do, whether good or ill, is assigned to individuals who stand before the judge, individuals whose link to the corporations—whether as owners, managers, employees, customers, or simply citizens in general—we do not even know.

What we face here is, to use the language of philosophy, the question of the moral agency of corporations, of whether collective entities such as corporations can be treated as moral agents in ways analogous to the ways we treat individuals in their roles as moral agents. But while we may use the language of philosophy, this is not just a philosopher's problem. In fact, I will address it here primarily as a problem confronting contemporary religious faith and practice, one that is actually an element in—although it is not directly addressed by—three recent mainline Protestant documents on justice and the economic order.

But first we must be clear on the issue of moral agency and its significance. Of the many ideas involved in this issue, the key one for us is the idea of moral accountability or moral responsibility. Clearly, the most familiar way of holding parties accountable is by treating them as moral agents—that is, as actors who can perceive various possible courses of action in a given situation, weigh them in relation to multiple considerations, including moral ones, choose among those options on the basis of those considerations, carry out such choices, and then be held accountable for their actions. "Moral agency" then refers only to an actor's capacity to act either morally or immorally, as distinguished from the total moral incapacity of such amoral forces as mad dogs, mental incompetents, hurricanes, and machines.

The complexity of this model of responsibility or accountability, even when applied to the easiest case of "normal" human individuals, can be seen in the continuing debates about it in law, philosophy, theology, and ordinary conversation. We multiply these complexities when we apply this model to groups or corporate entities such as business corporations.

One way to avoid such complexities would be simply to treat the individuals within corporations, but not the corporations themselves, as moral agents. However, there are several reasons to reject this suggestion. One is the simple matter of consistency. In ordinary conversation the idea of corporate moral agency and responsibility seems to pose few problems when applied to government, churches, labor unions, and various other institutions. The burden of proof would therefore seem to be on those who would maintain that there is something unique about business corporations that exempts them from this concept of corporate or collective moral agency.

Furthermore, if we see only individuals as moral agents, then moral concerns must be brought to the corporation from the outside and grafted onto individuals' corporate roles rather than arising from within the corporation itself. This is an unfair burden for individuals and an unjustified "pass" for corporations on moral matters. This would also mean that those proposing the use of corporate resources to serve the common good or economic justice would always bear the burden of proof and would most likely prevail only when they could tie such use directly to corporate self-interest. Finally, to address moral reasons and arguments only to individuals would mean that individuals dismissing such appeals could then use the massive resources of modern corporations to pursue interests contrary to society's with moral impunity.

What would it mean to treat corporations as moral agents? At mimimum it would mean three things: (1) challenging corporations themselves to perform certain actions and observe certain policies because they are morally correct, even when they conflict or seem to conflict with other legitimate corporate interests; (2) addressing moral arguments to those corporations with the expectation that they will, simply as moral arguments, weigh significantly in corporate decision-making; and (3) holding corporations accountable rather than just trying to constrain them by various sanctions and incentives.

Various objections to treating corporations as moral agents have been raised by both philosophers and economists. Some argue that the corporation is simply not a collective entity that can decide and act as a unit and that it therefore cannot be held accountable as a unit. Others argue that even if the corporation does act as a single entity, the sort of entity it was designed to be—one oriented to the generation of profit—makes it immune to considerations not directly related to that goal. In most cases moral considerations would be disqualified on this ground. A third argument not necessarily incompatible with the previous one is that one need not even bring in moral considerations to direct the self-interested corporation toward societal interests, since the alchemy of the free competitive marketplace will transform the dross of all participants' self-interest into societal good.

But despite these and other more common-sense objections, there is considerable support in various quarters of the larger society for treating corporations as moral agents. The law grants corporations standing as artificial persons and recognizes in them certain powers analogous to those exercised by individuals or natural persons: the capacity to act as an entity, to be a party to lawsuits, to own land and enter into contracts, and to exercise certain rights under the Constitution and under statutory law. In all of these cases corporations are seen as agents, even as moral agents. In many cases corporations' own credos and statements of purpose cast them in the role of moral agents working to serve consumers and the society in ways going beyond those strictly dictated by profit alone. Johnson and Johnson, Borg-Warner, and ServiceMaster, for example, have all made such commitments publicly.

The growing conviction that society is an integrated, interdependent whole in which each of the parts receives from others crucial benefits not strictly earned or otherwise deserved provides good grounds for opposing any significant locus of power—whether political, economic, cultural, or otherwise—that attempts to go its own purely autonomous way undisciplined by societal concerns. We give no other major segment of society—such as the professions, education and the universities, government, and the military—carte blanche to serve only its own self-interest. We hold all of them accountable to the public interest. It is not clear why business should be treated any differently. Of course, such accountability can be enforced from the outside, but only at great cost both to the larger society and to the entity on which it is imposed. Much more desirable for all concerned is the corporation's recognition of itself as a moral agent, since this will often lead to the development of internal structures of moral accountability.

Recent Christian Statements on Economic Justice

Economic Justice for All, the Catholic bishops' pastoral letter, deservedly received considerable attention as it moved through three preliminary drafts to its final form. Less widely heralded have been similar documents from several mainline Protestant denominations. Of these documents, only three approach the length and complexity of the Roman Catholic document: "Christian Faith and Economic Life" by the United Church of Christ, and two documents by the Presbyterian Church (U.S.A.)—"Christian Faith and Economic Justice"[2] and "Toward a Just, Caring and Dynamic Political Economy."[3] These documents share with the pastoral the conviction that the economies of the United States, and of the world, as judged by Christian standards do not currently serve people and communities as they should. These documents are written to promote a better understanding of the biblical, the Christian, and the denominational heritages in matters of economic justice, to promote among church members a better understanding of the current economic situation and of the structural dynamics underlying it, and finally to make recommendations to help alleviate the problems identified.

Effective recommendations must reflect an understanding of the problems addressed and must suggest plausible corrective actions. But they must also address those parties or institutions, those agents, best able to take effective action. Furthermore, they must address such agents in ways and on grounds most likely to move them to action. The agents addressed by these documents include the government, business corporations, the churches themselves, and individuals in their various roles in the economy. In the difficult area of addressing business and business corporations, however, these documents leave considerable work to be done. Given the role and influence of business corporations in the American economy and in the shaping of American society in general, it is imperative that we undertake this task. Among the documents treated here, the longer and more complex Roman Catholic document provides the most helpful starting points. But even it leaves much to be done.

Shared Ground

All of these documents agree on the significance of business activity in contemporary society and on the danger it poses of distorted priorities (PC, 1985, 304). They further agree that large business corporations increasingly dominate our economy. The Presbyterians note that we have moved into a third phase of industrial capitalism that they call the transnational stage, in which "capital has become much more mobile internationally" and "economic power in some key areas has become increasingly concentrated." This concentration is reflected in the fact that "more than seventy percent of all U.S. private economic activity—production and finance—is controlled and operated through 800 transnational corporations." Fourteen million firms share the other thirty percent. Four hundred "U.S. based transnational corporations account for fifty percent of our national gross product" (PC, 1984, 184, 186-87). Both the Presbyterians (PC, 1984, 190) and the United Church of Christ (UCC, 121; cf. par. 255)[4] note that of the 100 largest economic entities in the world, only 59 are nation-states. The rest are transnational corporations.

These facts of corporate presence and power are not only recorded but noted with concern. There is concern that the size and mobility of these corporations will enable them to escape regulation by nation-states (par. 280; UCC, 84), that corporate goals will sometimes override concerns about the common good. The profit motive alone, the bishops assert, is not sufficient to guide corporations to the common good (pars. 94, 234, 256).

It is crucial to note, however, that generally corporations are not made into stereotypical villains. The UCC document may flirt with this possibility in its updated version of the parable of the great judgment cited at the beginning of this chapter (UCC, 298ff.). And when the UCC document twice refers to "powers and principalities" that must be resisted (UCC, 47, 291) without naming any of them, readers must wonder if corporations are not among the most likely candidates. Nevertheless, business corporations are treated quite gently overall. They are never specifically named in the repeated mention of "social sin . . . embodied in systems and structures . . . interwoven into institutions" (UCC, 46). The economic problems currently facing the United States and the world, all agree, are overwhelmingly institutional and structural problems. The pivotal issue, then, is whether and how business and business corporations, as major elements in the current economic structures, are to be addressed so as to enlist them in the cause of economic justice.

The most general ground in these documents for assigning responsibility for economic justice to business and corporations is the asserted correlation between power and accountability. In a section titled "Those Who Wield Power Must Be Accountable," the Presbyterians insist that "All power, whether economic, political, or ecclesiastical, whether personal, corporate or governmental, needs appropriate checks and balances for accountability." Those wielding power are accountable to "the values and [must] serve the well-being of the community" (PC, 1985, 244, 246). The Catholic bishops affirm this same correlation for large corporations and financial institutions. But what is significant in terms of my discussion is that they conclude this affirmation by placing the burden of accountability largely on the managers of those corporations rather than on the corporations themselves (par. 111).

There is general agreement on the inadequacy of the current structures of accountability for corporations (par. 298; PC, 1985, 301-4), whether political (UCC, 84) or legal (par. 305), whether deriving from the workings of the market (UCC, 102, 107, 141, 190; PC,

1985, 505) or the general economic system (UCC, 147; PC, 1984, 227). This leads to calls for new and more adequate structures of accountability (PC, 1985, 572; par. 110; UCC, 122). But do these documents go beyond this call and help indicate what such structures might look like and how they might be implemented? In the previous section we have noted some of the difficulties of applying the moral-agency model to corporations. Yet if business and corporations are to be enlisted in the pursuit of economic justice beyond those ways supported by their own self-interest, either we must treat them as moral agents with all the puzzles involved, or we must resort to the various ways we have of controlling nonmoral agents—appeal to self-interest or even instinct, and the application of coercion and, in extreme cases, termination. Business corporations may certainly insist that economic justice is not part of their business. But if we deny them that disclaimer, as all three documents treated here do, it seems unlikely that they would choose to be treated as nonmoral agents in any of the ways just cited, with the possible exception of appeals to their self-interest. But history clearly shows that such an appeal alone is rarely adequate to protect crucial societal interests.

Given these various grounds for addressing business corporations as moral agents, do these documents really go only part of the way in treating business corporations as moral agents? And if so, why have numerous businesspeople felt after reading these documents that the corporations were there being criticized for moral failure? One important reason for this disagreement about the documents' view of corporate moral agency is that the documents never directly address this question. Their positions must be extrapolated from indirect evidence.

Clearly, these documents are critical of the current economy and thus of its major elements such as business corporations, of an exclusive focus on profit (pars. 256, 289), of unbridled market mechanisms (UCC, 102, 107, 114, 190; PC, 1985, 414, 505, 561; par. 282), and so on. But this alone does not establish that corporations are being portrayed as moral agents that can rightly be blamed and punished for past failure, or urged to moral responsibility concerning future performance. Rather, they seem to be treated almost as natural forces or powers that must be carefully observed and sometimes restrained but that are not themselves subject to direct moral appeal.

It is important to note here that whatever the problems involved in the idea of corporate moral agency, these documents do address other corporate entities as moral agents. The Catholic bishops maintain that both the society itself and the government have moral responsibilities (par. 18, PM; par. 122; cf. PC, 1985, 256). Similarly, in all these documents the churches themselves both speak as and are addressed as moral agents with a responsibility, a calling to serve others (UCC, 262-83; pars. 339-58). Labor unions (pars. 66, 107, 303), families, and voluntary associations (PC, 1985, 279-84) are also addressed as moral agents having moral obligations. Thus any failure of these documents to adequately address business corporations as moral agents does not derive from the inability to conceive of groups or institutions as such agents.

There is one final note of caution about drawing conclusions about corporate moral agency in these documents. Several elements found in them suggest some form of agency. These include assertions that corporate actions have produced unfortunate results; the insistence that we must find ways to alter those actions and their outcomes; the challenge to people within corporations to act individually as moral agents, to direct corporate actions toward morally desirable outcomes; and finally, references to corporations as agents or actors. In none of these elements, however, is the agency implied necessarily *moral* agency.

Documents of the UCC and the Presbyterian Church (U.S.A.)

Both the UCC and the Presbyterian documents begin to lay adequate groundwork for a theory of corporations' moral agency when they speak of the accountability of institutions as well as of individuals under "God's household rules" and the "Christian principles of economic justice" (UCC, 47, 50, 123; cf. PC, 1985, 508, 571-73). But such passages almost always refer to institutions generally and rarely if ever to business corporations as such.

In speaking of ways to affect corporate behavior, these documents overwhelmingly invoke either appeals to corporate self-interest through various incentives, taxation policies, or other forms of government intervention (UCC, 122, 195; PC, 1985, 505). Alternatively, there are suggestions about possible new ways to run corporations involving reconceptualized "corporate roles, ownership patterns, and modes of operation in relationship to the wider society" (UCC, 123; cf. PC, 1985, 292, 516-17).

Unfortunately, these documents show no interest in the significant moral differences between a sense of responsibility internal to corporations and regulations constraining corporations from the outside. Thus when they speak of an ethic for corporations, they seem to envision one endorsed by individuals and the society at large, its directives then being imposed on the corporation from the outside by various appeals to corporate self-interest. Furthermore, none of these Protestant documents suggest how corporations could be addressed directly on moral grounds (UCC, 196-97, 208; cf. PC, 1985, 572-81).

The Presbyterians not only do not address corporations directly as moral agents but go a considerable way toward obscuring their accountability. "In a practical manner," they insist, "it is absolutely impossible to separate the government from the economy, the public sector from the private." But rather than assigning equal responsibility to government and business for economic justice, they take a position that permits the corporations virtually to escape assessment. Discussions of the private sector focus on voluntary associations or on what is required of managers of corporations but not on what is required of corporations as such (PC, 1985, 279, 272, 296). Significantly, in this same passage, government as such is addressed with regard to its responsibilities, but in comments about the corporate sector it is the individuals, the managers, who are the focus.

Repeatedly the Presbyterians' presentations of the tensions and conflicts involved in the pursuit of economic justice put the focus on individual moral agency. As owner, the Christian might settle for less than maximum profits in light of other important goals, but as manager of the assets of others, could the Christian properly follow the same course? There is also reference to what individuals have received from the society and thus of what they owe in return (PC, 1985, 300, 322). But there is no parallel discussion of what corporations have received and now owe.

Perhaps most telling on the matter of corporate moral agency is what is not said. In the section on the corporations in the UCC document (UCC, 117-23), there is no clear indication that the corporations are themselves seen as moral agents. And, as already noted, in that document's conclusion, "The Parable of the Present and Future Great Judgment" (UCC, 298-303), corporations are not portrayed as having any moral being of their own, as themselves being accountable moral agents. Of course, it is hard to imagine the Divine Judge's sending the corporations either into eternal punishment or to the reward of the faithful. But we must either find a way around those difficulties or take seriously the apparent fact that corporations are not moral agents and then find other ways to enlist their resources in our pursuit of economic justice. These documents have not made a clear, consistent choice between these options. The uncertainty—even ambivalence—of these documents on the issue of corporate moral agency and accountability is best summarized in one of the Presbyterians' few direct statements on the issue: "Per-

haps democracy now requires the same kind of popular accountability for large business institutions that it has always required for
government institutions. That may be a scary thought to some of us,
but the times require us to consider it" (PC, 1985, 310).

The Bishops' Pastoral Letter

When we turn to the Catholic bishops' letter, we meet many of the
same themes and difficulties in the treatment of business corporations as moral agents, as accountable to the larger society. At the same
time, however, the bishops go at least two significant steps farther in
this matter.

First, the bishops assert more clearly than their Protestant
counterparts the appropriateness of corporate participation in the
pursuit of economic justice and the hope for its realization: "All the
economic agents in our society, therefore, must consciously and
deliberately attend to the good of the whole human family" (par. 324;
cf. pars. 110, 121). This general hope for corporate involvement is applied specifically to such areas as unemployment and self-help projects for the poor (pars. 159, 200). The moral standing of corporations
is enhanced by passages that put business on a moral footing parallel to that of other corporate moral agents. Speaking of the three
moral meanings of work, the bishops assert that "these three moral
concerns . . . should . . . govern the activities of the many different,
overlapping communities and institutions that make up society:
families, neighborhoods, small businesses, giant corporations, trade
unions, the various levels of government, international organizations
and a host of other human associations including communities of
faith" (par. 98; cf. par. 76). Thus both national and transnational corporations are thought to have significant roles to play with regard to
justice and solidarity (par. 116).

At the same time, it is not evident that the bishops have a
firm, clear sense of the business corporation as moral agent. In their
discussions of subsidiarity, a principle governing the role of various
sectors of society that mediate between the individual and the largest
forms of organization such as national governments, business corporations receive little attention. For example, their discussion of subsidiarity in paragraph 124 refers to the roles only of individuals and
smaller communities. And in their discussion of "some of the persons
and institutions whose work for justice will be particularly important
to the future of the U.S. economy," they devote sections to working
people and labor unions, owners and managers, and citizens and
government, but none to business or business corporations as such

(pars. 101-24; cf. par. 308). This is a glaring omission in a discussion of the U.S. economy.

In brief, the bishops acknowledge that present structures of corporate accountability to the larger community are inadequate (par. 298), yet they are ambivalent about the moral status of business and business corporations; accordingly, the bishops resort to strategies described earlier. Apparently more comfortable with individual moral agency and accountability, they tend to "individualize" issues of corporate responsibility and accountability by assigning them to individuals in the corporation, chiefly managers (par. 111) but also owners and investors (pars. 106, 110, 113, 354). While such individuals do indeed have responsibilities in matters of economic justice, matters related to their Christian vocation (pars. 111, 117), our current question is whether individual responsibilities can stand in the place of corporate responsibilities.

The bishops repeatedly note the desirability of external—primarily governmental—intervention to move business toward the goals of economic equity and justice (pars. 118, 154-56, 162-63), even suggesting that "transnational corporations should be required to adopt . . . a code" concerning the development and equitable distribution of their benefits (par. 280). Whether this is seen as a way of instilling a sense of moral agency in corporations or simply as another form of external control is unclear.

Finally, in their fourth chapter, the bishops propose what they call "A New American Experiment: Partnership for the Public Good," which they hope will extend democracy from the political arena into economic and business sectors. This experiment includes new modes of corporate governance and control, benefit sharing, and profit sharing, including broader and more local ownership (pars. 300, 310).

Whether these suggestions are offered in lieu of or simply to supplement a theory of corporate moral agency is not made clear. Given that relatively little is finally said about the corporations themselves being moral agents, the former possibility is the more plausible one.

The second way in which the bishops move toward fulfilling one of our three criteria for treating corporations as moral agents is by taking a potentially major step beyond our other documents. This step consists of the various ideas scattered through the letter that serve as moral grounds for holding corporations accountable and that can be addressed to corporations as good moral reasons for concerning themselves with the common good and economic justice. These considerations do not rely on coercion or other sanctions related to corporate self-interest to be persuasive; they are simply morally relevant observations about the actual situation of business corporations. In the current political economy, the bishops argue, corporations are already quasi-public institutions and therefore cannot legitimately pursue their self-interest at the expense of larger societal interests (par. 280). Parties other than owners and managers have made contributions to and have stakes in corporations and their actions that must be acknowledged in corporate decision-making (par. 298). The capital and other resources available to corporations are not their own creations but are in part the result of labor's contributions (pars. 113, 303), so that business and financial institutions are best seen as trustees, not owners (par. 112). Corporations, like all other economic agents, are elements in an extensively interdependent world of limited resources requiring that all moral agents attend to one another's needs and rights (pars. 298, 324).

Thus the Catholic bishops offer us two resources beyond those found in the Protestant documents for strengthening any theory of corporate moral agency already at work. One is their explicit (although not always consistent) placing of business corporations on a moral par with other corporate entities—family, government, religious congregations, unions—that are widely recognized as having a duty to pursue economic justice and the common good. The other is the series of observations about the nature and current situation of corporations that can serve as moral grounds for challenging corporations to become responsible moral agents.

Religious and Theological Implications

The issue of corporate moral agency is not only of moral and practical significance; it also has religious and theological implications. In terms of the application of religious vision to contemporary issues, there is the matter (also addressed in this section by Larry Rasmussen) of how realistic we are about the centers of power in contemporary society and how directly we address to them imperatives arising from our faith. All the documents treated here agree that modern business corporations are major centers of power. Addressing them as moral agents is the most promising and least disruptive way to enlist them in the cause of economic justice, since other ways suggested involve either the costly use of coercion or appeals to corporations' self-interest, which in the long run are potentially counterproductive. Thus, articulating a plausible theory of corporate moral responsibility is a potentially valuable step in enlisting the power, influence, and resources of business corporations in the cause of economic justice.

Seen from another perspective, we confront here the issue of human responsibility. To establish a theory of corporate moral agency that holds such entities responsible for their use of corporate power is, among other things, to assert that we are accountable for our actions, whether as individuals or as members of communities or corporations; that our responsibility goes beyond what we as individuals directly do in whatever roles we play and extends to the policies and actions of corporate entities to which we lend our support; and that such modes of joint action give neither us nor the entities into which we form ourselves immunity from the moral norms that should shape our life together in community.

Finally, we meet here the issue of divine sovereignty, for in asserting a theory of corporate moral agency and responsibility, we assert that God's sovereignty and moral will, partly expressed in the norms of justice informing these documents, reach human agents regardless of the modes in which they act, that God's sovereignty and moral will reach human creations such as corporations through which or as which we act. We profess that there are no principalities and powers—whether primordial and uncreated or humanly contrived—that escape the sovereignty of the one just God.

What must be added to these documents in the area of corporate moral agency to do justice to the moral, practical, religious, and theological matters at stake here? Put most briefly, we would have to treat business corporations as moral agents by doing three things: (1) stating publicly what moral expectations we have of corporations in the area of economic justice, just as these documents do with regard to individuals, governments, and churches; (b) backing those expectations with moral reasons arising from the corporations' complex role in contemporary society, a role consisting of rights and duties and in part defined by the benefits they receive from the society; and (c) making clear that although those expectations and reasons are of necessity addressed to certain individuals within the corporations, they bring moral responsibility to bear not only on those individuals but also on that corporate entity recognized in law that those individuals together help constitute but which in its powers and resources transcends them. Only in this way can the moral imperative of economic justice reach beyond individual consciences and into those larger and more complex corporate entities that currently structure—even dominate—so much of our lives, particularly our economic lives.

If we cannot do this, we face a situation unfortunate in

several respects. We will have to persuade individuals that they have a moral obligation to work for economic justice, that they even have such an obligation when they act within, through, for, or as a corporation, but that the corporation itself is an amoral entity not bound by any such obligations. It is not clear how this can be anything but confusing, even disorienting, for morally sensitive people working in corporations.

In the absence of a plausible theory of corporate moral agency, we will also have to try to move this society and this world toward greater economic justice without being able to count on the active, consistent assistance of the dominant economic agents in our national economy and in much of the world economy—modern business corporations. At best we will receive their assistance when it coincides with corporate self-interest, or when it can be coerced by external sanctions. At worst we will need to overcome their resistance to economic justice when corporate self-interest leads them to ignore it or even to act against it. To consent to this situation would be tantamount to acknowledging that achieving economic justice within current economic structures is highly unlikely, if not impossible.

Part 4 | *Roman Catholic Perspectives on American Economic Life*

16 | *Roman Catholic Perspectives on American Economic Life*

Suddenly American Catholicism has become fashionable among religious and secular intellectuals. The signs of this new preoccupation with Catholic life and thought are all around us. Although it is not surprising that Pope John Paul II's tour in 1987 across the southern United States should have attracted such intense media interest, the increasingly sophisticated press coverage of the semi-annual meetings of the National Conference of Catholic Bishops is something new. Ideological controversies among American Catholics that once would not have merited a moment's notice are now meticulously scrutinized for what they tell us about our collective state of soul. Internal theological disputes, such as Father Charles E. Curran's struggle over the Catholic Church's traditional teachings on sexual ethics, are now matters of public concern. Interested Protestant observers, ranging from Richard John Neuhaus to Robert Bellah,[1] in various ways have even suggested that now may be "the Catholic moment" in our nation's history.

This new and somewhat unexpected interest in things Catholic comes at a time when the contours of American religious history seem to be shifting. However much Neuhaus and Bellah may disagree on other matters, both are acutely aware of the relative and apparently long-term decline of the so-called mainline churches of liberal Protestantism. This decline has left a vacuum at the center of American public life, which Neuhaus analyzes as "the naked public square" and Bellah attributes to the corrosive forces of "utilitarian and expressive individualism." Much of the new concern about American Catholicism stems from the hope that somehow the Catholic community, with its unique traditions of communal and social responsibility, may be able to step into this vacuum and help renew our public life as a nation. Among the signs that the Catholic community may be preparing to take up this role is the recent pastoral letter of the National Conference of Catholic Bishops, *Economic Justice for All: Catholic Social Teaching and the U.S. Economy.*

Seen in this context, the team of Catholic scholars involved in this project bear a special relationship to the bishops' letter. For even apart from the expectations raised among our non-Catholic fellow citizens, we must cope with the letter's claim to represent the bishops' authoritative interpretation of Catholic social teaching, a tradition to which the members of the team hold themselves accountable. Like many other American Catholics, we have experienced the process of drafting the pastoral letter as occasioning a renewal of faith as well as a heightened sense of possibility and commitment perhaps unequaled since Vatican II burst on the scene almost a generation ago. One of the team members, Charles Wilber of the University of Notre Dame, played an important role in advising the bishops' drafting committee, while others in our group in one way or another contributed to the public moral dialogue provoked by the various drafts of the letter. So our team starts with a sense of familiarity with the letter that is not necessarily part of the experience of the other teams.

Whether or not "the Catholic moment" has arrived, each of us is eager to see the bishops succeed in their effort to exert religious moral leadership in our pluralistic society. Each of our essays, of course, is to some extent critical of the letter, but on the whole we are in basic sympathy with the bishops' intentions as well as their overall view of both Catholic social teaching and the American economy. Typically our strategy has been to pursue the suggestions indicated by the letter rather than to fundamentally challenge them, while pressing them further in the direction of greater consistency. We cannot claim, however, that our perspectives are representative of the full range of lay Catholic opinion on the pastoral letter. For there are voices to both the left and the right of the letter that express serious objections either to the bishops' analyses of the economy or to one or another points in their interpretation of Catholic social teaching.

Nevertheless, the essays that follow try to break new ground by exposing what is essential if the bishops are to take the lead in renewing the American public dialogue. Interestingly enough, no one on the Catholic team was particularly concerned to defend any of the specific policies advocated in the letter. Instead, our interest was focused on the overall sense of direction outlined by the bishops, especially their admittedly sketchy proposal for a new American experiment in democracy. While Wilber, Charles Strain, and Dennis McCann explored various aspects of the ideological and policy debate with opponents, real or imagined, of the bishops' experiment, Ann O'Hara Graff underscored the profoundly practical challenge involved in living out the experiment's underlying biblical anthropology, especially in a world of religious and secular institutions where sexism has yet to be fully confronted. What unites the four essays is a common appreciation for the communitarian vision ever more clearly emerging from the Catholic social teaching in America. But what is the context which enables us to understand that vision?

American Catholicism stands delicately balanced on two distinct legacies, that of the American Revolution and that of the Roman Catholic tradition. Often in our history thoughtful American Catholics have experienced these two legacies as opposed to one another, yet also as holding forth the hope of some creative synthesis at some future time. The American Revolution was the first of the world's successful struggles against European imperialism; the fight was not just about who shall rule but how a people might come to rule themselves. But at the heart of this revolution was a radically new conception of the role of organized religion in society, one that could not have been farther from the traditional expectations of Roman Catholicism. For its part, the Roman tradition found itself increasingly hostile toward and isolated from the revolutionary currents that America symbolized. As the revolution consolidated itself and in turn became a tradition, the Catholic Church romanticized its past and that of premodern Europe and dreamt wistfully of the restoration of papal supremacy throughout the civilized world. By the time that successive waves of immigration had created a sizeable Catholic population in the United States, the religious and ideological conflict between these two legacies was at its height.

Catholic social teaching, the most likely point from which to expect a creative synthesis between the two, should be seen not as running counter to the Roman church's anti-revolutionary legacy but as firmly rooted within it. For in its classic formulations, best epitomized by the papal encyclicals of Popes Leo XIII and Pius XI, Catholic social teaching offered a utopian vision of human community explicitly differentiated from liberal, individualistic, and a variety of collectivist models. From this standpoint Catholic social teaching protested the manifold indignities against individuals apparently created by modern forms of industrial and social organization. Although the vision was preached in season and out by various

Catholic activists over the first half of this century, rarely were these efforts based on any appreciation of American cultural history. And yet the American republic of artisans, tradesmen, and yeoman farmers envisioned by Thomas Jefferson and many of the founders of this country is just as utopian as anything aspired to in Catholic social teaching. Like the Catholic fantasy about premodern Europe, this Jeffersonian model of the commonweal pursued a dream of freedom from the exigencies of modern industrialism. For despite its revolutionary origins, or perhaps because of them, the American dream is also communitarian.

Here, then, is the point of creative synthesis, from which it makes sense to consider seriously the bishops' proposal for a new experiment in democracy. Although some form of communitarian vision is common to both legacies, in this country the bishops have boldly reshaped the anti-revolutionary tradition of Catholic social teaching into a vehicle of postrevolutionary protest. Catholic social teaching, so transformed, can thus help all Americans understand just how far we have yet to go before the communitarian vision becomes reality. The new experiment that the Catholic bishops propose may thus be seen as authentically American. It cannot be dismissed as an embarrassing impertinence any more than their appeal to our fellow citizens' basic sense of fair play can be discounted as naive or patronizing. The call for experiment can be taken seriously, for it stems from a new appreciation of just how much we the people of this nation have in common, despite our diverse origins in various communities of faith.

Any attempt to rethink Catholic social teaching as an expression of this new perspective will require the emergence of a new style of American Catholic intellectual inquiry. Those who would contribute to a creative synthesis that fully reflects the communitarian vision animating both the American Revolution and Roman Catholic tradition must be at home with this nation's culture and the unfinished business that defines our sense of national purpose. Although the new style will continue to be intensely Catholic, theological reflection will occur at the center of our common American struggle to understand and renew that sense of purpose. No longer can American Catholic intellectuals confine themselves to a European cultural ghetto, however convenient such might be for the church worldwide.

The peculiar strength of these essays, then, lies in their willingness to consider Catholic social teaching outside the confines of the old Catholic ghetto. Each in its own way reflects a significant engagement with the challenge of modern industrialism and tries to point out how the communitarian vision might be enlisted to trans-form the social and economic institutions in which we are fated to live. Yet precisely because each of these essays is also trying to over-come prevailing forms of religious and ideological polarization, each assumes that the current economic situation is basically unstable and therefore open to new possibilities. Of course, the Catholic team may be wrong, and their bishops' new American experiment may amount to no more than wishful thinking. Have we properly framed the theoretical and practical issues involved in any new experiment in democracy? Have we enabled the reader to understand self-consciously American Catholic contributions to the nation's public dialogue? Have we given good reasons for thinking that the bishops' strategy of political and economic reform is still possible within our current institutional system? If this is to be "the Catholic moment" in our nation's history, these difficult questions will have to be posed, and American Catholic intellectuals will have to provide satisfactory answers to them.

17 | *Beyond Madison and Marx: Civic Virtue, Solidarity, and Justice in American Culture*

Charles R. Strain

Human dignity and solidarity. These two concepts, undeniably, create the harmonic tension, the point–counterpoint within *Economic Justice for All,* the U.S. Catholic bishops' pastoral letter. Dignity, the bishops argue, can be realized only in community, through patterns of mutual determination. For its part, solidarity is governed by the norm of dignity. Forms of community in any sphere—familial, social, political, or economic—that do not enhance the dignity of all participants are unjust (pars. 28, 79-80). However, while the first concept is clear, if abstract, the second—solidarity—is rhetorically ambiguous. It evokes, and clearly is intended to evoke, the traditional Catholic communitarian vision of a human family ordered in organically related social structures. But the document ignores the repressive connotations of that patriarchal and hierarchical vision. Simultaneously the term elicits the theme of solidarity with the oppressed central to Latin American liberation theology. Yet the document implicitly rejects a liberationist analysis of society.

How, then, are we to interpret the bishops' richly evocative concept of solidarity? Is the vision of the social order that it projects theoretically defensible and practically possible? Of course, this second question is what finally matters, unless we are to condemn the bishops to irrelevancy. So I will treat the first question schematically in order to be able to devote my attention primarily to the charges of those who would answer the second with a blunt negative.

Forms of Solidarity

At the heart of the pastoral letter lies the conviction that "human life unfolds 'between the times,' the time of the first creation and that of a restored creation" (par. 53). This conviction is the source of the hope and the realism that characterize all of the bishops' pronouncements (par. 55). Four forms of solidarity derive from the theological articulation of this vision. *Natural solidarity* expresses the implicit unity of the human species. Religious vision and human wisdom cohere in the recognition that we are social animals. Friendship and community are more than the context for self-realization—they are the condition for it (par. 65). Natural solidarity, shattered by an idolatrous quest for absolute power and unbounded wealth, will be renewed in the coming of God's kingdom (par. 33).

Thus the bishops view human life perfected in *eschatological solidarity*. In negative terms this vision is expressed in the parable of the last judgment (Matt. 25:31-46). Failure to acknowledge and to achieve community with the poor and the oppressed is to refuse God's summons, to exclude God's presence in one's life (par. 44). In a positive vein the document portrays the Spirit of Christ struggling in and through human history to restore progressively the shattered bonds of solidarity, a labor that will be completed only at the end of time (par. 64).

Meanwhile, to live between the times is to experience two linked forms of solidarity in action: "Christian communities that commit themselves to solidarity with those suffering and to confrontation with those attitudes and ways of acting which institutionalize injustice will themselves experience the power and presence of Christ. They will embody in their lives the values of the new creation while they labor under the old" (par. 55).

This third form of solidarity is, in my judgment, the most distinctively and strongly Catholic element in the bishops' vision. The appropriate label for it is *sacramental solidarity*. The church at worship and in commitment to justice becomes a visible sign of the eschatological destiny of all creation (par. 331). Without romanticizing poverty, without manipulating the poor as the means for the rest of us to experience divine grace, the bishops express their incarnational sense that our moral involvements, our political struggles against injustice, can be spiritually transformative.

The religious sentiment of solidarity demands effective action (par. 43) if it is not to become sentimentalism. *Political solidarity,* then, is the necessary complement to sacramental solidarity. According to the bishops, "The virtues of citizenship are an expression of

191

Christian love more crucial in today's interdependent world than ever before. These virtues grow out of a lively sense of one's dependence on the commonwealth and obligations to it. . . . Solidarity is another name for this social friendship and civic commitment that make human moral and economic life possible" (par. 66).

Justice is the frame of political solidarity. Beyond safeguarding the minimal conditions for community embodied in civil and economic rights, justice calls us to enhance the power of all to participate fully in the productive life of society (pars. 73, 80).

There are those, in this book as elsewhere, who take issue particularly with the bishops' progressive eschatology, filtered as it is through their incarnational and sacramental sense of solidarity. Many have argued that the bishops, disregarding the resistance of concentrated power to social transformation and overlooking the persisting ambiguity of even our best efforts and achievements, fall prey to theological as well as political recklessness. "Really nothing is wrong with the bishops' recent pronouncements," evangelical theologian Kenneth Kantzer concludes ironically, "that a stiff dose of Augustine . . . would not cure."[1]

My own sense is that the document eminently defends itself against its theological critics. Where the religious and secular critics gang up, however, is in attacking the bishops' interpretation of *political solidarity.* If their charges on this score are valid, the bishops' position—however theologically defensible—is indeed condemned to practical irrelevance. So we must concentrate our attention upon the fourth form of solidarity.

Madison and Marx on the Attack

All sorts of objections have been raised concerning the bishops' concept of political solidarity. We can give coherence to these criticisms and simultaneously sharpen the debate by allowing them to gravitate to two opposing positions—the Madisonian attack and the Marxist attack on the letter. Like two magnetic poles, these radically different objections are undergirded by a common force. It is a shared focus on the relationship of power and solidarity. The bishops clearly place themselves within the American tradition of political rhetoric and practice, claiming to be about the "unfinished business" of democracy. Thus the first critique arises from within the American tradition of political discourse itself. It contests the theoretical foundations and the political realism of the bishops' new experiment in democracy. The second critique, however, sees the bishops as all-too-American in their espousal of a piecemeal analysis and a pragmatic, reformist politics. From this viewpoint the problem with the bishops' position is that it is no new experiment at all but merely a new variation of the old liberal politics.

The Madisonian critic argues that to maintain the illusion of a homogeneous, organic society conveyed in the concept of solidarity is to scorn the genius of American politics. Through the arts of check and compromise, we pacify competing interests rather than hoping to abolish them. What the bishops refuse to recognize is what Madison, especially in *The Federalist* No. 10, confronted without flinching—solidarity will always be confined to factions. Given the diversity of human desires and the unbounded character of human ambition, no universal harmony of interests is possible. The unchecked solidarity of a faction, especially a majority faction, is a basic threat to liberty.

The bishops' appeal to civic virtue, to a commitment to the commonweal, is no escape from the perils of factionalism. Madison and the other Federalists argued that public virtue, while extremely necessary, would always be in short supply, especially in a republic whose egalitarian ethos unleashed ambition in every person and undermined conventional patterns of deference to authority. How can the bishops claim to further the business of democracy when they ignore the crisis that nearly shipwrecked the American Confederation before fairly leaving port? In the midst of the crisis that led to the Constitutional Convention, George Washington wrote to John Jay, "We have, probably, had too good an opinion of human nature in forming our confederation."[2] Wouldn't sober realism demand that the bishops heed these admonitions of our founders?

Those critics of the pastoral letter influenced by a Marxist perspective, although not necessarily advocating a Marxist solution, view the bishops as reluctant prophets. Having stared into the moral abyss which is capitalism, they retreat into moral platitudes. Both the letter's rhetoric of solidarity and its organic model of society obscure the class conflicts that thwart the movement of genuine reform. Universal solidarity, argues Gregory Baum, is an eschatological goal the realization of which demands a very *partial solidarity* of and with the oppressed. Partial solidarity is more than a preferential option for the poor that depends upon the goodwill of those who wield power. It acknowledges that the historical conditions for universal solidarity depend upon a fundamental redistribution of power and that, consequently, the common good conflicts with the immediate interests of some classes within society.[3]

Failure to confront the systemic reality of capitalism causes the bishops to fritter away their moral capital in fragmentary diagnoses and piecemeal treatment of the symptoms of our economic ills. Moreover, a truly systemic analysis would uncover the power of economic institutions to alter "individual motivation, character and experience," creating behavioral patterns that are resistant to purely moral appeal. Is it the case, Gar Alperovitz asks, that reconstituting "a more moral, humane, and deeply rooted vision of community" will enable us one day to "bend the existing capitalist system to meet these ends"? Can fundamental change occur "which does not explicitly challenge the main institutions and operating assumptions of American capitalism? If so, what arguments—other than wishful thinking—sustain that belief?"[4]

From Solidarity to Subsidiarity

These classic but obviously conflicting objections force a deeper reading of the bishops' letter. Nothing in that document, I suggest, supports the supposed dichotomy of virtue and interest that lies at the heart of the Madisonian critique. Nor does it, grasped as a whole, imply the dissociation of moral conversion and institutional transformation attacked and overthrown in the second line of criticism. Instead, glimmers of an alternative understanding—never fully developed—of the transformative power of numerous small-scale institutions operating democratically emerge especially in Chapter Four of the letter.

The bishops have gravitated to a fully pluralistic understanding of solidarity that has more in common with Thomas Jefferson and Alexis de Tocqueville than with Madison or Marx. Jefferson's persistent concern to develop renewed and renewable forms of political self-determination led him to outline in a famous letter to John Adams a form of decentralized democratic participation that he had proposed in a bill placed before the Virginia legislature. The state was to be divided into wards, each of which would have its own free school, each of which would be responsible for a significant portion of government. In short, each ward would be a republic in miniature. Jefferson believed that experiences of education and local self-governance would have a transformative effect upon the majority of citizens, enabling them not to transcend all self-interest but to distinguish those among them who were able to subordinate private interest to public good. Unlike Madison, Jefferson could not accept the notion that civic virtue was so scarce that associations were necessarily factionalistic. With equal fervor, however, he insisted that virtue, to be effective, would have to be tutored and nurtured in democratic institutions. Ultimately, Jefferson defended this confidence in the educative power of democratic institutions by a theological interpretation of the implications of *natural* solidarity. "Indeed, it would have been inconsistent in creation to have formed man for the social state, and not to have provided virtue and wisdom enough to manage the concerns of the society."[5]

Like Jefferson, Tocqueville accented the tutoring role of local democratic associations developed spontaneously to meet a welter of contingencies. Within them civic virtue arises not in opposition to but out of self-interest:

> It is difficult to force a man out of himself and get him to take an interest in the affairs of the whole state. . . . But if it is a question of taking a road past his property he sees at once that this small public matter has a bearing on his greatest private interests. . . . The free institutions of the United States and the political rights enjoyed there provide a thousand continual reminders to every citizen that he lives in society. . . . At first it is of necessity that men attend to the public interest, afterward by choice. . . . By dint of working for the good of his fellow citizens, he in the end acquires a habit and taste for serving them.[6]

What both the Madisonian and the Marxist critics fail to understand is not the initial weakness of civic virtue compared with private interest but this mediating power of local associations. Here, this alternative tradition maintains, rises a countervailing force to the frozen motivational patterns which, so the Marxist claims, imprison a capitalist society. We are locked into neither factions nor classes.

Although it is grounded less in a vision of natural solidarity than in the bishops' incarnational sense of the redemptive possibilities latent in all human experience,[7] the principle of subsidiarity as it is articulated in the letter substantially accords with Jefferson's and Tocqueville's alternative model of social transformation. According to this principle, it is "a grave evil and disturbance of right order to assign to a greater and higher association what lesser and subordinate organizations can do" (pars. 99-100). The traditional wording of the principle retained in the letter betrays its origins in a hierarchical, organic model of society. Yet the kind of associations—ranging from worker management to community-development corporations—selected by the bishops as examples of the principle at work within the economic sphere ill fit that hierarchical model. The bishops have significantly shifted the meaning of the principle itself as they have tacitly aligned themselves with the Jeffersonian-Tocquevillian tradition.

Charles R. Strain

As with any such shift of meaning, those who effect it may not realize fully the implications of their own words. This is particularly the case if we ask what the consequences of the shift are for our understanding of justice and political solidarity. How can we tease out these unstated implications?

The principle as articulated in the letter breaks no less with the classic liberal model of justice, I suggest, than with the conservative organic model. A just society, Michael Walzer has argued, is based on no simple principle of fairness or equality. Each form of social good distributed in a society—from wealth and power to honor and love— demands its own principle of distribution. A master cellist does not, could not dole out her tutoring with a measuring cup to the plodding tyro and the budding musician. Education as a social good demands some combination of equality of opportunity and special treatment for those with demonstrated potential. Likewise, each form of association must develop operative principles of justice that accord with its structure and purposes. A family—unlike, say, a court—is unjust if it operates according to a principle of equal treatment for all. Nor would we call a family just if it operated according to a principle of fair exchange like a market. Rather, a child who needs more—of anything from loving attention to medical care—must be given more than children who need less.[8]

Walzer's argument uncovers the truly radical implications of the principle of subsidiarity. Viewed in this light, the principle repudiates two forms of political solidarity.

First, solidarity achieved by a process of social engineering directed by a central political authority—what the letter refers to as "statist" solutions to injustice (par. 121)—cannot possibly embody the complex justice required by this principle. Such measures inevitably fail to attune themselves to the inner workings of diverse social institutions. On the other hand, piecemeal reform—taking each social good and each form of association on its own terms—is compatible with a goal of systemic social transformation. It is, in fact, the only way to achieve a nontotalistic form of justice. To be sure, the bishops have neither analyzed nor prescribed remedies for each sphere of justice. Their approach is systemic in intent but not in scope.

Second, a thorough commitment to the principle of subsidiarity breaks with the nostalgia for a perfectly harmonious community that infects the organic, communitarian vision of society.[9] Commitment to political solidarity need not foster the illusion that we will soon be one big happy family.

The critics of the bishops may well be right in arguing, as Larry Rasmussen does in this book, that the bishops are "softly utopian."[10] I suggest, however, that neither they nor the bishops themselves realize the degree to which the letter develops its own antidote to this illusion. Subsidiarity is favored as a means of securing the maximum participation of all, which is another name for justice. Likewise, the bishops believe that cooperative endeavor within a plurality of social institutions is in the larger interest of all concerned. However, by stressing the role of subsidiary partnerships as the means to expand the democratic principle of *mutual accountability*, the letter simultaneously acknowledges the persistence of conflict and the unequal distribution of power within the multiple institutions that constitute society (par. 297). Apart from a wide dispersal of power both among and within a multitude of *social* institutions, as Tocqueville saw with a clarity that Madison lacked, the constitutional separation of powers in the *political* order will largely be a fiction and no firm bulwark against the proliferation of "democratic" forms of despotism.[11]

Conflict and the Spheres of Justice

Perhaps it is Madison who was shortsighted about the ambiguity of all forms of power, not just political power. Yet we have also, following Walzer, rejected the totalistic model for overcoming entrenched, oppressive power. There is no Archimedes' point upon which we can lever a complex form of justice into existence. Where does this leave us?

Walzer puts the dilemma bluntly. In each sphere of society and with each social good, some individuals or groups seek a monopoly. But in every society there is a dominant social good—caste position, religious knowledge, or wealth, to name a few that have existed in past societies. Those who possess this dominant good in large measure tend to commandeer other goods as well. Thus in medieval Europe those who monopolized the means of salvation claimed wealth and political power as well.

It is the use of one social good to control all the spheres of society that constitutes tyranny. Walzer argues that what ultimately galls is not the fact of disparities of income in a society that values wealth above all. Rather, it is that "the rich 'grind the faces of the poor,'" enforce a definition of humanity and conditions for acquiring all other social goods which depend upon the possession of wealth.[12]

We depend upon government to block the use of one good to claim all others—to outlaw, for example, the buying of votes or the selling of organs by people who are desperately poor but healthy to those who are wealthy but sick. But political power too can be commandeered. Apart from the vigilance of ordinary people working within their spheres of competence and maintaining a sense of what constitutes justice *within that sphere,* de facto tyranny is unavoidable.[13] I may have the means to endow a chair of religious studies at a prestigious university and the wish to install myself in it. What will prevent my accession on the basis of wealth alone will be not the law but the commitment of my peers to enforcing criteria for selection intrinsically related to the work of education.

Clearly, however, this model of a professional association enforcing appropriate standards has its limits. Those who monopolize, say, medical knowledge can transform their professional associations into the instruments of dominance. Mutual accountability must be maintained within each sphere and among spheres. Here again the principle of subsidiarity proves effective. When it is necessary to maintain boundaries among social spheres or to coordinate their efforts, government intervention can hardly be called statist. The bishops' demand for a mixture of decentralized and centralized actions to achieve economic justice may be the most realistic strategy of all.

Technological Change and Economic Democracy

This may be so, but the Marxist critic will not be silenced so easily. Is a "long march" through the multiple institutions of American life, transforming each on its own terms, even a remote possibility? The immediate answer is that the bishops offer us Christian hope grounded in their incarnational faith, not optimism rooted in some discernible trend. Nevertheless, a theoretical defense does not establis i the practical relevance of the bishops' hope. So I will analyze in this final section, all too schematically, one area *not* treated in the pastoral letter where economic justice is at stake—the technological revolution as it transforms the workplace.

However, the very phrase—"the technological revolution as it transforms the workplace"—represents a form of false consciousness now unfortunately embedded in the American psyche. Americans have come to believe, argues David Noble, that technologies arise through a process of natural selection. Objective science and the iron law of survival in the market act in tandem to insure the emergence of only the fittest technologies. Technological determinism, when combined with a reverence for the "miracles" of technology, creates the illusion that technology, apart from the achievement of any political—let alone religious—solidarity, creates *social* progress.[14]

Spellbound by our misplaced confidence in the power of technology to effect progress, we fail to realize that both the way we implement technologies and the very technologies we choose distribute power in ways that may be neither democratic nor just.[15] But a new generation of American historians is demonstrating both that no technological change is foreordained and that political purposes have frequently played a major role in steering such change. Consider the following example.

In his exhaustive study of the machine-tool industry after World War II, Noble dissects the struggles between the proponents of two forms of computer-assisted technology. The first, a "record-playback" system, depended upon programming by skilled craftsmen working on the shop floor. It promised to be an extraordinarily flexible technology effective for short-run production. However, it required close cooperation between management, engineers, and skilled laborers. The second, a "numerical control" system, depended upon programming by engineers. Machine tools, guided by numerical control, were made to operate at precision tolerances required in some advanced military equipment, like fighter airplanes, but unnecessary for most products. The system also reduced skilled craftsmen to machine tenders, except during the frequent breakdowns that plague this more "sophisticated" and certainly more expensive technology.

The factors that led to the choice of the second system by the industry are complex, but clearly productive efficiency was not the operative criterion. As the principal funder of research and development, the Air Force wanted a technology geared to its military goals and found the mode of production dictated by the numerical-control system more compatible with its own command-and-control authority structure. The engineers at Massachusetts Institute of Technology doing the research gravitated to the more complex technology. Managers and engineers in industry worried about the first system, which would significantly decentralize decision-making. And so the choice was made for numerical control, which created in its wake a particular distribution of power in the workplace.[16]

The experience of the machine-tool industry hardly deviates from the norm. Whatever the accomplishments of the first industrial revolution, which paved the way for an era of mass production, in America it led to the centralization of power in the hands of managers and engineers and to a significant de-skilling of workers. Just as the earlier transformation from an agrarian to a mercantile capitalistic economy had brought with it a particular division of labor along lines of gender, segregating women in the sphere of the home,

Charles R. Strain

so the industrial revolution created two false spheres, this time within the factory, excluding workers from decision-making power. (In Europe these divisions were far less rigid, and the new system of mass production retained significant vestiges of the craft production system.[17]) According to the model of justice that we discussed earlier, the segregation of power that grew in tandem with the new system of production, in some cases with the complicity of segments of the labor movement itself, was an instance of holding hostage one social good (a just distribution of power) to another (material well-being). In the name of economic efficiency, the democratic movement toward self-determination was halted at the factory gates.[18]

Now a number of economists are arguing that we are about to cross a "second industrial divide." They insist that no amount of labor concessions, conceivable increases in productivity, plant closures, or transfers to non-unionized parts of the country can make mass production in this country competitive with developing Third World production. Moreover, the contemporary marketplace clamors for highly specialized, tailor-made products. To survive, American manufacturers will have to develop a new system of production.

Flexible specialization, as this new system is called, frequently depends upon newly developed, computer-assisted technologies to allow rapid change from the short-run production of one specialized product to another. It is not the new technologies themselves that generate flexible systems of production. We have all too many examples of the implementation of reprogrammable, computer-assisted technologies (as in Noble's example of numerically controlled machine tools) in ways that reinforce an inflexible division of labor. Likewise, there are examples of even nineteenth-century technologies (such as those in the textile industry) and of modern, non–computer-assisted technologies (such as those in the production of specialty steels) that have been incorporated into flexible systems of production. No, what matters is first of all a relationship between machine and person that replicates that prevailing in traditional craft industries. The point is not to adapt the person to a specific task dictated by the structure of the machine but to allow the person to redesign the tool to achieve a multitude of purposes. As Michael Piore and Charles Sabel point out, "Production workers must be so broadly skilled that they can shift rapidly from one job to another; even more important, they must be able to collaborate with designers to solve the problems that inevitably arise in execution." This entails integration rather than segregation of the tasks of production from design to distribution. Close cooperation and decision-making on the shop

200

floor among managers, engineers, and workers is the lifeblood of the system. In short, flexible specialization demands a revolution in the workplace of precisely the sort rejected by the machine-tool industry.[19]

To effect a changeover to this new mode of production, government, business, and unions will need to collaborate in the devising and execution of retraining programs for workers. New industries employing flexible specialization must be incubated with significant assistance from local communities. Each of these forms of cooperation presumes virtue, restraint, a sense of solidarity—in short, "habits of the heart" alien to the economic era of mass production but now aligned with the nation's economic interest. Industries cannot dump older workers to avoid retraining costs. They cannot simply up and leave communities that have invested heavily in their development and still expect to salvage the climate of trust necessary to maintain their networks of cooperation. Unions must be willing to change outdated work rules and job classifications. All of this entails what Charles Wilber discusses later in this section as a commitment to "voice" versus "exit."[20] As Robert Reich explains in *The Next American Frontier*, "The notion that an atmosphere of civic membership and obligation is requisite for prosperity may seem quaintly old-fashioned in an age of robots and microcomputers. But the logic is timeless. Civic virtue is not a matter of charity or ethics; it is the adhesive of social and economic life."[21]

Here, too, nothing is foreordained. The history of America's economic institutions in the past century makes a conscious shift to flexible systems of production unlikely, however much it is in the nation's interest. We may well be the prisoners of the material successes and the power constellations of the system of mass production. Yet the history of American democratic associations in other spheres of society, as I have discussed it, suggests an alternative future. "It is [this] ideal of yeoman democracy," Piore and Sabel conclude, "that is most likely to catalyze American efforts to rebuild the economy on the model of flexible specialization."[22]

The prescriptions in the pastoral letter for a form of political solidarity grounded in the principle of subsidiarity accord strikingly with the economic promise of flexible specialization. Technological innovations can support the democratization of the workplace, but they cannot create the political will to achieve this end. Nor can a central authority simply ordain the complex patterns of cooperation and enhanced self-determination necessary to implement the new technologies. A new experiment in democracy is essential to achieve economic prosperity as well as economic justice.

We must begin that experiment fully aware that the kind of entrenched power exemplified in the case of the machine-tool industry may oppose our efforts. The genuine possibility of political solidarity does not eliminate factionalism. Economic democracy depends on a struggle to give new institutional shape to a deepened understanding of mutual accountability. It would be false hope and poor theology to assume that changing any single part will magically transform the whole. But the bishops, operating out of their incarnational hope, call us to begin in and through the associations that we already inhabit.

18 | *New Experiment in Democracy: Blueprint for Political Economy?*

Dennis P. McCann

If all we had to go on in trying to understand the American Catholic bishops' pastoral letter on the economy was the coverage given it in the nation's news media, we would probably be unaware of the bishops' call for a "new American experiment" in democracy. Media coverage, you'll remember, tended to take its cue from the fact that the first draft of the pastoral letter was released just the day after President Reagan's landslide victory over Walter Mondale. In that context, the letter was seen as a rehash of the policy debates that occasionally surfaced in the presidential campaign. It was either praised or criticized as further evidence that the American Catholic bishops merely represented "the left wing of the Democratic party at prayer." The later drafts of the letter didn't even receive that kind of treatment, because there were no major news stories on the media's agenda with which to give perspective to the letter's further development.

From the Catholic Church's point of view, this highly selective pattern of media coverage was most unfortunate, because it means that, although more people were exposed to Catholic social teaching through the coverage than through any of the church's own activities, the church failed to advance public dialogue about the U.S. economy much farther than it had already been taken by the pundits and politicians. Unlike the pastoral letter entitled *The Challenge of Peace: God's Promise and Our Response* (1983),[1] which received sustained press coverage throughout its development because of media interest in the nuclear freeze movement, the letter on the economy

203

Dennis P. McCann

was by and large taken up and then dropped when its "newsworthiness" was no longer apparent.

Like the others who have contributed to this book, I want to make sure that the pastoral letter will not lie quietly in the morgue assigned to it by the media. For a variety of reasons we find the letter far more interesting than the media apparently did. Like the other members of the Catholic working group represented here, I find in particular the bishops' vision of a new experiment, outlined in Chapter Four of the letter, more compelling than the various concrete policy proposals discussed in Chapter Three. In what follows, I hope to share with you the reasons why. In the wake of all the national self-examination on the nature of the original American experiment occasioned by the Iran-Contra affair, the Supreme Court nominations, and the Bicentennial of the U.S. Constitution, it makes sense to ask whether the nation's economic development and the problems generated by it require a new experiment in economic democracy.

My own question, however, is whether this call for an unprecedented social experiment amounts to a new model of political economy. Political economy, of course, refers to the relationship between the economy and society as a whole—in particular, the complex set of moral assumptions, legally enforceable rules, and political accommodations by which we structure the allocation and use of scarce resources for the continuance of our collective material existence. This set of relationships in our society is referred to as "modern industrial capitalism," since the management of such scarce resources is conducted primarily through business corporations responding to regulated market conditions. The question, then, is whether the new experiment in democracy advocated by the American Catholic bishops prescribes an alternative to capitalism. If not, what precisely is the point of the experiment? How will it reform capitalism or modify the set of social relationships that have made American capitalism possible? Will the results be an improvement over the current situation? My thesis is that the letter does not contain a blueprint for political economy. You will not find one in the Bible, and you cannot construct one from the biblical traditions developed in the letter. What we have is a set of priorities, an agenda, that may be brought to discussions of the existing economic order rather than a blueprint for an alternative to it. What this agenda means and why it makes sense to pursue it constitute the burden of my argument.

204

Understanding the Bishops' Experiment

The first mention of the new American experiment comes at the end of a crucial section of Chapter Two outlining what are called "moral priorities for the nation" (par. 95). Chapter Two as a whole is devoted to the Christian vision of economic life. It outlines the theological horizon and highlights the moral principles of Catholic social teaching as these have been brought into focus by the realities of the U.S. economy. The two most controversial aspects of this vision are the bishops' interpretation of the so-called preferential option for the poor (par. 52) and their expansion of the human-rights doctrine to include a package of "economic rights" (pars. 79-84).

Let us assume, as others have suggested in this book, that the option for the poor is a theological response to the distortions apparent in the U.S. economy, namely, the persistence—indeed, the growth—of poverty in what otherwise seems to be an economy of affluence. In this context, the option signals the church's discernment of the presence of God in the plight of the poor: "Whatsoever you do to the least of my brothers and sisters, that you do unto Me" (par. 44; cf. Matt. 25:40). The bishops' teaching on economic rights, on the other hand, represents a reiteration of certain theoretical developments in Catholic social teaching, especially since Vatican II.[2] Pope John XXIII's encyclical letter entitled *Pacem in Terris* had highlighted human rights as a central moral test for the tradition, and post-Vatican II statements such as Pope Paul VI's *Populorum Progressio* had underscored the global urgency of economic rights.[3] The pastoral letter, of course, presupposes this development and asks, in light of the religious imperative of an option for the poor, how these economic rights can be implemented. How, in other words, should our nation's moral priorities be changed, if both the Catholic faith and common morality require an expanded understanding of human rights?

The new American experiment is meant to answer this question. Inasmuch as the original American experiment in democracy did establish the framework of institutions guaranteeing civil and political rights, the bishops' proposal is to carry on a "similar experiment . . . : the creation of an order that guarantees the minimum conditions of human dignity in the economic sphere for every person" (par. 95). These minimum conditions include "the rights to life, food, clothing, shelter, rest, medical care and basic education." Spelling them out further, the bishops affirm a "right to earn a living . . . through remunerative employment, . . . a right to security in the event of sickness, unemployment and old age, . . . as well as the right to healthful working conditions, to wages and other benefits sufficient to provide individuals with a standard of living in keeping with human dignity, and to the possibility of property ownership" (par. 80).

Nor is this list of economic rights exhaustive. In the final section of Chapter Two, in which the bishops address specifically the rights and duties of various key groups in society, the letter reaffirms not only the worker's traditional "right to form unions and other associations" (par. 104) but also the businessperson's "right to private ownership of productive property" (par. 114) and, even more strikingly, "a right to an institutional framework that does not penalize enterprises that act responsibly" (par. 118). Unless the bishops' thinking is radically incoherent, the new package of proposed economic rights cannot mean the abrogation of these traditional economic rights. Nor, given the parallels rhetorically asserted between the old and the new experiments, can we suppose that the fulfillment of economic rights must be purchased at the expense of our hard-won civil and political liberties.

On the contrary. What is truly experimental about the new American experiment is precisely the bishops' desire to conserve the achievements of the American past even as we push on to greater economic justice for all. How is it possible, then, to implement a package of economic rights that has the right to employment as its centerpiece without sacrificing either the investor's right to private ownership of the means of production or labor's right to collective bargaining, both of which significantly affect an individual's chances of finding remunerative employment? How is it possible to guarantee a job for everyone who is willing and able to work without sacrificing America's constitutional legacy of civil and political liberties? The bishops' answer in Chapter Four is subtitled "Partnership for the Common Good." The experiment, in short, calls for a massive shift away from adversarial social relationships to cooperative social relationships. How can these rights be balanced so that none of them is sacrificed in principle? With a massive and institutionally creative commitment to social cooperation, or so the bishops hope.

At this point, even friendly critics may find it easy to belittle the bishops' proposal. After all, telling the American people that we can achieve economic justice if only we learn to cooperate with one another more effectively may seem like telling the fish that we could all live on land together if only they would learn to breathe air. Or as my grandfather used to say, "If wishes were horses, beggars would ride." But let's resist the temptation to take the easy way out. Is there more to the new American experiment than superficial exhortations to social cooperation? I think there is, though what it is, admittedly, is very elusive. What the bishops hope to achieve is clear: a transformation of U.S. economic institutions from the bottom up in favor of greater popular participation and social accountability. How they hope to achieve this goal is also fairly clear: they propose an across-the-board experiment in participatory democracy governed by the principle of subsidiarity. Their answer, in short, is appropriately pragmatic: we'll learn how to do it by doing it.

Thoughtful people, even notoriously pragmatic Americans, will not be satisfied with such an answer. Why should we restructure a system that, although not perfect, has worked tolerably well? The letter is particularly vulnerable to this rejoinder, for unlike radical critics of American capitalism, the bishops are fairly generous in their appreciation of the achievements of this system. So there must be some reasonable assurance that the experiment will leave us better off than we are now, both morally and economically. If you reread Chapters Four and Five of the letter, looking for such assurances, I believe you'll find them. They are both practical and theoretical.

The Bishops' Experiment: Practical Considerations

The first thing to notice about the proposed experiment is its remarkable consistency with the original American experiment in constitutional democracy. The bishops presuppose a federalist polity in its original sense—not the nightmare of centralized administration that the federal government evokes for many Americans but the founding vision of limited government achieved through a decentralized system of checks and balances. Accordingly, they envision the new experiment taking shape as a "public partnership" institutionalized at several levels, beginning with the local level and moving up to the national and international levels. Like Alexis de Tocqueville and other more recent observers, the bishops recognize the essential role of "mediating structures"—local communities and private voluntary associations—in preserving our freedoms and empowering us for effective social action (par. 308).[4] They do envision a positive and constructive role for the federal government, especially in coordinating the common effort at national economic planning, but it is appropriately circumscribed by the capacities and competencies that mediating structures are to foster at the state and local levels. The bishops insist that this federalist strategy is consistent with the traditional principle of subsidiarity developed in Catholic social teaching (pars. 314, 323), which I will discuss further on.

The organized learning of participatory democracy that the bishops propose is initially to take place in the public institutions with which we are most routinely familiar—namely, business corporations. The first proposal outlined in Chapter Four concerns "cooperation within firms and industries" (pars. 298-306). Here the bishops make common cause with many theorists of corporate management, who point out the productivity gains to be made by instituting new structures of shared accountability in the workplace: employee participation in managerial decision-making processes, profit sharing for all employees, full or partial employee ownership of the firm, and long-term job security.[5] Such reforms in the structure of corporate governance cannot help but transform the traditionally adversarial relations between labor and management. Although currently only a small percentage of American businesses have experimented in this direction, the bishops, like many business gurus, have a new set of expectations for the coming generation of entrepreneurs, who have the opportunity to make structural innovations precisely at the point when their businesses begin to grow. If their entrepreneurial success is seen to be related to their innovative managerial practices, then competitive pressures alone may help spread the new learning implicit in the bishops' experiment.

By looking first to business corporations, the bishops make two things clear about the overall objectives of this "partnership for the public good." One is that the experiment primarily concerns the creation of new wealth and only secondarily concerns its distribution. Throughout the letter, as I read it, the bishops acknowledge that increased economic growth based on greater productivity is the precondition for an advance in social justice for all. Their refusal to further intensify adversarial relations between rich and poor (par. 88)—or, in this case, between management and labor—suggests not that they have suddenly forgotten the lessons of the past but that for the present and future they realize just how counterproductive any needless intensification of social conflict can be. The bishops' experiment in participatory democracy proposes not an old-fashioned political mobilization of the masses in order to demonstrate for an increased share in a relatively stagnant national income pool. It promises instead a new kind of popular economic empowerment, the first result of which should be a steady increase in productivity capable of generating eventually dramatic overall gains in the national income. Of course, the bishops' point is well made: the required gains in productivity will come only through a more equitable restructuring of corporate governance and ownership.

By beginning with business, the bishops have also stumbled upon what, in my view, may be the real "grass-roots" level in any realistic scheme for participatory democracy in the American context.

There is something paradoxical about a society whose politics are formally democratic but whose basic modes of industrial production emphatically are not. Given that the majority of adult American citizens are employed by such organizations, it is not surprising that the habits of social interaction selectively reinforced by the ordinary work environment should carry over into all other aspects of public life, especially political life. If our politics have become at once both more passive and more adversarial—to such an extent that traditional calls for participatory democracy seem at best naive and at worst a sinister plot against the American way of life—then it makes sense to look for an explanation in the ways we organize ourselves for productive economic activity.[6] If the best we can do in the workplace is implement an authoritarian system based on restricted access to managerial "skills" and technocratic "expertise," we cannot be surprised that many citizens in practice regard the organs of political democracy as vestigial. The bishops' proposed experiment cuts to the heart of the problem of modern industrial democracy by insisting that industry itself must lead the way in promoting the habits of social cooperation, consensual decision-making, and shared accountability that make all forms of participatory democracy, political as well as economic, both possible and necessary.

So the partnership for the public good rests, to an intriguing degree, upon the willingness of entrepreneurs to experiment with innovative schemes of participatory management. Their motives for conducting such experiments no doubt will continue to be profit-oriented, but the strategies that promise the greatest gains in worker productivity will also fulfill some (though not all) of the economic rights advocated by the bishops. It is equally apparent, however, that innovative managerial practice is not enough to make the new experiment succeed. Unless the overall business climate, or incentive structure, is conducive to such experiments, individual entrepreneurs may feel that the risk is too great to warrant going very far on their own. Indeed, in Chapter Two the bishops already acknowledge this problem by insisting on the businessperson's "right to an institutional framework that does not penalize enterprises that act responsibly" (par. 118). Not surprisingly, then, Chapter Four of the pastoral letter considers the role of government and those mediating structures typically lumped together as nongovernmental organizations in fostering a business climate open to participatory democracy.

On the local and regional level, for example, the bishops endorse the idea of targeting business tax incentives to encourage job-creating investment in economically depressed areas. They also advocate experimenting with "community development corporations" that would coordinate various institutional resources and under-write projects that private entrepreneurs are unwilling or unable to take on. No doubt encouraged by the experience of church leaders responding to plant-closing crises in Youngstown, Ohio, and other cities, the bishops offer the services of the church in brokering the formation of broad-based community-development strategies (par. 311). Although the bishops don't emphasize the point, it is safe to assume that their hopes for local and regional cooperation will require the various mediating structures to scrutinize their own practices to see whether they too are consistent with the principles of participatory democracy.

At the national level, the bishops join both Pope John Paul II and a host of progressive American social philosophers in advocating a role for the federal government in national economic planning. If their argument here is to be made persuasively, they must be consistent with what they have proposed for individual corporations, local communities, and regional associations. There can be no successful experiment in participatory democracy that is grass-roots oriented at the local level but organized from the top down at the national level. A truly federalist attempt at national economic planning would have to be the culmination of local and regional efforts, both private and public.

Like many progressives, the bishops note the extent to which economic planning already is undertaken by both government and business in limited areas and for limited purposes. Their proposal is to coordinate the existing planning initiatives and focus them more coherently on three objectives. First, consistent with the overall thrust of the new experiment in democracy, the planning process must become an open-ended partnership involving all sectors of our society. Special-interest groups are urged to repress their special pleadings and focus instead on the common good, while government bureaucrats are asked to use their technical competencies to facilitate rather than inhibit genuinely public dialogue (par. 318). Second, mindful of the overall moral claim of the pastoral letter, which is symbolized by the option for the poor, the bishops urge all participants to make "the impact of national economic policies upon the poor . . . the primary criterion for judging their moral value" (par. 319). Third, in light of their previously expressed concern over the economics of war and peace, the bishops demand that the planning process remedy "the serious distortion of national economic priorities produced by massive spending on national defense" (par. 320).

It would take us too far afield to discuss the bishops' proposals at the international level. Let me simply note the consistency of these suggestions, especially the bishops' advocacy of strengthened multilateral institutions, with the principles already applied to the other levels.

As this outline of the experiment indicates, the bishops have produced something far more substantial than another homily recommending the virtues of social cooperation. In my estimation they have plotted a learning curve by which ordinary Americans can develop the habits of social cooperation, starting in the institutional setting that most routinely affects them—the workplace. Furthermore, as I have argued elsewhere, the process of drafting the pastoral letter itself may be construed as an important point on that learning curve, for the open hearings and discussions that contributed to the development of the letter challenged the church, both laity and clergy, to become facilitators of constructive public dialogue seeking the common good.[7]

The potential impact of these learning experiences—both the one undertaken by the church in drafting the pastoral letter and the one envisioned for experiment within business firms and industry—should not be underestimated. Those of us who are veterans of the civil rights movement of the 1960s and the various protests that have come in its wake have firsthand experience of the efficacy of such experimental learning curves. A generation ago, aided and abetted by the churches, we learned to expose the latent adversarial relations in our society that blocked the path to social justice. We learned, often through bitter experience, to confront the vested interests that made a sham of our aspirations for racial and sexual equality, peace with justice, and environmental integrity. I'm suggesting that now may be the time to embark on a new learning curve designed to dramatize a different lesson. Instead of continuing to sharpen our well-honed confrontation skills, perhaps now we should learn the technique of social cooperation.

If it is true that further progress toward economic justice will not occur apart from dramatic increases in sound economic growth and per-capita productivity, then the need for social cooperation above and beyond the confrontations of the immediate past should be obvious. The new American experiment, however, does more than merely point to the need; it offers us a plausible strategy for providing a majority of Americans with the opportunity to experience the rewards of meaningful collaboration and shared responsibility. At the same time, the participatory schemes proposed in the letter cannot help but produce a net gain in economic literacy in the population as a whole. Both of these are indispensable preconditions for a national

Dennis P. McCann

economic-planning process that succeeds in avoiding the pitfalls of centralized, bureaucratic domination.

Political Economy: Some Theological Reflections

So much for the practical promise of the new American experiment in democracy. But does it amount to a new model of political economy? Does the new experiment mean a radical departure from the political—and therefore inevitably economic—achievements of the original American experiment in democracy? I think not. As the previous outline of the bishops' proposals indicates, virtually everything currently envisioned for the new experiment builds upon institutional structures and strategies already exisiting in one or another sector of the economy as a whole. I believe that the new experiment could be conducted along the lines advocated by the bishops without any constitutional change whatsoever. Nor do the bishops, if I understand them properly, intend to propose a new model of political economy. At this point my argument must turn toward a theoretical analysis of an important principle of Catholic social teaching. In several places, like the pastoral letter itself, I have alluded to the principle of subsidiarity. I contend that although this principle may help to establish a typically Catholic agenda for social and economic justice, it does not provide a blueprint for political economy. A look at its historical origins and its theological presuppositions may suffice to make this point clear.

The principle of subsidiarity is a convenient piece of traditional Catholic jargon, one of those conversation stoppers to which all must respond, "Yes, yes, yes, subsidiarity, of course." The lip service, however routine, hardly illuminates the principle's radical meaning. Discussion of the state's "subsidiary function" first appeared in papal documents in *Quadragesimo Anno,* the 1931 encyclical letter of Pope Pius XI.[8] The principle mandates that social responsibilities that can be taken care of on the grass-roots level *ought* to be taken care of on that level and *ought not* to be interfered with by the state. *Quadragesimo Anno* makes this point in emphatically hierarchical terms: it speaks of "higher associations" and "subordinate organizations" in a manner reminiscent of medieval philosophy. But let me translate the essential point: government can justify itself only as a "subsidium," for its purpose is to give assistance to the flourishing of human beings in their interpersonal communities—hence the "subsidiary function" of the state.

The principle of subsidiarity was not lacking in some political functions of its own. *Quadragesimo Anno,* as many commentators have pointed out, must be read in the context of the Catholic Church's specific problems in the Italy of the 1930s. After having struggled for more than a decade with Mussolini's government over control of Catholic youth organizations and the nation's schools, the church had grown increasingly leery of Fascism. These issues are not discussed directly in *Quadragesimo Anno*, but the encyclical does bear indirect testimony to the lessons learned in the struggle. For although much of the economic program outlined by Pope Pius XI looks suspiciously like the theory and practice of "corporatism" espoused by Italian Fascists, the principle of subsidiarity pointedly draws the line on the overweening ambitions of the state.

You can see where I'm headed: in its original context the principle of subsidiarity represents a powerful protest against totalitarianism. Yet in this country the principle has been used by liberal and progressive Catholics to advocate the economic and social reforms of the New Deal era, and to argue, as the pastoral letter does, for their extension. Interpreted in a constitutional democracy that proclaims the virtues of individual liberty and limited government, the principle suggests that the federal government must take on new social responsibilities when people in community cannot otherwise flourish. On the other hand, neoconservative Catholics recently have appealed to this same principle to defend their support for the Reagan administration's attempts to cut back on welfare and social services. Here, too, the argument hinges on whether the various federal programs have actually enhanced the capacities of people to flourish in their own communities.

Given such a history of ideological flexibility, the principle of subsidiarity tends to be dismissed, even by the bishops, as little more than a political truism. But it is unwise to take subsidiarity so lightly. Although invoked several times in the letter, the principle never receives the kind of theological reflection that it deserves. Yet, as I have argued elsewhere,[9] the principle of subsidiarity itself is theologically grounded, and until this is generally appreciated, the bishops' new experiment in participatory democracy may be dismissed as just another holdover from the 1960s. It is not.

Taken as a whole, the theology underlying the letter is, not surprisingly, incarnational and Trinitarian. After all, this is a pastoral letter from the U.S. *Catholic* bishops. The Trinity is invoked: we find formulas about Father, Son, and Spirit, and this understanding of the reality of God is linked to the vision of authentic human community that the bishops hope to promote. Here are just two of the statements that testify to the pastoral letter's Trinitarian theological presuppositions:

Dennis P. McCann

> As disciples of Christ each of us is called to a deep personal conversion and to "action on behalf of justice and participation in the transformation of the world." By faith and baptism we are fashioned into a "new creature"; we are filled with the Holy Spirit and a new love that compels us to seek out a new profound relationship with God, with the human family and with all created things. (par. 328)

> The church is all the people of God, gathered in smaller faith communities, guided and served by a pope and a hierarchy of bishops, ministered to by priests, deacons, religious and laity, through visible institutions and agencies. Church is thus primarily a communion of people bonded by the Spirit with Christ as their head, sustaining one another in love and acting as a sign or sacrament in the world. By its nature it is people called to a transcendent end; but it is also a visible social institution functioning in the world. (par. 339)

But if you go beyond the pastoral letter itself and immerse yourself in the fine points of Trinitarian theology, quickly you will stumble upon highly abstract discussions regarding the relations of the Three Persons to one another within the Divine Mystery. My question is, What can we learn from these discussions regarding the divine pattern of authentic human community?

I am struck by the fact that Catholic theologians have usually characterized these relations as egalitarian and functional. In fact, we know about them only to the extent that there are distinct functions in the divine "economy of salvation" attached to each Person. Yet we must confess a perfect equality among the Persons, or they couldn't all be God. And a perfect community of Persons co-equally sharing in the Divine Mystery is precisely what Catholic theology traditionally affirms. God is Three-in-One. While the Trinitarian pattern thus is egalitarian and yet functionally differentiated within itself, considerations of hierarchy, interestingly enough, occur only in relation to us—that is, only in relation to the created order. God's relationship to creation becomes hierarchical, as the Mystery of Life is expanded to include finite persons like us in relation to the Divine Reality.

We could get lost in theological speculation at this point, but what I want you to consider is this: if society were to emulate the Trinitarian pattern, the burden of proof would be upon hierarchies. Hierarchies would be subsidiary to communities of human persons flourishing in fundamentally egalitarian reciprocities. Such an ideal of human community would be democratic in principle and would allow for further layers of organization, which necessarily become hierarchical at some point and in some way, but only to the extent necessary to sustain and encourage the flourishing of even more persons in community. Yet isn't that precisely the point of the principle of subsidiarity? Doesn't subsidiarity circumscribe the normative limits of managerial hierarchies, limits that it conceives in terms of the traditional Catholic vision of human persons flourishing in community?

I conclude that the principle of subsidiarity is theologically grounded, just as emphatically as the more obviously theological option for the poor. Subsidiarity, in other words, reflects the traditional Catholic understanding of the Trinity as a norm for the proper ordering of human social relationships. Although some Catholics may regard subsidiarity as old hat, it is old hat only if all you do is think about it. Were we to conduct a new experiment in democracy based consistently on the principle of subsidiarity, its radical implications would soon become apparent.

Yet the radical possibility that would emerge still would not amount to a blueprint for a distinct form of political economy; instead it would yield an agenda for political and economic change in any system. The principle of subsidiarity once provided a warrant for resistance to Italian Fascism, and in our own country it has served as a benchmark in controversies over the expansion and contraction of the New Deal welfare state. But just as effectively it has been used to bolster the ideology of Solidarity in Marxist-dominated Poland. In each of these different political economies, the principle of subsidiarity represents a fairly consistent agenda—in favor of decentralized power, in favor of social cooperation, in favor of schemes of empowerment for all workers, whether they take the form of free labor unions, profit-sharing programs, or innovative experiments with worker self-management. In each case, managerial hierarchy, however organized in either private or public enterprise, is justified only to the extent necessary, given the complexity of the overall process, to make sure that we all flourish together.

This is an *agenda* that is distinctively Catholic, theologically coherent, and well founded in Catholic tradition. Yet I have also insisted that this agenda does not constitute a *blueprint* for a political economy, because it has been pursued and can be pursued in a variety of political economies with the expectation of renewed progress toward authentically human community. The bishops' new experiment in democracy is just one possible strategy for implementing this perennially Catholic agenda.

19 | *Women and Dignity: Vision and Practice*

Ann O'Hara Graff

This essay is an exploration of the U.S. bishops' pastoral letter on the economy from the point of view of a Catholic, feminist theologian. I am concerned with two things: first, the vision of human dignity that the bishops articulate in the document, and second, the economic and political implications of that vision. I am primarily interested in the meaning of this vision and its practical effects on women. The vision of human dignity is an issue because women's experiences have so often been excluded when theologians portray "the person." So the question is, How have the bishops formulated their vision of human beings? What use have they made of Scripture and the Christian tradition, and how have they employed the present situation to inform them? This descriptive problem immediately becomes political. How is this vision effective in society and in the church, and how is it helpful or harmful to women? As a feminist theologian, I am interested in this critical relation between vision and practice because this interaction makes plain the ways in which the bishops call Christians, women and men, to live in the world.

A Biblical and Practical Vision of Human Dignity

That human dignity is the key category in the pastoral letter is evident when the bishops assert that "the basis for all that the church believes about the moral dimensions of economic life is its vision of the transcendent worth—the sacredness—of human beings. *The dignity of the human person, realized in community with others, is the crite-*

rion against which all aspects of economic life must be measured" (par. 28,
italics original). These two sentences contain the key to the bishops'
understanding of human dignity. First, it is a fact of human identity.
Second, it is somehow realized or not realized among us. As a theological fact, human dignity is inherent in our creation by God. This
sacredness or holiness is underscored by Scripture's assertion that we
are created in God's own image (Gen. 1:26-27; cf. pars. 28, 32). God is
the founder and guarantor of human dignity. Our dignity is also
linked to our place in the created world, as stewards who care for the
earth. Our vocation is to continue to unfold the Creator's gift
(par. 32).

Human dignity as sacredness is a given that must be recognized and responded to on a practical level. Thus the bishops evoke
the images of the covenant and the kingdom of God to contextual-
ize human dignity (pars. 35-44). The stipulations of Israel's covenant
form community. The covenant requires reciprocal responsibility,
mutual respect, truthfulness, mercy, compassion, and care for the
vulnerable. To these are joined worship and obedience to God. Jesus
intensifies this covenant vision. When he proclaims the kingdom, he
announces a community living according to the great commands of
love of God and neighbor.

In covenant and kingdom we glimpse the kind of community in which human dignity can be realized. Here dignity is a practice; it is something we bestow upon one another. Dignity entails
meeting our human physical needs as well as the needs of the heart
and the spirit. As the pastoral letter proceeds, it is clear that dignity
is bound up with the fundamental quality of our lives. It entails
having a winter coat, a warm meal, a decent place to live, and proper
care for our children (pars. 172, 177), as well as those less tangible but
critical concerns such as having the respect of others and having the
opportunity to enjoy our earth, our families, and God (pars. 141, 143,
337-38). Dignity, then, is characteristic both of our own lives and of
the kind of life we support for one another.

Moreover, both covenant and kingdom reveal a profound
concern for the poor. God questions Israel about provision for the
widow, the orphan, the stranger, the outcast (par. 38). Jesus tells his
followers that they must care for the least, the little ones. Jesus' message is that God has a special concern for the poor; the good news is
good for the poor (Luke 4:18; cf. par. 48). Thus the bishops state that
it is the poor who starkly reveal any society's commitment to human
dignity (pars. 24, 48-52). The condition of the wretched and the
powerless is the sign and the test of a society's justice.

Commitment to the poor is the essence of the challenge to

Christian discipleship (pars. 45-47). In imitation of Christ, the Christian vocation is to serve others, especially those in need. Such discipleship is of a piece with the bishops' vision of civic solidarity or the friendship and commitment to one another "that make human moral and economic life possible" (par. 66). Discipleship and solidarity in civic community entail a change of heart. The bishops call Christians to conversion out of a reverence for their own dignity and the dignity of others (pars. 45, 328). This lived spirituality includes an appeal to relinquish that which disproportionately benefits some so that all may be at least minimally secure. Clearly, this conversion is not simply personal. Dignity must characterize the community as a whole through the discipleship of the whole. The realization of human dignity in society is entirely dependent upon political and economic practice.

What the feminist affirms about this vision of human dignity is its practical nature. Feminist theologians seek a theology that works from experience and is accountable to experience as it struggles with the meaning of the Christian tradition. The biblical axiom of the dignity of the person both names our experience of human dignity and empowers the call to enact it. The very simplicity of this principle opens to a breadth of possible realizations in human lives. What is crucial, then, is how the bishops go on to formulate this vision of human dignity in practical terms, and what further practical consequences can be drawn from it. The feminist will be particularly concerned to see that the practical outworkings of the bishops' vision are responsible to the experiences of women.

An Alternative Vision of Dignity

This biblical, practical vision of human dignity just examined is an important theological development. It appears prior to an *alternative* statement that represents the classic Catholic formulation of the same problem. The two visions remain side by side. However brief, the presence of this alternative is a reminder of a powerful theological understanding of the person and the difficulties that attend it. The bishops say, "For human beings are created in God's image, and their dignity is manifest in the ability to reason and understand, in their freedom to shape their own lives and the life of their communities, and in the capacity for love and friendship" (par. 61). Reason, freedom, and love do not appear accidentally. They are the chief characteristics of the human being in the Catholic tradition. They ring through the theologies that span the centuries, such as those of Saint Augustine, Saint Thomas Aquinas, and Karl Rahner.

While at first these may appear easy to affirm—and a feminist does want to affirm them—one cannot do so naively. First of all, reason, freedom, and love must be contextualized. They are not abstract capacities; they exist within embodied human beings, and so are bound up in the complex reality that is any individual. Moreover, each person is a social, historical actor. Thus reason, freedom, and love are not only capacities; they are actions related to self and others. These considerations raise a series of problems.

First, reason simply as logical calculation is capable of building the neutron bomb, which can annihilate a human population without destroying the buildings. Such reason judges as irrational the social, embodied—indeed, emotional—reason of the women of Greenham Common, who give their daily lives as witnesses for peace. In the economic sphere, is not the "reasoned" decision to move a business to the Sunbelt often a decision about "the bottom line" without regard for the human cost? Might it not be considered irrational to weigh the needs of employees at least as highly as the profit/loss ledger? Feminists want to know how rational reason is when it operates in abstract, disembodied, asocial ways.

Feminists also know that women have long been taught not to trust their own reason. As Henry Higgins puts it, "Women are irrational—that's all there is to that. Their heads are full of cotton, hay, and rags." As long as women believe that their concerns are not credible in the public world, they will discount themselves. This inculcated self-doubt imposes a considerable social cost—namely, the loss of the plurality of women's alternative voices.

Second, questions can be raised about the capacity to freely determine oneself. Both feminists and blacks who have worked toward liberation know that the social, economic, political institutions operate to support white males so that they can make a wide range of choices about the disposition of their lives. Those same institutional arrangements have served to limit the choices of women and blacks. Moreover, both women and blacks have experienced the internalizing of a sense of inferiority that limits their freedom from within. A woman may tell herself that her musical gifts belong only in the family or the local community. Unable to even envision herself on the concert stage, she never attempts to be there. Again, the personal and the social, political, and economic realities (like the availability of conservatory scholarships and quality day care) are inseparably intertwined.

Finally, we can raise questions about women's experience of love. Can women, who have been socialized to seek approval and validation of their very identities from men, ever fully trust their experience of romantic love? Snow White and Cinderella tell us that a woman's whole history is bound to this love. This is not the essence of her lover's history, however. Similarly, how is a woman able to best actualize her love for her children when she has been socialized to recognize her love for them when she stays home but not when she goes to work? Again, her love is institutionalized—socially, politically, and economically.

These challenges to any too-glib assertion of the dignity of human beings as self-evident in the capacities of reason, freedom, and love offer some insight into the damaging way this classic Catholic tradition can operate to cover up the realities of human oppression. These challenges also illustrate why the bishops' move to a vision of human dignity that is fundamentally related to the practical experience of human life is critical if their theology is really going to be responsible to the realities of a wide variety of people's experiences, including those of women. Therefore, the issues raised by this alternative vision bring us again to the question of practice.

The Bishops' Recommendations concerning Women

The bishops are clear that since we as a community enable each other to live in dignity, justice demands that we establish a social situation in which at least a minimal level of economic security is insured for everyone (pars. 68-95). Only in this situation will a basic level of human dignity be possible in our society. The language of justice and rights that the bishops employ is moral and political; the content of their concern is economic. Throughout the pastoral letter, they also move beyond simple justice to call us to preferential consideration of the needs of the poor (pars. 86-92). The bishops recognize that there are important intersections between the creation of a just economy and the politics of our institutions (pars. 77, 80, 83 *inter al.*). Human dignity as an economic reality will require revisions in our social arrangements.

The first question, then, is, What does the pastoral letter already specify when it comes to economic justice and human dignity for women? The bishops' observations about the condition of women appear primarily in their treatment of the issues of employment (pars. 136-69) and poverty (pars. 170-215). The bishops note that large numbers of women are now in the labor market, both to utilize their talents and out of economic necessity (par. 144). Many families need incomes from both parents in order to survive. Other families depend on a single woman parent for livelihood (par. 144). Yet over 10 percent of female heads of household are unemployed (par. 140). Over one-third of their families are poor, and the statistics for minorities show that the poverty rate is over one-half (par. 178). Discrimination both in wages and in the kinds of job opportunities available to women persists (pars. 147, 179). In general, women earn only 61 percent of what men earn (par. 179). In other words, many women who work full-time remain poor, and often find themselves in jobs that offer little or no hope for advancement.

Child care increases the likelihood of female poverty, as the statistics on the female single-parent household already indicate. The fact that very few divorced women receive child support from their former husbands contributes to this condition (par. 180). (The bishops do not add that a divorced man often has more money to spend on himself, while his wife's income and that of the children plummets.) Child care also affects the state of married women. Women often interrupt their careers to give birth and attend to young children. Employers' anticipation that many women workers will interrupt their careers at some point to rear children may also adversely affect jobs available to women (par. 180).

The bishops call for an end to gender-based discrimination. They suggest pay equity, flex time, more job training, and affirmative action for women (pars. 167, 199). They urge social and tax policies that allow mothers of young children to remain at home. They lift up the need for quality day care when both parents work outside the home, and for parental leave policies that would maintain job security (pars. 207-8).

The bishops recognize major affronts to the dignity of women in the economic sphere. They alert us to the crushing way that economic factors operate against women who are single and who belong to racial minorities. They suggest some concrete responses that could foster dignity and justice for women. As a feminist theologian, I both applaud and push at this juncture. What is glaringly absent is any relation of the social, institutional politics of sexism (discrimination on the basis of sex) to the economic situation of women.[1] The same is true for racism. The statistical pictures the bishops offer do belong to the patterns of unemployment and poverty, but these are symptomatic of the insidious presence of institutionalized practices of sexual and racial discrimination.

I want to focus on the issue of institutionalized sexual discrimination. I want to argue that only if this matter is addressed is there any real hope of changing the economic situation of women. Sexism must be confronted if the God-given dignity of women is to be realized in practice. That dignity points toward reforming our institutions so that sexual equality, not bias in favor of males, is the norm.

In what follows I underscore the sexist patterns in our institutions that maintain women in disadvantaged economic positions. To illustrate my points, I offer several pictures of women and reflect on their situations. Let me note that while the bishops direct our attention to the poor,[2] I will work from the middle class, since more American women, including me, share that experience. However, some of the reality of and reasons for female poverty will be visible through this lens.

Wife and Mother at Home

First, let us picture woman as wife and mother at home. Imagine someone like the character Jane Wyatt played in "Father Knows Best." She is the ideal homemaker. She is organized in the kitchen, keeps a spotless house, cares tenderly for her husband and children, and is always there—and always in a fresh dress, earrings, and dewy makeup. She was the American "Mom" in the 1950s, and she remains so today for many people. (Does she appear in the shadows of statements 207 and 344-46 of the bishops' letter?) Underneath the romance, this woman is a worker. The work of the housewife is part of the system of labor in industrialized capitalism. Housekeeping, meal preparation, laundry, child care—all of these are an institutionalized part of the unpaid "shadow work"[3] that makes its partner institution of wage labor possible. The housewife frees her husband for his job.[4] Although apparently separated, the "public" male world of wage labor and the "private" female world of labor in the home developed together and depend upon each other.

This picture raises two distinct but related political issues. First, what are the dynamics of sexism within this system that assign roles, value, and limitations to men and women? Second, what of the institutions themselves, in which home provides both the support for and a market for industrialized technological production? (Ironically, the home is also the last refuge from the separate sphere of wage labor.) Should these institutions be maintained without modification?[5]

Women experience these two problems bound together. From the vantage point of the home, the woman herself lives in a relatively isolated world. Her household is increasingly an island as technology supplies the means for her to do most of her work alone. She and her small children live by themselves. This is particularly true today, in the late eighties, when fewer women are at home. Since other women in the neighborhood are at work, the woman at home is often without even the conversation and support of peers. Her husband goes out to work with others, while she functions as his private support system.

Furthermore, while from an objective viewpoint her work is absolutely necessary to the smooth functioning of daily life and the care of children, the dynamics of sexism rob it of value, so the woman often feels she is doing "nothing" and is ashamed to admit in public what she does. Certainly this isolation and disvaluing are an affront to the dignity the bishops seek to promote.

A second factor that this picture entails is that the mother bears a disproportionate share of parenting while the father bears the impoverishment of too little parenting. The ideal picture of the family has Dad home every evening and weekend, working only forty hours. In reality this is not the case for many families. Commuting cuts Dad's time at home, and many American families find his time even more curtailed. Consider the time committed by the doctor, lawyer, or academic who works well over sixty hours each week, or the relatively poorly paid restaurant manager or car salesman who works sixty to seventy-plus hours away from home. He is frequently absent both nights and weekends. Also, in some poorer families the father works two jobs to make ends meet. The mother is virtually left a single parent. She gets the kids up in the morning and puts them to bed at night without the help of her spouse, probably six days a week.

The structure of the present social and economic institutions is at the core of the problem. Rosemary Ruether points out that as long as a traditional workweek of forty hours or more provides adequate wages and necessary benefits, like health insurance, the present arrangement of dual, interdependent spheres will persist, together with their sexist dynamics.[6] Sharing the unpaid work at home and splitting the task of earning wages[7] remain a fantasy, while the economic facts are that two part-time salaries simply do not equal one full-time wage, nor do they supply benefits. Thus from a feminist perspective the obvious difficulty is not a matter of whether a husband "helps out" at home. Rather, the problem is one of the present arrangements of social and economic institutions. I will return to this point.

The Mother Who Works: Her Situation at Home

Continuing our exploration of woman as an economic actor, let us think about the middle-class working woman with a family. In the two-sphere economic world, this woman now has two jobs, one at home and one in the public workplace. Her job at home entails both housekeeping and child care. While some more "liberated" couples may share housekeeping, statistics show that most of the work still falls to the wife.[8] Therefore, she has to do one of two things about housekeeping: either do it outside her hours on the job or hire a housekeeper to help. Her outside job also presumes that an arrangement has been made for child care. If she is working more than part-time, beyond school hours, or has small children, she is paying someone else to care for her children. In sum, a middle-class woman is holding an outside job with one of the following arrangements: (1) she is working full-time or part-time and has both a housekeeper and a person helping with the children; (2) she is working full-time or part-time and has some child care, but does virtually all the housekeeping herself. In either situation, this woman is probably paying one or more other women to do portions of her work at home.

In other words, the female support that our present institution of wage labor depends upon continues. If one female abdicates a part of her expected role, she pays another, usually out of her own salary, to take her place. This second woman tends to be poorer than the woman who hires her and is often a member of a minority group. Since none but the wealthy can afford a full-time housekeeper, the working woman who pays another to clean periodically is still doing meal preparation, dishes, and ordinary cleanup each day. She simply moves from job to job. The woman who cannot afford any help is working even harder. Clearly, both the sexist hierarchy of our institutions and the institutions themselves present difficulties that call for reconsideration.

The Mother Who Works: On the Job

Once she has dealt with her work at home, what of the woman's job itself? While tremendous strides have been made in the wide employment of women in various fields, women's work remains based in jobs that mimic women's work at home and are part of the support structure for male work. Women are cooks, waitresses, clerks, typists, receptionists, hospital aides, teachers, nurses—all logical outgrowths of their nurturing roles. Women have entered more attractive professions, but the widest sector of women's work is in less attractive, low-paying support roles.[9] These jobs keep women relatively poor, especially if part of their income is also being spent on child care. Here further reasons for the feminization of poverty appear. It is coherent with the sexist politics of our economic way of life.

The bishops' own criterion of human dignity demands that we think about ways to adapt our social and economic institutions in order to end discrimination against women and secure the equality of the sexes. Rosemary Ruether suggests, for example, that we might adapt the American workweek to allow couples to share a fifty-hour week that would enable them to jointly receive wages and benefits comparable to those presently available for full-time work. With each of them working about twenty-five hours per week, they could also share parenting and housekeeping. Without this type of adaptation, Ruether argues, only a few wealthy women will be able to have both satisfying jobs and a family life.[10]

Children and a Community of Sexual Equality

If the institutions of work need to change in the new world of sexual equality, so too must the assumptions about children. The bishops' pastoral is not exceptional when it adverts to children primarily in relation to women (pars. 147, 178, 180, 207, 344). The fact is that children appear in public discussions as a kind of baggage that women entail. What is implicit is the depths of the unconscious presumption of a male public world, which calls attention to children primarily when men consider women. We need to encourage, in both presumption and practice, the consciousness that children belong to all of us. We all share in the responsibility for them; their care is a common concern. This is already manifest in some legal forms and in public education. It could be extended to neighborhood child-care arrangements, after-school programs, and day care at the workplace. The bishops share this dawning awareness (par. 208). Again, we look toward new social institutions. The possibility of a world of sexual equality as integral to human dignity presents us with new questions about the structure of human community for women, men, and children.

Birth Control and Human Dignity

I must also mention a subject the bishops avoided—birth control, notably in its artificial form. While the bishops mention the issue of population control (par. 287), they sidestep this matter. One can only assume that they did not want to encounter *Humanae Vitae*. Moreover, the presumptions of a male public world make the responsibility for sexual intercourse, like children, an entailment of women. As such, it is a "private" social concern, not a public one. But this is precisely what our exploration so far argues against. There is no isolated private world. Home and family are integrally related to our other social and economic institutions. Sexual practice is a social and economic matter. It is an aspect of human dignity, and the justice demanded by that dignity cannot be segmented.

The medical technology of birth control helps American families to choose the number of children they can support emotionally and financially. While the church may rightly warn that birth control can be abused for selfish ends, used responsibly it has many benefits. One is that families can be more financially secure and better able to provide for their children, especially in a situation of increasing costs. Women are able to work, whether primarily to benefit their families or to utilize their wider talents or both. Men and women may be better parents because they can give more attention to fewer children. (We should remember that not all adults have the requisite energy and gifts to parent large numbers of children.) Birth control, then, has a direct impact on the economic and emotional life of the family and on the ability of women to work outside the home.

The vision of human dignity as a practical reality must confront questions about birth control. It appears inconsistent that the church can urge a position that would cause some families great suffering, including plunging them into the poverty to which the bishops so strongly object. There is also little dignity in a mother at her wit's end and exhausted, pregnant again and trying to care for too many children already. Perhaps not a few of us Catholics were children whose mothers had that experience. In addition, having many children can deny a woman the opportunity for self-realization that work outside the home provides, a dimension of dignity the bishops promote (pars. 97, 137). Dignity demands that this issue be rethought.

Human Dignity and Work within the Church

Lastly we turn our attention to the church itself as an economic actor. The bishops take themselves to task in the pastoral letter (pars. 347-357). Yet, again, they largely fail to address the issue of sexism in the institutional system. Unfortunately, the Roman Catholic Church remains a paradigm of a patriarchal and sexist institution, despite the fact that its theological underpinnings have been destroyed.

The church's sexism is partially treated in the pastoral letter by the bishops' discussion of the rights of "employees" and the work of "laity and religious" (pars. 351-52). The situation is that male clerics are the employers, and that employees, whether religious or lay, are largely women. This is as true in the parish rectory and school as in the chancery and the diocesan agencies. The church provides a classic representation of a female support structure for an institution in which authority and visibility belong to males alone. Major decision-making power is hierarchically distributed among the male clerics. This system remains intact despite recent moves toward more conciliar practices. Money is also distributed in relation to this hierarchy. The bishops recognize the obligation to pay just salaries (par. 351), and they do recognize the obvious problem that those most poorly paid are the women whose work supports the institution, especially at lower levels (par. 353). They acknowledge that this is a function of discrimination (par. 353). While there have been real efforts to change wage scales, there is evidence of female poverty within the church itself as a direct result of sexism.

Furthermore, the bishops challenge young people to carry on the unpaid volunteer work that supports the life of the church (par. 352). They do not recognize this work as primarily the contribution of untold thousands of hours given by women to the institution. Without this, many parishes simply could not carry on. The churches survive on the regular use of female "shadow work" in the form of everything from ironing altar linens, to serving coffee after mass, to running the Christmas bazaar or the clothing drive, to offering assistance in the school classrooms or lunchroom, to attending school-board or parish-council meetings. This too must be recognized as coherent with the system of work we have been discussing. Women perform the necessary but disvalued housekeeping functions that keep parishes and dioceses alive.

The bishops are honest enough to address to themselves the same questions they address to the economy at large. The structure of the institution insofar as it participates in political and economic sexual exploitation must also be questioned, and on exactly the kind of grounds enunciated in the bishops' articulation of human dignity.

Conclusion

Elizabeth Janeway says that feminism is finally about a new humanism.[11] The bishops' vision of human dignity leads precisely to a new humanism that entails sexual equality in our social and economic institutions. This is an aspect of the solidarity they say must characterize our civic community. Anything less than this equality would admit that discrimination could be possible in the realm of our God-given dignity. Any such position is patently absurd.

For Christians this new humanism is a result of our deeper conversion to the visions of covenant and kingdom that the bishops describe. It is not only a matter of individual change of heart. It is a question of a social, institutional enactment of the dignity that we are given by God and to which we are unceasingly called. Only institutional change can practically manifest the dignity that the bishops say must characterize our entire society. The test of that dignity is our treatment of the least among us. Surely the condition of women is no small measure of our practice of dignity.

The bishops begin to name some of the many possible and necessary realizations of this dignity. I have continued in that vein so that the institutional realities that shape women's situation might become visible. This is where the hard work of social adaptation lies ahead.

I have explored these problems where those of us in the middle class know them best. Yet our situation already reveals multiple reasons for feminine poverty. It also points to the equally insidious—and for women, additional—burden of racism. As the institutionalized politics of sex must change with our economic structures, so too must those of race if we are to create the community of justice that the bishops' vision of dignity demands. When women of all classes and all races are free from the bondage of institutionalized forms of discrimination, then we will all more justly enact our identity as dignified people, made in the image and likeness of the God who is love.

20 | Individualism, Interdependence, and the Common Good: Rapprochement between Economic Theory and Catholic Social Thought

Charles K. Wilber

Possibly the most important difference between traditional economic theory and Catholic social thought is that the former is based on an individualist conception of society and the latter on a communitarian vision. That difference is based, in turn, on different assumptions of how independent or interdependent individuals are in society. If individual members of society are independent of each other, economic theory argues that pursuit of self-interest can lead to the common good. However, if interdependencies are the rule, not the exception, market failures make it impossible to attain the common good without intervention. Interdependencies mean that some individuals and groups have power over other individuals and groups. Public sponsorship of cooperation as a complement to market competition is a possible means to counter that power and to attain the common good.

The communitarian vision of the bishops engages macroeconomic realities most directly in Chapter Four, "A New American Experiment: Partnership for the Public Good." This is the most innovative section of the U.S. bishops' economic pastoral letter on the economy. I plan to show that recent developments in economic theory over the last fifteen years provide a solid rationale for the bishops' arguments.

Charles K. Wilber

The bishops' pastoral letter is fundamentally a moral document; it is not a treatise on economics. Concern for the effects of the U.S. economy on the lives of millions of human beings led to the issuance of the letter. The letter argues that concern for human dignity in social solidarity is at the core of Christian faith. Because economic institutions and policies have a major impact on human dignity, they are not only technical but moral concerns as well. Therefore, the bishops argue, every perspective on economic life that is human, moral, and Christian must be shaped by three questions: What does the economy do *for* people? What does it do *to* people? And how do people *participate* in it? In addition, the bishops argue that in the pursuit of the common good, special concern must be given to the economy's impact on the poor and powerless because they are particularly vulnerable and needy.

The concept of the common good is rooted in a communitarian vision of society.[1] Because of this, it emphasizes both the dignity of the human person and the essentially social nature of that dignity. Both civil and political liberties on the one hand and social and economic needs on the other are essential components of the common good.

Vatican II defined the common good as "the sum of those conditions of social life which allow social groups and their individual members relatively thorough and ready access to their own fulfillment."[2] The common good is not the aggregate of the welfare of all individuals. Rather, it is a set of social conditions necessary for the realization of human dignity that transcend the arena of private exchange and contract. For example, "such goods as political self-determination, participation in the economic productivity of an industrialized society, and enjoyment of one's cultural heritage can be obtained by an individual only through participation in the public life of society."[3] Such conditions or goods are essentially relational. To exist they must exist as shared. Claims on these goods are social rights such as the right to assembly, work, adequate health care, and so on.

In short, individuals have rights to those things necessary to realize their dignity as human beings. These rights are derived from a person's membership in a community, not from his or her status as an isolated individual. As the bishops say in the pastoral on the economy, "The virtues of good citizenship require a lively sense of participation in the commonwealth and of having obligations as well as rights within it" (par. 296).

In contrast, classical economic theory is rooted in an individualist conception of society. Society is seen as a collection of in-

dividuals who have chosen to associate because it is mutually beneficial. The common good is simply the aggregate of the welfare of each
individual. Individual liberty is the highest good. Traditional
economic theory attempts to provide a rigorous demonstration that
rational individuals, left free to engage in voluntary exchange, will
construct competitive market institutions that yield optimal levels of
individual freedom and material welfare. In the absence of market
failures, this economic theory of individual rationality indicates that
intervention by public authorities lowers efficiency and thus the level
of output.

What can we say about the justice of such free-market outcomes? Despite differences of opinion among economists, the free-
market argument is based on a procedural view of social justice.[4] In
this view the rules of the game justify the outcome and not vice versa.
Further, a just social process is one that rational individuals would
have unanimously agreed to in a Lockean state of nature.[5]

Building on the concept of interdependence and on the realization that economic actors never have access to the totality of relevant information (the concept of imperfect information), I argue in
the next section that economic theory can in fact provide a legitimate
basis for public and private cooperation to supplement the competition of the market process. Specifically, I argue that economic theory
can provide a basis for the type of cooperative partnership programs
derived from the common-good philosophy embodied in Chapter
Four of the bishops' pastoral letter.

Interdependence, Economics, and Moral Hazards

From Adam Smith to this day, mainstream economists have argued
that the best way to overcome scarcity and to increase personal freedom is to rely on the individual's pursuit of self-interest in a private-
property system regulated by the forces of market competition,
where the government simply acts as an umpire enforcing the rules
of the economic game. In order to maximize his or her income, each
person has to provide something (product, service, or labor) that
others want and are willing to pay for, and this will maximize overall production. As each individual attempts to become better off,
society, made up of the individuals living in it, benefits. Thus private
profit and public welfare become reconciled through the automatic
and impersonal forces of competition.

The result is not only a particular economics but also a particular social philosophy. It can be termed the "free market" or the
"laissez-faire" tradition within economics. This was the dominant

view of economics until the 1930s in both England and the United States, and after a forty-year eclipse it has once again become the dominant position in economics.

This theory of a free market economy has not remained unchallenged. There has been substantial scholarly work in economics over the past fifteen years that demonstrates that rational self-interest, under the conditions of interdependence and imperfect information, leads to socially irrational results.[6] Traditional economic theory assumed independence of economic actors and perfect information. However, the more realistic assumptions that one person's behavior affects another person's behavior and that they have less-than-perfect knowledge of what the other's behavior will be give rise to strategic behavior or what game theorists call "moral hazards." Some examples will be helpful.

The type of moral hazard known as the Parable of Distrust can be explained by the classic example of the real-estate agent who attempts to earn a quick profit by selling a house in an all-white neighborhood to a black family, hoping that other homeowners will panic and sell at below market values to the realtor. The realtor then resells the houses at full market values to other black families. Each white owner attempts to deal with the threat of falling market values (real or imagined) by selling quickly before the price falls even more. If all attempt this strategy, prices decline faster. Most white owners agree that the result is undesirable and irrational, but no one household on its own will refuse to sell. In effect, each household says it will not sell only if all the others do not sell. However, no agreement is reached.

This is a clear case in which the pursuit of individual self-interest results in both the group (white owners) and each individual being worse off than if they had cooperated. The problem is simple and common. The homeowners are interdependent and do not have perfect knowledge of what others will do. The resulting lack of trust leads to behavior that is self-defeating. Each homeowner would be better off if he or she agreed not to sell. But since each does not trust the others to honor an agreement not to sell, each would rather sell than be duped by being the only one not to sell.

Take the case of inflation. A labor union fights for a wage increase only to find that other unions also have done so, and thus the wage increase is offset by rising consumer prices. No one union alone can restrain its wage demands and maintain the support of its members. Business firms are caught in the same dilemma. They raise prices to compensate for increased labor and other costs only to discover that costs have increased again. Distrust among unions, among firms, and between unions and firms makes a cooperative agreement on price and wage increases impossible.

The case of recession is similar. As aggregate demand in the economy declines, each company attempts to cope with its resulting cash-flow difficulties through employee layoffs. However, if all companies pursue this strategy, aggregate demand will decline further, making more layoffs necessary. Most companies agree that the result is undesirable for each company and for the whole economy, but no one company on its own will maintain its work force. In effect, each company says it will not lay off its employees only if all other companies do not lay off their employees. Here as in the other cases, no agreement is reached.

These cases have two things in common. First, they all have a group with a common interest in the outcome of a particular situation. Second, while each individual attempts to choose the best available course of action, the result is not what any member of the group desires. In these cases the individual motives lead to undesired social and individual results. Adam Smith's "invisible hand" not only fails to yield the common good but in fact works malevolently.

Why is it so difficult for the individuals involved to make an agreement? The reason is basically economic—*exit* is cheap, but *voice* is expensive.[7] "Exit" means to withdraw from a situation, person, or organization. Exit depends on the availability of choice, competition, and well-functioning markets. It is usually inexpensive and easy to pursue one's own course of action—to buy or not, sell or not, and hire or fire on one's own. "Voice" means to communicate explicitly one's concern to another individual or organization. The cost to an individual in terms of time and effort to argue, persuade, and negotiate will often exceed any prospective benefit to that person.

In addition, the potential success of individual voices depends on the possibility of all members joining together for collective action. This leads to the "free rider" problem. If someone cannot be excluded from receiving the benefits of collective action, he or she has no incentive to join the group. This is the reason why union organizing is next to impossible in states that prohibit union shops (businesses in which if a majority of the workers vote for a union, *all* workers must join and pay dues).

The problem is further complicated by the possibility that what started as a simply self-interested or even benevolent relationship will become malevolent. Face-to-face strategic bargaining may irritate the parties involved if they perceive each other as violating the spirit of fair play. This can result in a response of hatred rather than mere selfishness. Collective action is unlikely if the members of the group hate and distrust one another.

Allan Schmid refers to the type of problem we have been discussing as a "social trap," which he defines as a situation where "micro-motives are not consistent with what individuals who share a common preference want to obtain as a long-run result." Under what conditions does the social trap occur? Schmid goes on to argue, "The micro-motive is supplied when there is some act under the individual's unilateral control that promises to produce some welfare improvement for that individual." The cases previously cited provide examples. According to Schmid, "The alternative line of action that would be consistent with the more preferred long-run result is marked by the fact that no matter how hard the individual tries, alone he can produce no net benefits or fewer than in the dominant activity."[8] The alternative line of action requires some level of trust to engage in the process necessary to reach group agreement. It is worth noting that in social traps, altruistic behavior by an individual will achieve nothing unless it changes the actions of others.

Thus, for an individual or organization to break out of a social trap requires a common consciousness of one's interdependence on others, the realization that the group is in fact more than a collection of individuals. This consciousness does not have to be benevolent or altruistic, although that undoubtedly would make collective action easier to attain. It certainly requires a degree of mutual trust. If malevolence arises, the trap will be strengthened.

Springing Social Traps

How can we spring the trap? The resolution of the problem must remain speculative. Even the most casual observer cannot help but see the persistence and intractability of many of these social traps. Some would argue that the notion of a social trap has become institutionalized—that is, part of the geology of American capitalism—and that it would be better to speak about social quicksand rather than traps that can be removed or avoided. However, laissez-faire or revolution are not the only possibilities. Neither appear any more practical or desirable than reform of the present system.

Let us look at three possibilities: (1) government regulation, (2) group self-regulation, and (3) the internalization of habits of non–self-calculating behavior, reinforced by cultural practices, so that short-run rewards become less important.

Let's look first at government regulation. Traditional economic arguments have left the impression that if government intervened in free-market exchanges only in those few cases of market failure—pollution, monopoly, and so on—ideal economic efficiency would result. However, as we have seen, there are so many "moral hazards" in everyday economic life that market failures of this type are ubiquitous. In these cases, private economic actors can benefit greatly from government measures for their protection. Because of interdependence and imperfect information, distrust leads the parties to self-defeating behavior. Certain kinds of government regulation—from truth in advertising to food and drug laws—can reduce distrust and thus economic inefficiency, making possible a gain for all concerned. But government regulation has its limits. The government will not necessarily succeed where the market fails. Where the regulated have concentrated power (electric companies, for example), the regulators end up serving the regulated industry more than the public. The ability of government to regulate is dependent on the willingness of people to be regulated. That is also the issue in the other two possible escapes from a social trap.

A second possible solution is self-regulation. For example, sellers could voluntarily discipline themselves not to exploit their superior information. This is the basis of professional ethics. Surgeons, for example, take on the obligation, as a condition for the exercise of their profession, not to perform unnecessary operations. The danger is that the professional association will end up protecting its members, including those who do not regulate themselves, at the expense of others. Again, unequal power is a problem. Organized consumer-advocacy groups might be a way to monitor professional associations so that they do not abuse their power.

The Kennedy administration's wage/price guidelines were a partially successful attempt to control inflation through eliciting the public encouragement of labor and management cooperation to limit wage increases to productivity increases. The cooperation broke down because of the fierce and growing struggle among social classes and occupational groups for larger shares of GNP. More formal cooperation between labor and management, monitored by government, might reduce the distrust that cripples their relationship.

This leads us to the final possibility—developing habits of non–self-calculating behavior, reinforced by cultural practices, so that short-run rewards become less important. As we have seen, efficient operation of markets requires something beyond calculated self-interest. Unfortunately, traditional economics has forgotten one of Adam Smith's key insights. It is true he claimed that self-interest will lead to the common good if there is sufficient competition, but also—and more importantly—he claimed that this is true *only* if most people in society accept a general moral law as the guide for their behavior.[9]

The assumption that self-interest in a competitive environment is sufficient to yield the common good is an illusion. An economy, capitalist or socialist, in which everyone—buyers, sellers, workers, managers, consumers, firms—constantly lied, stole, and committed fraud and violence would neither yield the common good nor function efficiently. Yet, pushed to its logical extreme, individual self-interest would suggest that since the individual is faced with interdependence and imperfect information, it is usually in his or her interest to evade the rules that guide the other players. Similarly, the "free rider" concept suggests that the individual best serves his or her interest by not cooperating in a situation of social interdependence if others do cooperate, for he or she will obtain the same benefits without any sacrifice. Why don't people always behave this way? The answer is not only fear of the police power of the state. Our tendency to maximize our material welfare at the expense of others is also inhibited by a deeply ingrained moral sense, one often based on religious convictions.

Peter Berger reminds us that "no society, modern or otherwise, can survive without what [Emile] Durkheim called a 'collective conscience,' that is, without moral values that have general authority."[10] Fred Hirsch reintroduces the idea of moral law into economic analysis: "Truth, trust, acceptance, restraint, obligation—these are among the social virtues grounded in religious belief which . . . play a central role in the functioning of an individualistic, contractual economy. . . . The point is that conventional, mutual standards of honesty and trust are public goods that are necessary inputs for much of economic output."[11]

The major source of this social morality has been the religious heritage of the precapitalist and preindustrial past. However, this legacy of religious values has diminished over time because of a twofold change. The repudiation of the social character and responsibility of religion has meant its banishment to a purely private sphere, and the elevation of self-interest as a praiseworthy virtue has in turn undermined that privatized religious ethic.

Capitalist development was far from conflict-free in the past. But one of its advantages was the absence of an identified villain behind the disruptions that occurred. Such changes resulted from the independent decisions of thousands of people acting upon their rational self-interest. None could rig the rules to his or her benefit, so inequalities appeared legitimate, and the undermining of religious values had no identifiable cause. The centrality of government today, however, provides a target for dissatisfaction. In such circumstances the legitimacy of inequalities and changes in values is open to challenge. The gradual disappearance of a moral consensus forces government to act as a substitute and to provide a context that will encourage principled action among the elite while at the same time ensuring acceptance of the outcome by the majority. Thus government must create or in some sense embody a "civil religion." But as Robert Bellah points out, "No one has changed a great nation without appealing to its soul, without stimulating a national idealism; as even those who call themselves materialists have discovered, culture is the key to revolution, religion is the key to culture."[12]

There is a central flaw in the current approach that calls for the pursuit of self-interest by individuals in the private sector but forbids it in the public sector. The expectation that public servants will not promote their private interests at the expense of the public interest reinforces the argument that the economy relies as fundamentally on moral behavior as on self-interested behavior. "The more a market economy is subjected to state intervention and correction," Fred Hirsch points out, "the more dependent its functioning becomes on restriction of the individualistic calculus in certain spheres, as well as on certain elemental moral standards among both the controllers and the controlled. The most important of these are standards of truth, honesty, physical restraint, and respect for the law."[13] But the more that self-interest progresses and the more that the original moral consensus of society is undercut, the less likely it is that these conditions are going to be met.

Attempts to rely solely on material incentives in the private sector and more particularly in the public sector suffer from two defects. First, stationing a policeman on every corner to prevent cheating simply does not work. Regulators are at a disadvantage in terms of relevant information compared with those whose behavior they are trying to regulate. Second, who regulates the regulators? Thus there is no substitute for an internalized moral law that directs people to seek their self-interest only in "fair" ways.[14] Paradoxically, reliance on external sanctions further undermines the remaining aspects of an internalized moral law.

In summary, the erosion of society's moral consensus under the onslaught of self-interest has important practical results. As Hirsch says,

> Religious obligation performed a secular function that, with the development of modern society, became more rather than less important. It helped to reconcile the conflict be-

Charles K. Wilber

tween private and social needs at the individual level and did it by internalizing norms of behavior. It thereby provided the necessary social binding for an individualistic, *non*altruistic market economy. This was the non-Marxist social function of religion. Without it, the claims on altruistic feelings, or on explicit social cooperation, would greatly increase, as was foreseen, and to some extent welcomed, by a long line of humanists and secular moralists. Less love of God necessitates more love of Man.[15]

Is it possible to rebuild a moral consensus wherein we relearn habits of non–self-calculating behavior? Yes, but we must rethink our view of people as simply self-interested maximizers. Economists have made a major mistake in treating love, benevolence, and particularly public spirit as scarce resources that must be economized lest they be depleted. This is a faulty analogy because, unlike material factors of production, the supply of love, benevolence, and public spirit is not fixed or limited. In fact, possibly the opposite. "First of all," points out Albert Hirschman, "these are resources whose supply may well increase rather than decrease through use; second, these resources do not remain intact if they stay unused."[16] These moral resources respond positively to practice, in a learning-by-doing manner, and negatively to nonpractice.

A good example is the system of blood collection for medical purposes in the United States compared with that in England.[17] In the United States we gradually replaced donated blood with purchased blood. As the campaigns for donated blood declined because purchased blood was sufficient, the amount of blood donated declined. In effect, our inclination to be benevolent toward anyone in need of blood began to atrophy from nonuse. In contrast, blood donations remained high in England, where each citizen's obligation to others was constantly emphasized.

People are capable of changing their values. In fact, a principal objective of publicly proclaimed laws and regulations is to stigmatize certain types of behavior and to reward other types, thereby influencing people's values and behavior codes. Aristotle understood this, noting that "lawgivers make the citizens good by inculcating habits in them, and this is the aim of every lawgiver; if he does not succeed in doing that, his legislation is a failure. It is in this that a good constitution differs from a bad one."[18]

It is here that the bishops' call for cooperation is most persuasive. The inculcation of habits of benevolence and civic spirit can be furthered by bringing groups together to solve common problems.

238

The growth of worker participation in management, the coming to-gether of local committees and business firms to negotiate plant clos-ings and relocations, the establishment of advisory boards on em-ployment policy that represent labor, business, and the public—these are steps toward a recognition that self-interest alone is insufficient. They foster mutual responsibility in a world where interdependence and imperfect information tempt individuals into strategic behavior that in turn generates distrust and self-defeating behavior.

Changing the environment from a competitive one to a cooperative one might provide the trust necessary for people to alter their behavior. This is not a call for altruism. Rather, it is an argument that it is possible to change the environment so that people will real-ize that their long-term interests require foregoing their short-term interests. In the next and final section of this essay I summarize worker management, a particular form of cooperation, and a specific instance of it—the industrial cooperatives of Mondragon in the Basque region of Spain.

Firms Owned and Managed by Workers: Mondragon

Firms owned and managed by workers are relatively new on the national scene in the United States, though some have existed at the local level for many years.[19] They have become important for several reasons. It is becoming clear that profitable plants are being closed, not just unprofitable ones. This is more common when the plant is a small part of a conglomerate holding company. The plant may be closed because even more profit can be earned if it is moved to a lower-wage area or if it is shut down for tax write-off purposes or for a variety of other non–production-related reasons.[20] In these situa-tions, purchase of the plant by the current employees preserves jobs, which makes such a purchase an attractive possibility. Now a legal mechanism, the employee stock ownership plan (ESOP), facilitates employee ownership by providing significant tax incentives to firms that adopt this plan.[21]

There is increasing evidence that worker-owned firms that incorporate employee participation and workplace democracy have rates of productivity at least as high as and frequently higher than those of traditional firms.[22] Thus worker-owned firms have been used to maintain employment at plants that otherwise would have closed and have been used to maintain and improve productivity as well as the quality of work life. In fact, all these factors are linked. As employees become owners and managers, the old distrust that led to shirking and excessive supervision can be reduced. The new environment enables people to see that the short-run advantage of shirking is outweighed by the negative impact on long-run productivity and profits in which they share. Free riding is still possible, of course, if the employees never coalesce as a group.[23]

Of particular interest as models for firms owned and managed by employees are the industrial cooperatives of Mondragon in the Basque region of Spain.[24] Their achievements are quite impressive. The first of the Mondragon cooperatives was established in 1958. Twenty years later the seventy cooperatives together had sales of over $750 million; one-fifth of these sales came from exports to other countries. Among the many goods produced are refrigerators and other home appliances, heavy machinery, hydraulic presses, steel, semiconductors, and selenium rectifiers. Among the cooperatives are the largest refrigerator manufacturer in Spain, a bank with over $500 million in assets, a technological research center, a technical high school and engineering college, and an extensive social-security system with health clinics and other social services.[25]

The ownership and management structures of the Mondragon cooperatives are especially interesting. Every new member must invest a specified amount in the firm at which he or she is employed. At the end of each year, a portion of the firm's surplus or profit is allocated to each worker's capital account in proportion to the number of hours worked and the job rating. The job-rating schedule allows for a quite narrow three-to-one ratio between the highest-paid and lowest-paid workers. The result is a pay scale quite different from that prevailing in private industry. In comparison, lower-paid workers earn more in the cooperatives, middle-level workers and managers earn the same, and top managers earn considerably less. Each cooperative's board of directors is elected by all the members, and the board in turn appoints the managers. There is a social council made up of elected representatives of the lowest-paid workers that negotiates with the board over worker grievances and other issues.

The purely economic results are impressive. When both capital and labor inputs are accounted for, the Mondragon cooperatives are far more productive in their use of resources than private firms in Spain. One study found that in the 1970s the average cooperative, in comparison with the 500 largest firms in Spain, used only 25 percent as much capital equipment per worker, but worker productivity reached 80 percent of that in private industry.[26] That is, with only one-fourth as much capital, each worker produced four-fifths as much output as his or her counterpart in private industry.

How might we explain this highly efficient labor force in the Mondragon cooperatives? Clearly, worker motivation plays a major part. As workers became owners and participated in management decisions, the incentives to shirk were lessened. It was not that workers became more altruistic. Rather, the structural environment made it easier for trust to develop. Strategic behavior declined as workers saw that their short-term individual interests could be in conflict with their long-term interests. Shirking might benefit them here and now, but productivity would benefit them over the long haul. The free-rider problem was controlled by the growth of group consciousness.

This latter is what makes it so difficult to transfer the Mondragon experience to the United States. Basque solidarity clearly has been an important factor in the cooperatives' success. But this may be a chicken-and-the-egg problem. Must we have the group consciousness first, or will the experience of ownership and management help create that consciousness? We do not know, but the continued deterioration of the industrial structure in the United States is creating the conditions for worker buyouts, which, if combined with the philosophy of economic democracy contained in the bishops' pastoral letter, could be used to build a new social consensus.

Notes

Notes to the Introduction

1. "Christian Faith and Economic Justice: A Paper Prepared for the General Assembly of the Presbyterian Church (U.S.A.) by the Council on Theology and Culture," in *Minutes of the 196th General Assembly of the Presbyterian Church (U.S.A.)* (New York: Office of the General Assembly, 1984), pp. 365-66; and "Christian Faith and Economic Life: A Study Paper Contributing to a Pronouncement for the Seventeenth General Synod of the United Church of Christ," ed. Audrey Chapman Smock (New York: United Church Board for World Ministries, 1987), p. 2.

2. Robert Samuelson, "Progress and Poverty," *Newsweek,* 24 Aug. 1987, p. 41.

3. Gar Alperovitz and Jeff Faux, *Rebuilding America: A Blueprint for the New Economy* (New York: Pantheon, 1984), pp. 139-40.

4. Neuhaus, *The Naked Public Square: Religion and Democracy in America* (Grand Rapids: Eerdmans, 1984), p. vii.

5. Neuhaus, *The Naked Public Square,* p. 28.

6. Drayton, "To the Virginian Voyage," in *New World Metaphysics: Readings on the Religious Meaning of the American Experience,* ed. Giles Gunn (New York: Oxford University Press, 1981), pp. 30-31.

7. Winthrop, "A Model of Christian Charity," in *New World Metaphysics,* pp. 53-54.

8. Booth, *Modern Dogma and the Rhetoric of Assent* (Chicago: University of Chicago Press, 1974), pp. x-xi.

Notes to Chapter 1

1. *The Evangelical–Roman Catholic Dialogue on Mission, 1977-1984,* ed. Basil Meeking and John Stott (Grand Rapids: Eerdmans, 1986), p. 33.

2. The existence of "a kind of *magisterium*" that operates in evangelical groups was acknowledged in the report of the missiological dialogue group; see *The Evangelical–Roman Catholic Dialogue on Mission,* pp. 23-24.

Notes to Chapter 2

1. Eidsmoe, *God and Caesar: Biblical Faith and Political Action* (Westchester, Ill.: Crossway, 1984), p. 98.

2. Eidsmoe, *God and Caesar,* p. 98.

3. Eidsmoe, *God and Caesar,* pp. 98-111.

4. Weakland, "The Church in Worldly Affairs: Tension between the Laity and Clergy," *America,* 18 Oct. 1986, p. 202.

5. See, for example, Brian Griffiths, *The Creation of Wealth: A Christian's Case for Capitalism* (Downers Grove, Ill.: InterVarsity, 1984); and Ronald H. Nash, *Poverty and Wealth: The Christian Debate over Capitalism* (Westchester, Ill.: Crossway, 1986).

6. See, for example, Sider's *Rich Christians in an Age of Hunger: A Biblical Study* (Downers Grove, Ill.: InterVarsity, 1977).

7. Griffiths, *The Creation of Wealth,* pp. 60-61.

8. See Bilheimer's *Spirituality for the Long Haul: Biblical Risk and Moral Stand* (Philadelphia: Fortress Press, 1984).

9. Kristol, *Two Cheers for Capitalism* (New York: Basic Books, 1978), pp. 65-67.

10. Kristol, *Two Cheers for Capitalism,* p. 67.

Notes to Chapter 3

1. See Rowland Croucher, *Recent Trends among Evangelicals* (Sutherland, Australia: Albatross, 1986), pp. 13-15.

2. Johnston, *Evangelicals at an Impasse: Biblical Authority in Practice* (Atlanta: John Knox Press, 1979), p. 151.

3. Fackre, "The Use of Scripture in My Work in Systematics," in *The Use of the Bible in Theology: Evangelical Options,* ed. Robert K. Johnston (Atlanta: John Knox Press, 1985), pp. 200-226.

4. Fackre, "The Use of Scripture in My Work in Systematics," p. 224.

5. Curran, "Relating Religious-Ethical Inquiry to Economic Policy," in *The Catholic Challenge to the American Economy: Reflections on the Bishops' Pastoral Letter on Catholic Social Teaching and the U.S. Economy,* ed. Thomas M. Gannon (New York: Macmillan, 1987), p. 48.

6. Pinnock, "How I Use the Bible in Doing Theology," in *The Use of the Bible in Theology,* p. 29.

7. Wells, "The Nature and Function of Theology," in *The Use of the Bible in Theology,* pp. 195-96.

8. Moberg, *The Great Reversal: Evangelism versus Social Concern* (Philadelphia: Lippincott, 1972).

9. Henry, *The Uneasy Conscience of Modern Fundamentalism* (Grand Rapids: Eerdmans, 1947), p. 68.

10. Niebuhr, *Christ and Culture* (New York: Harper & Row, 1956).

11. Tobin, "Unemployment, Poverty and Economic Policy," *America,* 4 May 1985, p. 359.

12. Niebuhr, *Faith and Politics,* ed. Ronald Stone (New York: George Braziller, 1968), p. 139.

Notes to Chapter 4

1. The Lay Commission on Catholic Social Teaching and the U.S. Economy, *Toward the Future: Catholic Social Thought and the U.S. Economy* (New York: American Catholic Committee, 1984), p. ix.

2. Novak, *The Spirit of Democratic Capitalism* (New York: Touchstone, 1982).

3. Griffiths, *The Creation of Wealth* (Downers Grove, Ill.: InterVarsity, 1984), p. 91.

4. Novak, *American Vision: Essay on the Future of Democratic Capitalism* (Washington: American Enterprise Institute, 1978).

5. Novak, *American Vision,* p. 25.

6. Novak, *American Vision,* p. 119.

7. Kuyper, *Lectures on Calvinism* (Grand Rapids: Eerdmans, 1931); Dooyeweerd, *A New Critique of Theoretical Thought,* 4 vols., trans. David H. Freeman and others (Philadelphia: Presbyterian & Reformed Publishing Co., 1953-58).

8. See, for example, Alan Gibbard, "What's Morally Special about Free Exchange?" *Social Philosophy and Policy* 2 (Spring 1985): 20-28.

9. An example of the argument to re-embed the economic system in the Judeo-Christian ethic can be found in Daniel Bell's *Cultural Contradictions of Capitalism* (New York: Basic Books, 1976). Evidence for the lack of adequate cultural values could be taken from Robert Bellah et al., *Habits of the Heart: Individualism and Commitment in American Life* (New York: Harper & Row, 1985).

10. *Toward the Future,* p. 10.

11. Griffiths, *The Creation of Wealth,* p. 63.

12. In *Dialogue on Wealth and Welfare: An Alternative View of World Capital Formation* (Oxford: Pergamon, 1980), Orio Giarini suggests the best alternative directions.

13. See *Reinhold Niebuhr on Politics,* ed. H. R. Davis and R. C. Good (New York: Scribner's, 1960).

14. Boulding, *The Economy of Love and Fear* (Belmont, Calif.: Wadsworth, 1973).

15. *Toward the Future,* p. 44.

16. Berger, *Pyramids of Sacrifice: Political Ethics and Social Change* (Garden City, NY: Doubleday, 1976).
17. See Charles Wilber's discussion in Chapter 20, pp. 231-34.

Notes to Chapter 5

1. There is no consensus among Third World specialists on the number of people suffering from absolute poverty. In 1980, for example, the World Bank estimated that 780 million in the Third World were living in this condition. More recently, the United Nations Food and Agricultural Organization has estimated that nearly 500 million people suffer from malnutrition, while the Overseas Development Council, which annually classifies countries on the basis of economic and social statistics, has estimated that some 1.3 billion people are living in conditions of extreme poverty.
2. Bellah, "Religious Influences on United States Foreign Policy," in *American Character and Foreign Policy*, ed. Michael P. Hamilton (Grand Rapids: Eerdmans, 1986), pp. 53-55.
3. Wolterstorff, *Until Justice and Peace Embrace* (Grand Rapids: Eerdmans, 1983), p. 97.
4. Sider, *Rich Christians in an Age of Hunger: A Biblical Study* (Downers Grove, Ill.: InterVarsity, 1977), p. 162.
5. Andre Gunder Frank, a leading critic of the modernization theory, has argued that prior to the expansion of modern capitalism, Third World nations were *undeveloped*. The integration of Asia, Africa, and Latin America into the world economy led to *underdevelopment*. See *Latin America: Underdevelopment or Revolution* (New York: Monthly Review, 1969), chap. 1.
6. The Lay Commission on Catholic Social Teaching and the U.S. Economy, *Toward the Future: Catholic Social Thought and the U.S. Economy* (New York: American Catholic Committee, 1984), p. 50.
7. Griffiths, *Morality and the Marketplace* (London: Hodder & Stoughton, 1982), p. 136.
8. Griffiths, *The Creation of Wealth* (Downers Grove, Ill.: InterVarsity Press, 1984), p. 13.
9. *On Human Work* (Washington: United States Catholic Conference, 1981), pp. 9-10.
10. *Toward the Future*, pp. 25-26.
11. Bauer, "Western Guilt and Third World Poverty," *Commentary* 61 (Jan. 1976): 22.
12. Singer and Bracken, "Don't Blame the U.S.," *New York Times Magazine*, 7 Nov. 1986, p. 34.
13. Darling, "How Humanitarianism Impedes Third World Development," unpublished lecture, Vienna, Va.
14. Novak, *The Spirit of Democratic Capitalism* (New York: Simon & Schuster, 1982), p. 185.
15. Harrison, *Underdevelopment Is a State of Mind: The Latin American Case* (Lanham, Md.: University Press of America, 1985), p. 2.
16. Novak, *The Spirit of Democratic Capitalism*, p. 302.

17. Robert Gilpin, *The Political Economy of International Relations* (Princeton: Princeton University Press, 1987), pp. 321-22.

18. Jack Shepherd, "When Foreign Aid Fails," *Atlantic Monthly,* Apr. 1985, pp. 41-43.

Notes to Chapter 7

1. A version of the story appears in Abraham J. Heschel's "Teaching Jewish Theology," *The Synagogue School* 28 (Fall 1969): 27.

2. See Michael Goldberg, "Two Letters on the Economy," *Christian Century,* 10 Apr. 1985, pp. 347-50.

3. See Saul Friedlander, *Pius XII and the Third Reich* (New York: Knopf, 1966); Carlo Falconi, *The Silence of Pius XII* (New York: Little, Brown, 1970); and Guenter Lewy, *The Catholic Church and Nazi Germany* (New York: McGraw-Hill, 1964). On the activities of Paul VI, especially with regard to help given to Nazi war criminals seeking to escape from Europe after World War II, see Ladislas Farago, *Aftermath: Martin Bormann and the Fourth Reich* (New York: Avon, 1974), pp. 196, 211-14, 241.

4. See Roger Brooks, *Support for the Poor in the Mishnaic Law of Agriculture: Tractate Peah* (Chico, CA: Scholars Press, 1983), pp. 33-35.

5. See Robert L. Katz, *Pastoral Care and the Jewish Tradition: Empathic Process and Religious Counseling* (Philadelphia: Fortress Press, 1985).

6. *Tractate Sota* 14a. All translations from the Talmud are derived from the standard English translation edited by I. Epstein (London: Soncino, 1936).

7. *Nostra Aetate: The Declaration on the Relation of the Church to Non-Christian Religions* was adopted by Vatican Council II in 1965. Paragraph 4 in particular relates to the Jews. See John Pawlikowski and James Wilde, *When Catholics Speak about Jews* (Chicago: Liturgy Training Publications, 1987), pp. 71-78.

8. Heschel, *God in Search of Man: A Philosophy of Judaism* (Philadelphia: Jewish Publication Society, 1955), pp. 273-74.

9. On "rights" in Jewish law, see Moshe Silberg, *Talmudic Law and the Modern State* (New York: Burning Bush, 1973), chaps. 6 and 7.

10. On the virtue of poverty and the sinfulness of wealth in medieval Judaism, see Yitzhak Baer, *A History of the Jews in Christian Spain* (Philadelphia: Jewish Publication Society, 1966), 1:261-77. On the rejection of the view that the poor are being punished by God with poverty, see Abraham Cronbach, "The *Me'il Zedakah*," *Hebrew Union College Annual* 11 (1936): 561; cf. pp. 518-20. In the Talmud, see *Erubin* 41b, *Nedarim* 64b, *Baba Bathra* 116a. On the stigmatization of the poor in the American Protestant tradition, see Martin Marty, *Righteous Empire: The Protestant Experience in America* (New York: Dial Press, 1970), pp. 110, 150.

11. *Midrash Exodus Rabbah* 31:12, 14; *Midrash Rabbah—Exodus,* trans. S. M. Lehrman (London: Soncino, 1939), pp. 391-92.

12. *Midrash Vavosha,* in *Beit Ha-Midrash,* ed. Adolf Jellnick (Jerusalem, 1938), 1:55. There is no standard English translation of this text.

13. Heschel, *God in Search of Man*, p. 377.

14. The letter does mention the problems of the prevention of poverty (nos. 161, 196) and the economic dangers potentially and actually affecting the economically solvent (nos. 17, 172), but it does not explore them to any significant degree, since it concentrates almost exclusively on the plight of the poor and the unemployed.

15. Rashi is an acronym for Rabbi Solomon Izhaki, the most important medieval Jewish commentator on Hebrew Scriptures. See *The Pentateuch and Rashi's Commentary—Leviticus*, trans. A. Ben Isaiah and B. Sharfman (New York: SS & R Publishing, 1949), p. 265.

16. See Tzvi Marx, "Priorities in Zedakah and Their Implications," *Judaism* 28 (Winter 1979): 80-90.

17. *Kethubot 67b.*

18. "Re'eh," *Sifre on Deuteronomy,* par. no. 118, ed. L. Finkelstein (New York: Jewish Theological Seminary, 1969), p. 177. An English translation by Rueven Hammer was published by Yale University Press in 1986.

19. Maimonides, "Laws Regarding Gifts to the Poor," in *Mishnah Torah—Book of Agriculture,* trans. Isaac Klein (New Haven: Yale University Press, 1979), p. 77.

20. *Peah 8:8.*

21. See the rabbinic commentary on Psalms, *Midrash on Psalms,* trans. William Braude (New Haven: Yale University Press, 1959), 1:437; and *The Fathers According to Rabbi Nathan,* trans. J. Goldin (New Haven: Yale University Press, 1955), p. 171.

22. See Meir Tamari, *With All Your Possessions: Jewish Ethics and Economic Life* (New York: Macmillan, 1987), pp. 51-60, 83-125, 280.

23. *Midrash Pesikta Rabbati,* trans. William Braude (New Haven: Yale University Press, 1968), p. 514. See also Solomon Schecter, "Notes of Lectures on Jewish Philanthropy," in *Studies in Judaism: Third Series* (Philadelphia: Jewish Publication Society, 1924), pp. 238-76.

24. This citation is from the medieval German Jewish work entitled *Sefer Hasidim—The Book of the Pious,* ascribed to Judah the Pious, currently unavailable in a standard English translation. There are two standard Hebrew editions of this work based on different manuscripts. In the one edited by Jehudah Wistinetzki (Frankfurt: Wahrmann, 1924), see par. 1345, p. 331; in that edited by R. Margaliot (Jerusalem: Mosad Ha Rav Kook, 1960), see par. 415, p. 297.

25. *The Fathers according to Rabbi Nathan,* chaps. 3, 26. In the Talmud, see *Kethubot* 68a.

26. In the Talmud, see *Gittin* 7a, *Kethubot* 50a. In Maimonides' code, see "Laws Regarding Gifts to the Poor," pp. 77-78.

27. See Abraham Cronbach, "The Gradations of Benevolence," *Hebrew Union College Annual* 16 (1941): 163-87.

28. On *gemilut hasadim* and *tsedakah* in the Talmud, see *Sukkah* 49b.

29. *Kethubot 67a.*

30. See Tamari, *With All Your Possessions,* pp. 242-77.

31. Maimonides, "Laws Regarding Gifts to the Poor," p. 85.
32. See Abraham J. Karp, *Haven and Home: A History of the Jews in America* (New York: Schocken, 1985), pp. 7-8.

Notes to Chapter 8

1. See Elliot N. Dorff, *Jewish Perspectives on the Poor* (New York: American Jewish Committee, 1986).
2. See Roger Brooks, *Support for the Poor in the Mishnaic Law of Agriculture: Tractate Peah* (Chico, CA: Scholars Press, 1983); and Louis Newman, *The Sanctity of the Seventh Year: A Study of Mishnah Tractate Shebiit* (Chico, CA: Scholars Press, 1983).
3. See Joel Roth, *The Halakhic Process: A Systemic Analysis* (New York: Jewish Theological Seminary, 1986).
4. This section is entirely a reflection upon Steven S. Schwarzschild's "Karl Marx's Jewish Theory of Usury," *Gesher* (1978), pp. 7-40. Published in an obscure journal, this essay is a brilliant, ground-breaking exposition of the roots of socialist thinking in traditional Jewish sources—e.g., on money-lending as idolatry.
5. Cf. Psalm 15. This psalm is often recited at Jewish funerals.
6. *Mishnah Sh'vi'it* 10:3, in *The Mishnah*, trans. Herbert Danby (London: Oxford University Press, 1933); cf. *ibid.* 10:8; Maimonides, *Hilhot Sh'mitah* 7:3, 9:4, 10:5; and S. Zeitlin, "Prosbol: A Study in Tannaitic Jurisprudence," *Jewish Quarterly Review* 37 (1947): 341-62.
7. B. T. *Gittin* 34b-36b in *The Talmud*, ed. I. Epstein (London: Soncino, 1936).
8. B.T. *Baba Metzia* 75b.
9. Cf. B.T. *Baba Metzia* 63b, 64a, 65b, 68b, 74a.
10. Cf. Hayim Soloveitchik, "Halakhah in Exile," *Proceedings of the American Academy of Jewish Research* 38/39 (1972).
11. Chapters 159-77 of *Yoreh Deah*.
12. Schwarzschild cites *Cant. R* 1.5-6 and *Exodus Rabbah* 48:2, but I have been unable to find these references.
13. In *Ahavat Chesed*, trans. L. Oschry (New York: Feldheim, 1967), pp. 144-48.
14. Following David Hoffman's Hebrew commentary on the books of Leviticus and Deuteronomy, these citations from the Babylonian Talmud should be consulted: *Rosh Hashanah* 9a, 9b, 26a; *P'shahim* 51b, 52b; *Arachin* 28b, 29a, 32b, 3a, and 3b; *Baba Kama* 116b, 118a, 140a, 141a, and 141b; *Baba Metsia* 60b, 70a; *Kiddushin* 14b, 21b, 38b; *Moed Kattan* 3a; *Gittin* 36a; *Sanhedrin* 39a.
15. Buber, *Paths in Utopia*, trans. R. F. C. Hull (New York: Macmillan, 1950).
16. Cf. the important studies of Isadore Twersky: "Some Aspects of the Jewish Attitude toward the Welfare State," *Tradition* 5:137-58; and *Studies in Jewish Law and Philosophy* (New York: Ktav, 1982), pp. 108-29. See also Steven Schwarzschild's "A Note on the Nature of Ideal Society—A

Rabbinic Study," in *Curt Silberman Festschrift*, ed. H. A. Strauss and H. K. Reissner (New York: Federation of Central European Jews, 1969), pp. 86-105; and Schwarzschild's classic "The Economic Views of Maimonides," originally published in 1941, now available in *Ancient and Medieval Jewish History,* ed. Salo W. Baron (New Brunswick, N.J.: Rutgers University Press, 1972).

Notes to Chapter 9

1. Wise, *Challenging Years: The Autobiography of Stephen Wise* (New York: G. P. Putnam, 1949), p. 110.
2. Wise, *Challenging Years*, p. 97.
3. Melvin I. Urofsky, *A Voice That Spoke for Justice: The Life and Times of Stephen S. Wise* (Albany: SUNY Press, 1982), p. 360.
4. Wise, *Challenging Years*, pp. 97, 311.
5. Holmes, "The Paradox of Rabbi Wise," *Opinion: A Journal of Jewish Life and Letters* 19 (May-June 1949): 4.
6. Heschel, cited in Byron L. Sherwin, *Abraham Joshua Heschel* (Atlanta: John Knox Press, 1979), p. 13.
7. Niebuhr, cited in *Abraham Joshua Heschel: Exploring His Life and Thought*, ed. John C. Merkle (New York: Macmillan, 1985), p. xiii.
8. Heschel, *The Prophets* (Philadelphia: Jewish Publication Society, 1962), p. 21.
9. Heschel, *The Prophets*, pp. 24, 22.
10. Heschel, *The Prophets*, pp. 198-200.
11. Heschel, *The Prophets*, pp. 213, 218.
12. Bernard W. Anderson, "Coexistence with God: Heschel's Exposition of Biblical Theology," in *Abraham Joshua Heschel*, pp. 59-60. See also Heschel, *God in Search of Man: A Philosophy of Judaism* (New York: Farrar, Straus & Giroux, 1955), chap. 28.
13. Heschel, *The Insecurity of Freedom: Essays on Human Existence* (New York: Schocken Books, 1966), pp. 160-61.
14. Heschel, *The Prophets*, p. 364.
15. New Jewish Agenda, "National Platform," *Agenda Newletter*, 1982, p. 1.
16. *Agenda Newsletter*, pp. 1-8.
17. Michael Lerner, "TIKKUN: To Mend, Repair and Transform the World—The Founding Editorial Statement," *Tikkun: A Quarterly Jewish Critique of Politics, Culture & Society* 1 (1986): 3, 5.
18. Waskow, *The Bush Is Burning: Radical Judaism Faces the Pharaohs of the Modern Superstate* (New York: Macmillan, 1971), p. 26.
19. Ruether, *Sexism and God-Talk: Toward a Feminist Theology* (Boston: Beacon Press, 1983), pp. 22-33, 61-64.
20. Waskow, "Making the Jubilee Our Own," *Genesis 2: An Independent Voice for Jewish Renewal* 16 (Feb. / Mar. 1985): 11.
21. Waskow, *These Holy Sparks: The Rebirth of the Jewish People* (New York: Harper & Row, 1983), p. 73.

22. *These Holy Sparks,* pp. 77-78.
23. *These Holy Sparks,* p. 197.

Notes to Chapter 10

1. Schulweis, *The Single Mirror of Jewish Images: The Pluralistic Character of Jewish Ethics* (Los Angeles: University of Judaism, 1982).
2. The first quote is from the Jerusalem Talmud, *Kiddushin,* end of tractate; the second quote is from *Pirke Avot* 6:4.
3. Kristol, "Christianity, Judaism, and Socialism," in *Reflections of a Neoconservative: Looking Back, Looking Ahead* (New York: Basic Books, 1983), p. 316.
4. Biale, *Power and Powerlessness in Jewish History* (New York: Schocken Books, 1986), pp. 32-33.
5. Walzer, *Interpretation and Social Criticism* (Cambridge: Harvard University Press, 1987), p. 91.
6. Ignatieff, *The Needs of Strangers* (New York: Viking Press, 1985), p. 141.
7. Robert Pear, "Poverty Rate Dips as Median Family Income Rises," *New York Times,* 31 July 1987, A12.

Note to Chapter 11

1. Kenneth T. Jackson, *Crabgrass Frontier: The Suburbanization of America* (New York: Oxford University Press, 1985), pp. 91-92.

Notes to Chapter 12

1. For this approach to the letter, as well as for later comments on method, I am indebted to the work of my colleague, Beverly W. Harrison, "Social Justice and Economic Orthodoxy," *Christianity and Crisis* 21 (Jan. 1985): 513-15; and "Response to Lee Cormie's 'The U.S. Bishops on Capitalism,'" unpublished presentation for the Liberation Theology Working Group of the American Academy of Religion.
2. What Ernst Troeltsch wrote at the turn of this century remains a remarkable list of social effects of this revolution:

> Where this spirit [of gain for the sake of gain] predominates it makes all values abstract, exchangeable, and measurable; it mobilizes property and, in a way of which no one hitherto had dreamed, advancing beyond the merely natural dependence of life, it groups together the economic values and the possibilities which they contain. The economic system based on money depersonalizes values, makes property abstract and individualistic, creates a rational law of trade and possessions, raises men above natural conditions of life, unites its fortunes with forethought, intelligence, and calculation, replaces the idea of Prov-

idence and the spirit of mutual help and solidarity of those who are bound together in loyalty to one another, by products which are at all times ready for use; it produces great differences in possessions and in needs, and leads from the simple standpoint of the consumer to an active production of artificial values and conditions. It is the cause of the development of formal abstract law, of an abstract, impersonal way of thinking, of rationalism and relativism. As a result it leads to a restless and changing social differentiation which is based not upon the unchanging land, but upon accidental accumulations of money which can change anything into anything else. The personal relationships depending on nature and on social groups are dissolved; the individual gains an abstract freedom and independence, and, on the other hand, deteriorates into unknown forms of dependence which seem to be the powers of superior common sense and the sum of attractive possibilities. The individual makes up for the loss of concrete individuality, that is, of an originality which is definitely differentiated and secured by corporate relations, by abstract individualism; that is, by the assertion of individual powers, from which it builds up rationally unions, group fellowships, institutions, and enterprises, and to which it makes conditions rationally serviceable.

The Social Teachings of the Christian Churches, trans. Olive Wyon (Chicago: University of Chicago Press, 1981), 1:250-51.

3. Niebuhr, *Moral Man and Immoral Society: A Study in Ethics and Politics* (New York: Scribner's, 1932), p. 15.

4. Walzer, *Spheres of Justice: A Defense of Pluralism and Equality* (New York: Basic Books, 1983), p. 122.

5. Tocqueville, cited in Allan Bloom, *The Closing of the American Mind: Education and the Crisis of Reason* (New York: Simon & Schuster, 1987), pp. 85-86.

6. The phrase is Cornel West's, one he uses in *Prophesy Deliverance: An Afro-American Revolutionary Christianity* (Philadelphia: Westminster Press, 1982), and other of his writings.

7. This discussion of church and its relationship to reigning power is much indebted to the work of John Howard Yoder, specifically "The Constantinian Sources of Western Social Ethics," in *The Priestly Kingdom: Social Ethics as Gospel* (Notre Dame, Ind.: University of Notre Dame Press, 1984), pp. 135-50.

8. Hellwig, *Jesus: The Compassion of God* (Wilmington: Michael Glazier, 1965), p. 81.

Notes to Chapter 13

1. For the truth of such a caricature in light of a more comprehensive account of differences, see James M. Gustafson, *Protestant and*

Roman Catholic Ethics (Chicago: University of Chicago Press, 1978), esp. pp. 1-29.

2. Weakland, "The Church in Worldly Affairs: Tensions between Laity and Clergy," *America*, 18 Oct. 1986, p. 203.

3. Weakland, "The Church in Worldly Affairs," pp. 203, 215.

4. Hollenbach, "Human Work and the Story of Creation Theology and Ethics," in *Laborem Exercens: Co-Creation and Capitalism*, ed. Oliver S. Williams, C.S.C., and John W. Houck (Washington: University of America Press, 1983), p. 60.

5. For a fuller discussion, see my book entitled *Sacramental Ethics: Paschal Identity and the Christian Life* (Philadelphia: Fortress Press, 1987), esp. pp. 98-101.

6. See Thomas W. Ogletree, *Hospitality to the Stranger* (Philadelphia: Fortress Press, 1985), pp. 1-8, 35-59.

7. On Bonhoeffer and arcane discipline, see Bruce C. Birch and Larry L. Rasmussen, *The Predicament of the Prosperous*, ed. Howard Kee (Philadelphia: Westminster Press, 1978), pp. 186-93. On domestic rituals, see Philip Turner, "Spirituality in the Parish: An Anglican Perspective," unpublished paper, 1987.

8. John Paul II, "Homily at Yankee Stadium," *Origins*, 25 Oct. 1979, p. 311.

Notes to Chapter 14

1. These statistics and all others on the current U.S. poverty population are taken from U.S. Department of Commerce, "Money Income and Poverty Status of Families and Persons in the United States: 1985," *Current Population Reports*, series P-60, no. 154 (Washington: Government Printing Office, Aug. 1986).

2. Weber, *The Protestant Ethic and the Spirit of Capitalism* (New York: Scribner's, 1958), p. 172.

3. Gilder, *Wealth and Poverty* (New York: Bantam Books, 1981), p. 87.

4. Erol R. Ricketts and Isabel V. Sawhill, "Defining and Measuring the Underclass," Urban Institute Working Paper, Dec. 1986.

5. In 1987 a single person living alone and eligible for SSI could receive a maximum grant of $340 per month.

6. Judith M. Gueron, *Work Initiatives for Welfare Recipients* (Manpower Demonstration Research Corporation, Mar. 1986).

Notes to Chapter 15

1. "Christian Faith and Economic Life: A Study Paper Contributing to a Pronouncement for the Seventeenth General Synod of the United Church of Christ," ed. Audrey Chapman Smock (New York: United Church Board for World Ministries, 1987), par. 300, 302. Hereafter this work is cited parenthetically in the text as "UCC," followed by paragraph numbers.

2. "Christian Faith and Economic Justice: A Paper Prepared for the General Assembly of the Presbyterian Church (U.S.A.) by the Council on Theology and Culture," in *Minutes of the 196th General Assembly of the Presbyterian Church (U.S.A.)* (New York: Office of the General Assembly, 1984), 364-99. Hereafter this work is cited parenthetically in the text as "PC, 1984," followed by paragraph numbers.

3. "Toward a Just, Caring and Dynamic Political Economy: Report of the Advisory Council on Church and Society's Committee on a Just Political Economy," *Minutes of the 197th General Assembly of the Presbyterian Church (U.S.A.)* (New York: Office of the General Assembly, 1985), 332-68. Hereafter this work is cited parenthetically in the text as "PC, 1985," followed by paragraph numbers.

4. In this chapter I will refer to *Economic Justice for All* via the abbreviated form consistently used in this text. Thus any reference in parentheses that is preceded simply by the abbreviation *par.* is a reference to the bishops' letter. I am also following the established form for citing the pastoral message preceding the letter.

Note to Chapter 16

1. Bellah et al., *Habits of the Heart: Individualism and Commitment in American Life* (Berkeley and Los Angeles: University of California Press, 1985); and Neuhaus, *The Catholic Moment: The Paradox of the Church in the Postmodern World* (New York: Harper & Row, 1987).

Notes to Chapter 17

1. Kantzer, "Pastoral Letters and the Realities of Life," *Christianity Today*, 1 Mar. 1985, p. 13.

2. Washington to Jay, 15 Aug. 1786, cited in Gordon S. Wood, *The Creation of the American Republic, 1776-1787* (New York: W. W. Norton, 1969), p. 472. For the historical background to the Madisonian critique, see Wood's text. For a contemporary attack on the proponents of civic virtue, see John Patrick Diggins, *The Lost Soul of American Politics: Virtue, Self-Interest, and the Foundations of Liberalism* (Chicago: University of Chicago Press, 1984).

3. Gregory Baum, "Class Struggle and the Magisterium: A New Note," *Theological Studies* 45 (1984): 690-701; and "A Canadian Perspective on the U.S. Pastoral," *Christianity and Crisis*, 21 Jan. 1985, pp. 516-18.

4. Alperovitz, "The Coming Break in Liberal Consciousness," *Christianity and Crisis*, 3 Mar. 1986, pp. 62-63.

5. Jefferson to Adams, 28 Oct. 1813, in *The Portable Thomas Jefferson*, ed. Merrill D. Peterson (New York: Viking Press, 1975), pp. 533-39. For Jefferson's differences with Madison over the theory and practice of democracy, see Jefferson to Madison, 20 Dec. 1787, ibid., pp. 428-33.

6. Tocqueville, *Democracy in America*, trans. G. Lawrence, ed. J. P. Mayer (Garden City, N.Y.: Doubleday, 1969), pp. 511-13.

7. Dennis P. McCann, *New Experiment in Democracy: The Challenge for American Catholicism* (Kansas City, Mo.: Sheed & Ward, 1987), p. 57.

8. Walzer, *Spheres of Justice: A Defense of Pluralism and Equality* (New York: Basic Books, 1983), pp. 3-10.

9. Cf. Christopher Lasch, "The Communitarian Critique of Liberalism," *Soundings* 69 (Spring/Summer 1986): 63-67.

10. See Larry Rasmussen's discussion in Chapter 12, pp. 134-37.

11. Tocqueville, *Democracy in America*, pp. 112-16, 667-76.

12. Walzer, *Spheres of Justice*, pp. xiii, 10-13.

13. Walzer, *Spheres of Justice*, pp. 15-17; and Lasch, "The Communitarian Critique of Liberalism," pp. 67-72.

14. Noble, *Forces of Production: A Social History of Industrial Automation* (New York: Oxford University Press, 1986), pp. 144-45. For the historical development of this "facile faith," see Leo Marx, "Does Improved Technology Mean Progress?" in *Technological Change and the Transformation of America*, ed. Steven E. Goldberg and Charles R. Strain (Carbondale, Ill.: Southern Illinois University Press, 1987), pp. 23-36.

15. Langdon Winner, "Do Artifacts Have Politics?" *Daedalus* 109 (Winter 1980): 121-36.

16. Noble, *Forces of Production*, pp. 144-92.

17. Brian G. Sullivan, "The Challenge of Economic Transformation: Forerunner of Democracy," in *Technological Change and the Transformation of America*, pp. 92-94; and Michael J. Piore and Charles F. Sabel, *The Second Industrial Divide: Possibilities for Prosperity* (New York: Basic Books, 1984), p. 5.

18. Cf. Walzer, *Spheres of Justice*, pp. 291-303.

19. Piore and Sabel, *The Second Industrial Divide*, p. 273; cf. pp. 258-80; and Robert B. Reich, *The Next American Frontier* (New York: Times Books, 1983).

20. See Charles Wilber's discussion in Chapter 20, p. 233

21. Reich, *The Next American Frontier*, p. 280.

22. Piore and Sabel, *The Second Industrial Divide*, p. 306.

Notes to Chapter 18

1. National Conference of Catholic Bishops, *The Challenge of Peace: God's Promise and Our Response* (Washington: United States Catholic Conference, 1983).

2. David Hollenbach, *Claims in Conflict: Retrieving and Renewing the Catholic Human Rights Tradition* (Ramsey, N.J.: Paulist Press, 1979).

3. *Pacem in Terris* (nos. 4-27) and *Populorum Progressio* (nos. 43-80), in *Justice in the Marketplace: Collected Statements of the Vatican and the U.S. Catholic Bishops on Economic Policy, 1891-1984*, ed. David M. Byers (Washington: United States Catholic Conference, 1985).

4. Peter L. Berger and Richard John Neuhaus, *To Empower People: The Role of Mediating Structures in Public Policy* (Washington: American Enterprise Institute, 1977).

5. Thomas J. Peters and Robert H. Waterman, Jr., *In Search of Excellence: Lessons from America's Best-Run Companies* (New York: Harper & Row, 1982).

6. Robert A. Dahl, *A Preface to Economic Democracy* (Berkeley and Los Angeles: University of California Press, 1985).

7. See my book entitled *New Experiment in Democracy: The Challenge for American Catholicism* (Kansas City, Mo.: Sheed & Ward, 1987).

8. *Quadragesimo Anno* (nos. 79-80), in *Justice in the Marketplace*.

9. McCann, *New Experiment in Democracy*, pp. 131-39.

Notes to Chapter 19

1. Teresa Amott, "Women and the Economy: A Missing Viewpoint," *Probe* 12 (May/June 1985): 2.

2. See Chapter 14 in this volume.

3. Ivan Illich, *Gender* (New York: Pantheon, 1982), pp. 45-60.

4. Rosemary Ruether, "Toward New Solutions: Working Women and the Male Workday," *Christianity and Crisis*, 7 Feb. 1977, p. 3.

5. Ruether, "Toward New Solutions," pp. 5-6.

6. Ruether, "Toward New Solutions," pp. 5-7.

7. One wants to add "in the workplace" here. Note how our language covers up the reality of woman's work. Again, she does "nothing."

8. Ethel Klein, *Gender Politics* (Cambridge: Harvard University Press, 1984), p. 171.

9. Elizabeth Janeway, *Cross Sections: From a Decade of Change* (New York: William Morrow, 1982), p. 88.

10. Ruether, "Toward New Solutions," pp. 3-8.

11. Janeway, *Cross Sections*, p. 104.

Notes to Chapter 20

1. See David Hollenbach, *Claims in Conflict: Retrieving and Renewing the Catholic Human Rights Tradition* (New York: Paulist Press, 1979); Josef Pieper, *The Four Cardinal Virtues* (Notre Dame, Ind.: University of Notre Dame Press, 1966); and Jacques Maritain, *The Person and the Common Good* (New York: Scribner's, 1947).

2. *Gaudium et Spes*, no. 26, in *Proclaiming Justice and Peace: Documents from John XXIII to John Paul II*, ed. Michael Walsh and Brian Davies (Mystic, Conn.: Twenty-Third Publications, 1984).

3. Hollenbach, *Claims in Conflict*, p. 147.

4. The laissez-faire advocates among economic theorists base their argument, sometimes inaccurately, on *Anarchy, State and Utopia* by Robert Nozick (New York: Basic Books, 1974). Economic theorists of a more liberal orientation find John Rawls' work more congenial. See *A Theory of Justice* (Cambridge: Harvard University Press, 1971).

5. See F. A. Hayek, *Law, Legislation, and Liberty*, 2 vols. (Chicago: University of Chicago Press, 1976).

6. See George A. Akerlof, *An Economist's Book of Tales* (Cambridge: Cambridge University Press, 1984); Kenneth E. Boulding, *The Economy of Love and Fear* (Belmont, Calif.: Wadsworth, 1973); Fred Hirsch, *Social Limits to Growth* (Cambridge: Harvard University Press, 1978); Albert O. Hirschman, *Exit, Voice, and Loyalty: Responses to Decline in Firms, Organizations, and States* (Cambridge: Harvard University Press, 1970); Andrew Schotter, *Free Market Economics: A Critical Appraisal* (New York: St. Martin's Press, 1985), pp. 47-88; and A. Allan Schmid, *Property, Power, and Public Choice: An Inquiry into Law and Economics* (New York: Praeger, 1978).

7. See Hirschman, *Exit, Voice, and Loyalty*; and *Rival Views of Market Society* (New York: Viking Press, 1986), pp. 77-101.

8. Schmid, *Property, Power, and Public Choice*, pp. 162-69.

9. See Smith, *Theory of Moral Sentiments* (London: Henry Bohn, 1861); and *The Classical Economists and Economic Policy*, ed. A. W. Coats (London: Methuen, 1971). The importance of such a moral consensus has been widely recognized. Cf. Gary Wills, "Benevolent Adam Smith," *New York Review of Books*, 9 Feb. 1978; Edward C. and L. F. Banfield, *The Moral Basis of a Backward Society* (Glencoe, Ill.: Free Press, 1958); and James C. Scott, *The Moral Economy of the Peasant: Rebellion and Subsistence in Southeast Asia* (New Haven: Yale University Press, 1976).

10. Berger, "In Praise of Particularity: The Concept of Mediating Structures," *Review of Politics* 38 (July 1976): 134.

11. Hirsch, *Social Limits to Growth*, p. 141.

12. Bellah, *The Broken Covenant: American Civil Religion in a Time of Trial* (New York: Seabury, 1975).

13. Hirsch, *Social Limits to Growth*, pp. 128-29.

14. This casts new light on the recent attempts to construct theories of justice that base moral law on rationality rather than religion. See Rawls, *A Theory of Justice*, and the literature spawned by that work.

15. Hirsch, *Social Limits to Growth*, pp. 141-42.

16. Hirschman, *Rival Views of Market Society*, p. 155.

17. See Richard Titmuss, *The Gift Relationship: From Human Blood to Social Policy* (London: Allen & Unwin, 1970).

18. Aristotle, *Nicomachean Ethics*, 1103b.

19. The best known and most studied of these firms are the plywood cooperatives in Oregon and Washington. See K. Berman, *Worker-Owned Plywood Companies* (Pullman, Wash.: Washington State University Press, 1967).

20. Barry Bluestone and Bennett Harrison, *The Deindustrialization of America* (New York: Basic Books, 1982).

21. U.S. Congress Joint Economic Committee, *Broadening the Ownership of New Capital: ESOPs and Other Alternatives*, 94th Congress, 2nd session (Washington: U.S. Government Printing Office, 1976).

22. Henry M. Levin, "Issues in Assessing the Comparative Productivity of Worker-Managed and Participatory Firms in Capitalist Societies," in *Participatory and Self-Managed Firms: Evaluating Economic Performance*, ed. D. Jones and J. Svejnar (Lexington, Mass.: D. C. Heath, 1982);

R. Oakeshott, *The Case for Workers' Co-ops* (London: Routledge & Kegan Paul, 1978); and K. Friden, *Workplace Democracy and Productivity* (Washington: National Center for Economic Alternatives, 1980).

23. See B. Thurston, "South Bend Lathe, E.S.O.P. on Strike against Itself?" *Self-Management* 8 (Fall 1980): 19-20.

24. See Henry M. Levin, "The Workplace: Employment and Business Intervention," in *Handbook of Social Intervention*, ed. E. Seidman (Beverly Hills: Sage Publications, 1983); A. G. Johnson and W. F. Whyte, "The Mondragon System of Worker Production Cooperatives," *Industrial and Labor Relations Review* 31 (1977): 18-30; and H. Thomas and C. Logan, *Mondragon: An Economic Analysis* (Boston: Allen & Unwin, 1982).

25. Levin, "The Workplace," pp. 511-12.

26. Henry M. Levin, "Raising Employment and Productivity with Producer Cooperatives," in a work not yet titled, ed. P. Streeten and H. Maier (London: Macmillan, forthcoming).